M000278904

"Our younger generations need to kı
the pioneers of the Church of God i

**Bishop Chandler D. Owens, Presiding Bishop,
Church of God in Christ Worldwide**

"This valuable book should be in the hands of every member of the Church of
God in Christ."

Bishop C. L. Anderson, First Assistant Presiding Bishop

"God gave Bishop C. H. Mason an anointing to preach powerfully, to heal the
sick, and to sing out in spontaneous worship. May we covet the same anointing
that transformed thousands in his day."

Bishop J. Neaul Haynes, Second Assistant Presiding Bishop

"We are the descendants of a mighty move of God that began at Azusa Street.
This book will help us to pass on an equally dynamic spiritual life to our succes-
sors, taking the Church of God in Christ into the next century."

Bishop P. A. Brooks, Secretary, General Board

"Church leaders would do well to emulate the dynamic spiritual life of our founder,
Bishop C. H. Mason."

Bishop O. T. Jones, Jr.

"Every pastor in our denomination and beyond should have a worn and well-
read copy of this book."

Bishop Charles E. Blake, Sr.

"Bishop C. H. Mason knew that a dynamic encounter with God propelled him
into effective ministry. May we also pursue God wholeheartedly, believing Him
to empower us for service."

Bishop Roy L. H. Winbush

"In order for us to transform our society, we must be faithful to the vision of our
founder, Bishop C. H. Mason."

Bishop Leroy R. Anderson, Assistant Secretary

"Bishop Clemmons reminds us that our denomination was forged in the fires of
a pentecostal revival that continues to impact our society today."

Bishop Gilbert E. Patterson

"You will be inspired to hunger and thirst for God as you read the biography of
Bishop C. H. Mason."

Bishop L. E. Willis

"May God grant us a return to Azusa Street where barriers of color, race, sex, and social status were demolished by the power of the Holy Spirit and may the Church of God in Christ lead the way."

Bishop Samuel L. Green, Jr.

"God enabled Bishop C. H. Mason to lead both blacks and whites in an interracial fellowship at a time when segregation permeated our society. May we likewise tear down walls of separation."

Bishop W. W. Hamilton, General Secretary

"Years of research make this one of the most thorough documentaries of our denomination that I have ever seen."

Bishop Frank O. White, Financial Secretary

"Bishop Clemmons paints a realistic picture of the dynamics that gave birth to our denomination."

Bishop Samuel L. Lowe, Treasurer

"Our roots establish our legacy and provide the springboard for the future. This documentation is a must for this generation and the generations to come."

Mother Emma F. Crouch, Supervisor, Women's Department,
Church of God in Christ, President, International Women's Convention

"This is must reading for every seminary student preparing to minister in the Church of God in Christ. This will be extremely valuable to students of church history regardless of denomination."

Dr. H. Vinson Synan, Ph.D., Dean of the School of Divinity,
Regent University, Virginia Beach, VA

"Finally, a documentary written by a black historian/theologian and a lifelong member of the Church of God in Christ. Bishop Clemmons' perspective is insightful, informative, and refreshing."

Dr. William C. Turner, Ph.D., Professor of Theology, Duke Divinity
School, Duke University, Durham, North Carolina

"This book tells the amazing story of a fledgling movement that became a powerful presence in our inner cities in just a few decades."

Dr. Dorothy Webster Exumé, Ph.D., Missionary to Haiti

"Allow Bishop C. H. Mason's vision to grip you, to challenge you, and to change you."

Raymond C. Pierce, J.D., Deputy Assistant Secretary,
U.S. Department of Education, Office for Civil Rights

BISHOP C. H. MASON
and the Roots of the Church of God in Christ
CENTENNIAL EDITION

DEDICATION

To my parents,
Bishop Frank and Mrs. Pauline Clemmons,
and other pioneers of the Church of God in Christ.

ABOUT THE AUTHORS

B ishop Ithiel C. Clemmons is a member of the General Board (Presidium) of the Church of God in Christ. He is the Church's historian and for many years has overseen the Prayer Initiative of the Church of God in Christ.

Bishop Clemmons is the Jurisdictional Prelate of Eastern New York First Jurisdiction, Pastors First Church of God in Christ, Brooklyn, New York; and COGIC Cathedral, home of Wells Memorial Church of God in Christ, Greensboro, North Carolina.

He is Adjunct-Professor of African-American Religious Studies at Regent University, Virginia Beach, Virginia. He is sometimes lecturer at the Duke University Divinity School. Bishop Clemmons is also Chairman of the Executive Committee of the Pentecostal/Charismatic Churches of North American (PCCNA), a member of the Planning Committee of the North American Renewal Service Committee (NARSC) for the Harry Emerson Fosdick Convocation convening at Riverside Church, New York City in 1997. He is a member of the Board of Directors of the LeMan Corporation of Longwood, Florida. As a scholar, Bishop Clemmons is a past president of the Society for Pentecostal Studies (SPS).

He holds masters degrees in Education and Divinity and also doctoral degrees in Divinity and Church Planning from Union and New York Theological Seminaries in New York. He has been awarded numerous honorary degrees from various colleges and universities including the Doctor of Divinity from the Charles Harrison Mason Seminary at the Interdenominational Theological Center in Atlanta, Georgia.

Dr. Adrienne M. Israel, who wrote Chapter 7, is an associate professor of history and intercultural studies at Guilford College in Greensboro, North Carolina, and a member of the Church of God in Christ. She earned a doctorate degree in history from the Johns Hopkins University and holds a master's degree in African studies and a bachelor's degree in English from Howard University. A native of Massillon, Ohio, she has worked as a journalist and freelance writer. Her current work in progress is a biography of nineteenth century Methodist holiness evangelist Amanda Berry Smith.

ACKNOWLEDGMENTS

Most pastors I know, especially pastors of the black church, are frustrated that their primary obligations allow so little time for serious and sustained writing. The late William Orlando Carrington, who was for many years pastor of First AME Zion Church in Brooklyn, New York and one of my mentors, seemingly wrote with such ease, depth, and style. I have not been so gifted, although Dr. Carrington insisted that it was for him more a matter of time management and sustained hard work than giftedness.

In the pastoral ministry, as one prepares to preach once, twice, and often three times weekly and sometimes thrice in one day, illuminations occur, insights clarify, and convictions crystallize. Ministers write articles for weekly bulletins and periodicals. Ideas for books form in the mind. These are put on back burners, however, as the tyranny of the urgent takes over and immediate duties demand priority. Time gets away, hundreds of pages of broodings and ruminations never become the clearly organized, sequentially ordered chapters of a publication. This has been my continual nemesis.

These pages are the modest fruit of reading, reflection, dialogue, and pastoral work in urban and suburban settings that has absorbed me for over a decade. I am indebted to so many persons in so many places that to list them all would be virtually impossible.

A special thanks to the members of my local church who helped me to complete research on the Church of God in Christ. My dissertation – and this book, which resulted from it – could not have been completed without their help. To my wife Clara Clemmons, to Jeanette Jones, Ora Clark, the Reverend Melvin Robinson, and to all professional leaders holding management positions in education, health care, mental health, and religion, I say thank you!

I am deeply indebted to Dr. Paul Smith, pastor of First Presbyterian Church, Brooklyn, New York, my official and faithful mentor in this project His rare gifts as a teacher – and unusual ability to synthesize, inspire, and connect – combined rigorous critique with positive motivation and uncompromising integrity to carry me through difficult periods.

I must also acknowledge the significant contribution of Dr. Adrienne M. Israel, who wrote Chapter 7. I thought it best that a chapter detailing the foundation of the women's department be written by a woman.

Several seminary faculty members generously gave their time to read successive revisions of these pages. Out of their large stores of wisdom they suggested helpful changes to strengthen the content of this book. These persons are Dr. Dale Irvin; Dr. Angela Askew, New York Theological Seminary; Dr. Gayraud S. Wilmore, recently retired but busier than ever at the Interdenominational Theological Center in Atlanta, Georgia; Dr. Robert T. Handy, church historian par excellence, with whom I studied for the Ph.D., now retired from Union Theological Seminary, New York, but whose patient, person-affirming temperament has kept me focused over several years of initial struggle; Dr. James M. Washington and

Dr. James Cone of Union Theological Seminary; Dr. James A. Forbes, now senior minister of The Riverside Church, New York; and Dr. Cornel West, Harvard University. I am indebted to these younger colleagues. Their critical intellectual reflections, prodigious writings, and personal friendships have been immensely helpful.

I am greatly indebted to Lt. Col. Dr. Douglas J. Nelson (USA Chaplain Corps, Ret.), now a United Methodist pastor in San Antonio, Texas. Doug and I have been close companions since we were first-year divinity students at Union Seminary in the mid-1950s. I am especially grateful for his marvelous doctoral dissertation on Bishop William J. Seymour and the Azusa Street revival and his written consent to quote from his work. Some in the pentecostal publications establishment would rather see this valuable work remain unpublished, but it sheds important light on the beginnings of our denomination.

Dr. Cheryl Townsend-Gilkes, professor of sociology at Colby College, Waterville, Maine, first alerted me that the intense theological controversies that split the forming National Baptist Convention and precipitated the reorganization of the black church were in fact religious language for a much wider debate of cultural retentions and ethnic identity: the fine print of black religious and social organization. Dr. Gilkes' unstinting sharing of her findings has been of inestimable value. Any planned published works on the Church of God in Christ must take into account her primary research and sociological insights.

I have also worked with several black holiness-pentecostal scholars who are themselves writing histories of black holiness-pentecostal church bodies, theological thought, and ethics of the movement. They are Dr. Leonard Lovett, pioneering dean of C. H. Mason Seminary at the Interdenominational Theological Center; Dr. William C. Turner, professor of theology at Duke University School of Theology; Dr. Robert M. Franklin, professor of ethics at

Emory University, Candler School of Theology, now with the Ford Foundation; Dr. David Daniels, professor at McCormick Theological Seminary; and Dr. Alonzo Johnson, professor of religion at University of South Carolina and pastor of Bowman Chapel Church of God in Christ. Their helpful insights and critiques are reflected in these pages. I give thanks to all of them.

Not only has Jeanette Jones been an immensely resourceful site-team member, she has untiringly organized and typed the many drafts of this manuscript and assisted in the difficult editing process. A special thanks to Sandra Nealy, my secretary, who assisted Mrs. Jones. A special thanks also to Susan Rogers, whose journalistic skills helped me to smooth out many a preacher-style run-on sentence. Thanks also to Dr. Barbara Withers of Friendship Press for her editorial expertise.

I pay tribute to the members of First Church of God in Christ, Brooklyn, New York, and to the members of Wells Memorial Church of God in Christ, Greensboro, North Carolina, who with much grace and forbearance had to adjust and readjust to an apparently eclectic pastoral style.

I am grateful for the warm friendship of my colleagues on the General Board (Presidium) of the Church of God in Christ. They are faced with the awesome but meaningful challenge of guiding this growing and evolving fellowship into the twenty-first century, its second 100 years. A special thanks to the Secretary of the Board of Bishops, the Bishop Ted Thomas of the First Jurisdiction of Virginia and his lovely wife Charletta, who helped me to locate documents of Bishop Mason's founding of the Church of God in Christ in Virginia. (Bishop Mason founded the church while on his way from the Azusa Street revival back to Memphis, Tennessee in April 1907.)

A special thanks to Pastor James C. Austin, Sr., and the staff of the St. Luke Church of God in Christ with whom I have worked over the past three years to produce an audiovisual work for the C.

H. Mason Foundation entitled " C. H. Mason–Legacy of a Leader."
In a family setting much like a Jewish Seder, the life and work of C.
H. Mason and the Church of God in Christ unfolds. The audiovisual has been distributed throughout the Church of God in Christ
as Sunday school and discipleship training items.

I must express thanks to Professor Odie Tolbert of Memphis
State University for his diligent, successful work in having Mason
Temple designated a historical landmark by the Tennessee Historical Preservation Commission. His insights and perspectives are of
great value.

These years of toil and struggle have been particularly hard
on my wife and family. Yet they have supported, prayed for, and
strengthened me. For this I am eternally indebted and grateful.

BISHOP C. H. MASON

and the Roots of the Church of God in Christ

CENTENNIAL EDITION

Bishop Ithiel C. Clemmons

BISHOP C. H. MASON

and the Roots of the Church of God in Christ

CENTENNIAL EDITION

Copyright © 1996 by Bishop Ithiel C. Clemmons

Second Printing

ISBN 1-56229-451-2

Pneuma Life Publishing
P. O. Box 10612
Lanham, MD 20721
1-800-727-3218

CONTENTS

FOREWORD

Twenty-five years ago, I had the pleasure of meeting Bishop Ithiel C. Clemmons at a Youth Congress of the Church of God in Christ. Being a third-generation Church of God in Christ member, I was excited by his insights into Church of God in Christ history back then. Now with the advent of his book, *Bishop C. H. Mason and the Roots of the Church of God in Christ*, I am even more excited by his accomplishment. This book is an amazing feat, for it presents the disparate pieces of Church of God in Christ history in a sound narrative for the first time, providing the general reader and the Church of God in Christ membership with an interesting introduction to Church of God in Christ leaders and achievements.

With this publication, Bishop Clemmons has catapulted the Church of God in Christ into a new era of visibility. Now to the many queries from around the world for information about the Church of God in Christ this book can serve as an adequate response. Drawing upon his lifelong collection of research, Bishop Clemmons joins the ranks of denominational historians. Within the historiographies of pentecostalism and African-American Christianity Bishop Clemmons fits within the "school" defined by James

Tinney, Leonard Lovett, Cheryl Townsend-Gilkes and Cheryl Sanders. He argues for the African-American roots of pentecostalism and slave religion as the basis of the African-American Christianity which finds expression in pentecostalism.

This book tells the story of the Church of God in Christ in an engaging and thoughtful manner, crafting a story about the Church of God in Christ's accomplishment of forming a major denomination from the few churches which reorganized in 1907 in Memphis, Tennessee as a pentecostal denomination. The genius of Bishop Charles Harrison Mason is lauded; the verve of the many Church of God in Christ men and women who "preached out" churches is heralded; and the spirituality which birthed a vital prayer, preaching, prophetic, and gospel music tradition is brought into focus. The outstanding ministry of Bishop Mason is finally interpreted for the general public. The book introduces readers to the great women and men who mentored Bishop Mason, shaping the vision which Bishop Mason would forge within the Church of God in Christ as well as the men and women who made the Church of God in Christ an international denomination.

Bishop Clemmons informs the reader of the critical role the Church of God in Christ played during the formative era of the pentecostal movement. He notes that the Church of God in Christ is the first major denomination to emerge from the interracial and ecumenical Azusa Street Revival. Bishop Mason had an advisory relationship with Bishop William Seymour, the leader of the Azusa Street Revival. Bishop Mason also embodied early pentecostal spirituality-combining prayer with prophetic action-which marked the Azusa Street Revival. In addition, the Church of God in Christ institutionalized the interracial vision of the Azusa Street Revival. Regarding the interracial vision, Bishop Clemmons shows why the vision collapsed locally and nationally with the rise of white congregations and denominations which recruited white Church of God in Christ clergy and laypeople.

Bishop Clemmons shatters the stereotypes of the early Church of God in Christ as either a large collection of prayer bands or an overly emotional group of "holy rollers" with his discussion of the interracial moral vision of Bishop Mason, the political vision of Bishop Henry Louis Ford, and the female leadership visions of Mothers Lizzie Roberson and Lillian Brooks Coffey. Bishop Clemmons argues that the larger vision of these Church of God in Christ leaders reflected the early pentecostal vision of the Azusa Street Revival which sought societal transformation through encounters with the Holy Spirit. He also argues against interpretations of the Church of God in Christ as a privatized form of Christianity. According to Bishop Clemmons, societal change must serve as the larger framework to interpret Church of God in Christ ministry. Connected with this social vision is the Church of God in Christ commitment to minister to the poor in the United States. He explains the expressive, jubilant dimension of the Church of God in Christ as more than the religiosity of the poor and the uneducated. According to Bishop Clemmons, Church of God in Christ spirituality and worship flow out of Bishop Mason's commitment to Scripture and the faith experience of Christian slaves called slave religion in the scholarly literature.

The book introduces the readers to the pioneers and giants of the Church of God in Christ besides Bishop Mason, offering snapshots of great leaders such as Bishops E. R. Driver, O. T. Jones, Sr., J. O. Patterson, L. H. Ford, and C. D. Owens and Mothers Lizzie Roberson and Lillian Brooks Coffey. This book includes a wonderful chapter by Dr. Adrienne Israel on women in the Church of God in Christ. Dr. Israel lodges the women's ministry of the Church of God in Christ within the holiness and pentecostal movements, the black self-help movement, the women's suffrage movement, and the West African male and female leadership tradition. Through his inclusion of the portraits and Dr. Israel's chapter, Bishop Clemmons presents a fuller picture of the Church of God in Christ leadership.

More than a narrative of chronological events, the book instructs the reader into theological themes which shape the denomination. Bishop Clemmons offers the readers the holiness distinction between justification and sanctification-justification involves forgiveness of sin and reconciliation with God and sanctification entails being freed from the "power and root of sin" and the restoration of the image of God within the Christian. Throughout the book Bishop Clemmons accents the Wesleyan focus on love as the core of sanctification, especially with Seymour and Mason's joining of love and glossolalia. Bishop Clemmons isolates the origins of the Church of God in Christ within the Baptist holiness movement, which Bishop Charles Price Jones and Mason led in the mid-South, correcting the histories which place the Church of God in Christ within the Methodist holiness movement.

Bishop Clemmons marks 1968 as the dividing line between the two major periods with Church of God in Christ history. Until 1968, the Church of God in Christ was shaped by the first generation which held on to the early pentecostal vision, especially during Bishop Mason's tenure (1897-1961). After 1968, the Church of God in Christ was shaped by the second generation which consciously sought to modernize the denomination. With the passing of the first generation of the Church of God in Christ from the leadership of the denomination this book offers a longer view of the denomination besides the personal experiences and memories of the current membership. The richness of the Church of God in Christ tradition is now available for perusal. During this era of retrieval when Christians across denominations are searching their past, this book can stand at the center of the discussion about retrieving the best of the Church of God in Christ past. Bishop Clemmons has created this book in such a way that it is more than nostalgic reflection. His study of the Church of God in Christ past is presented in a manner which embodies a vision of the Church of God in Christ future.

As the Church of God in Christ stands at the brink of the twenty-first century pondering its role in the new arena of national and global leadership within the Christian world, Bishop Clemmons challenges the Church of God in Christ to think critically about its unique contribution to the Church as well as her mission in the world. For him the national and global role of the Church of God in Christ is intertwined with the mission which is nourished by the heritage bequeathed by the great Church of God in Christ pioneers.

While the book does not claim to be exhaustive, it does present an engaging history of Bishop Mason and the development of the Church of God in Christ. With this book Bishop Clemmons inaugurates a new era for the Church of God in Christ scholars in the denomination, demonstrating the constructive role they can play in advancing the best of the tradition and the realm or kingdom of God. Bishop Clemmons' book will definitely serve as the text that all serious students of Church of God in Christ history will have to consult first and a gift to those seeking insight into that history.

Dr. David D. Daniels
Associate Professor of Church History
McCormick Theological Seminary
Chicago, Illinois

INTRODUCTION

The Church of God in Christ (Memphis, Tennessee) is probably the largest pentecostal denomination in the United States and certainly the one with the most direct historical connection to Bishop Charles H. Mason, Elder William J. Seymour, and the Azusa Street revival (1906-1911) – the most significant single event in the historical origins of modern pentecostalism.

This book, distilled from a research project for my dissertation, endeavors to survey historically, analyze theologically, and view critically the distinctive features and resources within the humble beginnings of this church tradition. I will attempt to outline the inaugural vision of Mason and Seymour, including the social and political implications of its pentecostal formulation of Christian theology.

The vision of Mason and Seymour, which lies at the root of the pentecostal movement in general and the Church of God in Christ in particular, provides the criteria for evaluating the ministry of contemporary Church of God in Christ churches.

In the late 1950s, James Baldwin, the famed novelist/essayist, was white America's inside eye on the black holiness-pentecostal churches. Like blacks generally, especially the black scholars of that period, Baldwin tended to accept the white stereotypes of black sects and cults.[1] In an autobiographical address at the World Council of Churches General Assembly at Uppsala, Sweden in 1962, Baldwin talked candidly about his love/hate relationship with Christianity, pentecostalism generally, and black holiness-pentecostalism in particular. He acknowledged that the culture of pentecostalism was highly significant and indelibly imprinted upon him, yet its naivete about life appalled him and drove him away.[2]

In the first decades of the twentieth century, the black holiness-pentecostal leaders planted and nurtured great churches through their vision of the pentecostal empowerment of the poor for personal survival and social growth. What challenges face them in the closing years of the twentieth century? Black holiness-pentecostalism must reconsider the pneumatological vision of those founders. Moreover, they must ascertain how it ought to be broadened to effect social transformation so that life can be both spiritually empowered and humanized in the ghettoes of this nation.

1

ABOUT THE FOUNDERS

The Church of God in Christ has a rich spiritual heritage, dating back more than a hundred years. If we are to experience the faith that the early members experienced, we must look to the legacy of the founders.

In the late nineteenth century, through the dynamic preaching of Charles Harrison Mason and the prolific writings and hymnology of Charles Price Jones, sanctified or holiness congregations bearing the name of the Church of God in Christ sprang up throughout the South and Southwest. Mason and Jones changed the religious landscape in the black community and broadened the black religious experience. Thus, a major new black denomination was founded in 1897.

Charles H. Pleas, Charles Mason's first holiness convert, gives the clearest and best eyewitness account of the formative years of the Church of God in Christ. He wrote in 1955:

The closing years of the last century and the early years of the present century heralded what was then thought to be an insignificant religious upheaval. That period . . . extended from 1894-1906.

The Church of God in Christ has progressed to such proportions in its organization, and its influence has reached such a capacity in the church world, that it has become very necessary to tell more of its history than is generally known.

There have been many who were very critical about whether this faith was a mere cult that could not stand the ravages of time and opposition. However, its accomplishments have been so pronounced that the public has come to acknowledge it as one of the most potent factors in the development of Christianity and the promulgation of the gospel of the kingdom of God.

It has also been realized that the principles for which it stands are forever enduring and that they claim the attention of honest hearts in the quest for truth.[1]

From the seventeenth through the nineteenth century, most blacks in the United States encountered Christianity through Baptist or Methodist churches. What appeared to be an insignificant religious upheaval among some poor, obscure blacks in the Delta region of Mississippi became in fact a major reorganization of the black church in America and a major bearer of pentecostal spirituality in the twentieth century.[2]

I've quoted extensively from the late Bishop Charles H. Pleas regarding the formative years of the Church of God in Christ for several crucial reasons. Charles Pleas was an adult before he learned to read or write, but his acquired skill at both, along with his phenomenal memory of dates, times, places, circumstances, and scenery, were legendary in his lifetime. At age ninety, he knew the full roster of every baseball team in both the National and American leagues. He could reel off the batting averages and status of every major league player in 1960. A veritable walking encyclopedia of the denomination's founding personalities and events, Pleas is the only historian of the Church of God in Christ who gives adequate recognition to the vast contributions of Charles Price Jones.

This autobiographical quotation illustrates the reliability of Charles Pleas' eyewitness accounts.

> I was saved in October 1896, through the preaching of the Church of God in Christ's founder, Elder C. H. Mason, who is now Senior Bishop, whose Spirit-filled gospel led me into the ministry. I give credit to him and his associates whose teachings encouraged and informed; and that gospel gave my hungry soul the much needed strength that enabled me to resist the evils and to press for the mark of the high calling of God in Jesus Christ.
>
> I was not blessed with a mother and father as many others. I was raised as an adopted child by my uncle, Charles Pleas, Sr., with the assistance of his wife, Nancy Redman Pleas, and his mother (my grandmother), Martha Pleas. Having no education, they could not read, could not write, and they were not encouraged to give me what they did not have. Therefore, I was greatly hindered in the way of schooling. I took it upon myself to "bootleg" my education. (I must confess that I am in the bootlegging business until now . . .)[3]

Charles Pleas' account of his sanctification during Elder Charles Mason's week of revival in Natchez, Mississippi – and the organizing efforts that followed – helps us understand both the religious and cultural reasons for the rise of the Church of God in Christ. The varied themes – the struggle among black Baptists over the issue of sanctification, the violence surrounding the founding of the Church of God in Christ, and the principal persons – are all present in his narrative.[4]

Charles Harrison Mason (1866-1961)

Historians agree that Charles Harrison Mason, was, from 1897-1961, the dominant figure in shaping the life, witness, and structure of the Church of God in Christ.[5] Mason was born on September 8, 1866, just north of Memphis, Tennessee, on the Prior Farm, which is today the town of Bartlett. Prior Lee, after whom the plantation, Prior Farm, was named, had slaves in Jackson Mississippi and in Tennessee. He was a wealthy member of First Baptist Church of Jackson, Mississippi — a church founded in 1834 with 34 blacks and 13 whites. Prior Lee's slaves manufactured and laid the bricks for the earliest edifice of the First Baptist Church of Jackson, Mississippi, and founded the Mt. Helm Baptist Church in 1867, following the Civil War. I will discuss these churches later in this chapter.

Mason's parents, Jerry and Eliza Mason, were former slaves and devout members of the Missionary Baptist Church. They suffered the widespread, devastating poverty affecting blacks following the Civil War. Mason's mother "prayed fervently for her son, that he would be dedicated to God."

As a boy Mason prayed earnestly with his mother, asking "above all things for God to give him a religion like the one he had heard about from the old slaves and seen demonstrated in their lives." This yearning for the God of his forebears underlies the dynamic of his life.

When Charles was twelve, a yellow fever epidemic forced Jerry Mason and his family to leave the Memphis area for Plumersville, Arkansas. There they lived on John Watson's plantation as tenant farmers. The plague claimed Jerry Mason's life in 1879. During those fearful and difficult days, the young Mason worked hard with little chance for schooling.

In 1880, just before his fourteenth birthday, Mason fell ill with chills and fever. His mother despaired of his life. In an astounding turn of events, however, Mason was miraculously healed on the first Sunday in September 1880. He and his mother went to the Mt. Olive Baptist Church near Plumersville, where the pastor, Mason's half-brother, the Reverend I. S. Nelson, baptized him in

4

an atmosphere of praise and thanksgiving. Mason went throughout southern Arkansas as a lay preacher, giving his testimony and working with souls on the mourner's bench, especially during the summer camp meetings.

Ordination and Unhappy Marriage

Despite being licensed and ordained to preach in 1891 at Preston, Arkansas, Mason held back from full-time ministry to marry Alice Saxton, a daughter of his mother's best friend. To his great disappointment and distress, Alice bitterly opposed his ministerial plans and divorced him after two years. Mason fell into such grief and despair that at times Satan tempted him to take his own life. Mason remained unmarried while Alice was alive.

Following his heart-rending divorce, Mason resolved to get an education. That same year Meyer and Brothers of Chicago published the widely read volume, *An Autobiography: The Story of the Lord's Dealing with Mrs. Amanda Smith, the Coloured Evangelist*. A disciple of John Inskip, Amanda Smith (1839-1915) became one of the most influential, widely traveled, and respected black holiness evangelists of the nineteenth century. Her life story swept many blacks, especially in the South, into the holiness movement, including Mason, who claimed the grace of divine sanctification after reading her autobiography.

Mason preached his first sermon on sanctification at Preston, Arkansas. He chose as his text 2 Timothy 2:3, which begins, "Thou therefore endure hardness, as a good soldier of Jesus Christ." Mason often quoted this sermon, and he, in fact, endured much hardship throughout his life.

Preparation for Ministry

On November 1, 1893, Mason entered Arkansas Baptist College, founded by Elias C. Morris, pastor of Centennial Baptist Church at Helena, Arkansas, and president of the Arkansas Baptist State Convention. Mason was deeply disturbed by the new higher criticism in biblical interpretation that Charles Lewis Fisher, a top graduate of Morgan Park Seminary (now the University of Chicago Divinity School), had brought to Arkansas Baptist College. Having both hermeneutical and cultural suspicions of the methods, philosophy, and curriculum at this institution, Mason decided that the college would be of no help in preventing the loss of Slave Religion's vitality because of its assimilation into the culture at large. He left in January 1894.

Mason met Charles Price Jones in 1895 and found that they had much in common. Sharing similar views and a zeal for God, they immediately became friends and colleagues in ministry. Jones was a natural leader and Mason, by now a dynamic preacher, had no trouble following him. Mason described Jones as a man who was "sweet in the Spirit of the Lord, who prayed much."[6]

Charles Price Jones (1865-1947)

Charles Price Jones was born in Texas Valley near Rome, Georgia on December 9, 1865. The piety and prayer life of his mother, a slave of William Jones of Floyd County, Georgia, deeply influenced him. She died in 1882 when he was seventeen.

Like many young people of his generation, Jones found himself alone, making his way in a hard, hostile society. He had learned to read, write, and think under the tutelage of J. E. Gush, a young man of Talledega College, and a woman named Ada F. Dawson. Jones traveled through Tennessee and as far west as Kansas City, finding various menial jobs from laboring for contractors to working on road-building dumps. Converted at Cat Island, Tennessee in October 1884, he began teaching Sunday school on the very day Elder J. D. Petty baptized him. That same fall, Jones began to preach.

Early in his ministry he was inspired to go to Africa and "teach the Africans the way of God." He went to Helena, Arkansas to

6

consult with Elias C. Morris, pastor of the Centennial Baptist Church. Morris persuaded him, as he had other young men, to go to college.

Gifted for Ministry

Jones entered Arkansas Baptist College at Little Rock, Arkansas, on January 3, 1888. He soon impressed A. M. Booker, the president of the college, and Charles Lewis Fisher, academic dean, as a young man of tremendous talent. Only six months later he was elected pastor of Pople Creek Baptist Church. In October 1888, Fisher ordained him at Mt. Zion Baptist Church in Little Rock. The very next month Jones was elected pastor of St. Paul Baptist Church, also in Little Rock. From 1888-1891, he pastored both the Pople Creek and St. Paul churches while continuing his college work, graduating in 1891.

That same year he accepted a call to Bethlehem Baptist Church at Searcy, Arkansas, and also became the editor of the *Arkansas Baptist Vanguard*. His gifts attracted the attention of denominational leaders, who elected him corresponding secretary of the Arkansas Baptist State Convention and a trustee and auditor of the Arkansas Baptist College. Few in the denomination made greater progress in shorter time.

Just how powerful was Jones' preaching? His final message to the Arkansas State Convention, after he accepted the call to Tabernacle Baptist Church at Selma, Alabama, made a deep impression. He preached with such conviction that men in that great assembly wept, sobbed, and cried, "Stop him, stop him."[7]

For two and one-half years, he pastored at Tabernacle Baptist, becoming a popular preacher, singer, and evangelist. Jones says that at Selma he found himself in need of a "deeper experience of grace and a larger power."

> As I asked God for His grace, He demanded that I let Him sanctify me; which I did. I fasted and prayed three days and

nights. He then sanctified me sweetly in His love. New visions of Christ, of God, of truth were given me. The earnestness of the Spirit was mine.[8]

Early in 1895, Jones accepted the call to Mt. Helm Baptist Church of Jackson, Mississippi. On two previous occasions – after conducting annual revivals there in 1893 and 1894 – he had declined their invitation. In those days Charles Fisher, William Bacote of Marion, Alabama, and other strong black Baptist leaders were his close companions. These were men of wisdom, godliness, and training.

Holiness Controversy

Jones' preaching on holiness and sanctification had begun in 1895 at the General Baptist Association meeting in Vicksburg, Mississippi. Jones published his first booklet in 1896, a treatise on 1 Corinthians 12 entitled: "The Work of the Holy Spirit in the Churches."[9]

In 1896, the General Baptist Association of Mississippi convened at Mt. Helm Baptist Church at Jackson, Mississippi, with Jones as the host pastor. Some controversy around the nature of holiness was stirred. Sometime after the association meeting, Jones felt led by the Lord to call a holiness convention. He had already begun to publish and distribute a bimonthly newsletter, *The Truth*, which became the special organ of the call for a holiness convention to be held at Mt. Helm Baptist Church.

The meeting began Sunday, June 6, 1887, and continued two weeks. Among those attending were Jones, Mason, W. S. Pleasant, J. E. Buris, T. J. Hardy, R. H. Morris, E. W. Butler, W. T. Nickerson, and H. Funches. These participants studied the Bible and prayed night and day. The convention itself became the first independent thrust of Jones and Mason, with representatives from Alabama, Arkansas, Georgia, Illinois, Missouri, North Carolina, Tennessee, and other states.

Jones claimed, "Our movement was entirely interdenominational and in spirit anti-sectarian. The sick were healed, the blind were made to see, the afflicted were blessed.... Black and white, Jew and gentile sought God together."[10]

In that period, Charles Mason emerged as a strong influence on the brethren, accepting and preaching holiness. Jones and Mason became the major bearers of the holiness doctrine among black Baptists, causing major upheavals in Baptist churches in Mississippi, Tennessee, and Arkansas.

Understanding the Conflict

Jones' and Mason's challenge to the black Baptist Associations during the late 1890s resembled conflicts that occurred when Wesleyan perfectionism departed from the older Calvinist position [1880s and 1890s] – a conflict that became very bitter. In the 1890s, existing denominations failed to meet the demands of the emerging new era of the Spirit that the proponents of holiness doctrine felt to be drawing to a close. As a result, new perfectionist sects proliferated in the United States. Various groups among black Baptists proved to be no exception. As Charles H. Pleas said, "The fight was on." Note this observation by Wesleyan scholar Albert C. Outler:

> Salvation is carried on by "convincing grace," usually in Scripture termed "repentance," which brings a larger measure of self-knowledge (of our need of grace), and a farther deliverance from the heart of stone. Afterwards, we experience the proper Christian salvation, whereby "through grace" we are "saved by faith," consisting of those two grand branches, justification and sanctification.
>
> By justification we are saved from the guilt of sin and restored to the favor of God; by sanctification we are saved from the power and root of sin and restored to the image of God. All experience, as well as Scripture, shows this salva-

9

tion (this restoration of the image, which is the human power to respond to God's initiatives) to be both instantaneous and gradual.

It begins the moment we are justified, in the holy, humble, gentle, patient love of God and man. (For Wesley, early and late, the essence of sanctification is the gift, power, and fruit of love – love to God above all else, and love to neighbor – that is every child of God in all the world to whom we can be loving.) It gradually increases from the moment as a "grain of mustard seed . . ." but gradually "puts forth large branches" and becomes a great tree; till in another instant the heart is cleansed from all sin and filled with pure love to God and man. (Note that Wesley consistently defines sin as the violation of known laws of God – which is to say, voluntary and deliberate.) But even that love increases more and more, till we "grow up in all things into him that is our head"; "till we attain the measure of the stature of the fullness of Christ."[11]

Jones and Mason introduced into the black Baptists' Calvinist doctrinal framework the Wesleyan perfectionist doctrine of sanctification.

The Lutherans and Calvinists had taught that the human condition, apart from grace (what they called the natural man), was truly hopeless. Wesley agreed with their conclusion but disputed the assumption that a Christian life should continue to exhibit sinfulness. Wesley preached:

[There] is no excuse for those who continue in sin and lay the blame upon their Maker by saying: "It is God only that must quicken us; for we cannot quicken our own souls." For allowing that all the souls of men are dead by nature, this excuses none, seeing there is no man that is in a state of mere nature; there is no man, unless he has quenched the Spirit, that is wholly void of the grace of God.

No man living is entirely destitute of what is vulgarly called "natural conscience." But this is not natural. It is more properly termed "preventing grace." Every man has a greater or less measure of this, which waiteth not for the call of man.... So that no man sins because he has not grace, but because he does not use the grace which he hath.[12]

From 1896-1899, the holiness conventions, revivals, and periodicals of Mason and Jones split the Baptists. In a few cases, the Methodist were also divided by the development of independent "sanctified" or "holiness" congregations and associations. Mason, Jones, and their colleagues attracted vehement opposition from the National Baptist Convention and, finally, expulsion.

In search of direction for these independent "sanctified" congregations, Mason prayed and studied Scripture. Sometime during this period, while walking along a certain street in Little Rock, Arkansas, Mason received the revelation of a name, "the Church of God in Christ" (1 Thess. 2:14; 2 Thess. 1:1).

Mt. Helm Baptist Church

To fully comprehend the events that led to the conflict and eventual split between Jones, Mason, and the black Baptist leadership, one must understand the history of Mt. Helm Baptist Church where Jones began his "deeper spiritual labors" among the people. The church, then in its sixtieth year as a black religious community, began as the slave church, First Baptist Church of Jackson, Mississippi.

In 1835, Prior Lee made it possible for the colored people to worship in the basement of a newly erected white Baptist church. The slave congregation complied with the law, which required them to have in their congregation two or three responsible white persons who generally met with them. The pastor of the white congregation administered the ordinances of the church.

A peculiar coincidence gave rise to early sunrise prayer meetings among the slaves. White men with dogs patrolled the city all night to see that no Negroes walked or assembled without written consent of their master. Early in the mornings, the patrols would fall asleep. Therefore, on Sunday morning the slaves would slip out of their quarters, gather at the church and have early prayer meetings.

These congregational and worship arrangements continued until the Civil War, when the white congregation of the First Baptist Church of Jackson, Mississippi suspended their services. At the defeat of the Confederacy, the colored people praised God with drum and fife in the basement of the church, their accustomed place – infuriating the deacons of the white congregation. The need for their own place of worship forcibly presented itself to the black congregation.

Thus, in 1867, a man named Helm gave the colored Baptists of Jackson a lot for a church. The white citizens contributed generously. Deacons Jack Bass, John Lee (who was among the first charter members of the Church of God in Christ at Lexington, Mississippi in 1897), Clerk Henry Mayson, James Penchance, Peyton Robinson, Charles Rollins, Ned Slaughter, and Frank Shepherd named the newly formed church the Mt. Helm Missionary Baptist Church.

The Reverend Marion Dunbar pastored the congregation from its organization in 1867 to 1890. Through his ministry hundreds added their names to the membership. After the death of Dunbar, the Reverend E. B. Topp served until 1893 when the congregation split, with 210 members following Topp to form the Farish Street Baptist Church.

In 1893, the Reverend Charles Lewis Fisher left Tabernacle Baptist Church in Selma, Alabama to become pastor of Mt. Helm. Dr. Fisher found the church in a state of great debt and confusion. He led the congregation in the building and furnishing of a parsonage.

Patrick Thompson, a Hebrew and Greek scholar specializing in church history, became the fourth pastor of Mt. Helm Missionary Baptist Church, succeeding Fisher (1894-1895).

In February 1895, Charles Price Jones succeeded Patrick H. Thompson at Mt. Helm with a determination to build the congregation spiritually.[13]

Perfectionism Divides the Church

Jones' "deeper spiritual labors" at Mt. Helm took a strange turn. He began to lift up the theme of Christian perfection using Matthew 5:48, "Be ye therefore perfect, even as your Father which is in heaven is perfect." Many members entered a new covenant to strive with God's help toward godly perfection. Jones' motto for those living the "higher Christian life" was, "Christ all in all; no more I, but Christ."

Jones continued to build his reputation as a powerful and persuasive preacher, a writer of tracts, prolific hymnologist, and gospel songwriter.

By the turn of the century, Jones' Wesleyan perfectionist ideology had stirred a storm of protest among black Baptists. Years later, Jones admitted he was possibly extreme in his fight. He felt the times demanded it. Conflicts began at the Mt. Helm Baptist Church and moved outward until they had to be dealt with by the National Baptist Convention leaders.

Between the holiness conventions of 1897-1898, Jones' message and style divided the Mt. Helm congregation. Dissenters were rooted in Calvinist Baptist theology and were turned off by Jones' strong methods of leadership. His controversy with Mt. Helm was as much caused by his personality as his theology.

During the holiness convocation held at Mt. Helm in 1898, Jones moved to change the name of the church from Mt. Helm Missionary Baptist Church to Church of Christ Holiness. Mt. Helm

13

Church went to court, and the struggle between the Jones' faction and the Mt. Helm faction lasted a year.

During that time, controversy over the doctrine of sanctification engulfed the Mississippi Negro Baptist Convention, finally involving the entire leadership of the newly formed National Baptist Convention.

It is interesting to observe that 100 years after the debates about the doctrine of sanctification among black Baptists, in the waning years of the last decade of the twentieth century, a grandson of the Church of God in Christ, the charismatic Dr. Paul S. Morton (whose father was one of the Church of God in Christ bishops), has founded the numerically exploding Full Gospel Baptist Churches Fellowship within the National Progressive and American Baptist Conventions. This time the debates are not over the doctrine of sanctification, but over a constellation of theological and polity issues that include the pentecostal experience with speaking in tongues and the ordination of women.

Breaking from the Baptists

The records imply that the doctrine of Christian perfection or sanctification, as it was called among black Baptists and Methodists, was the issue that underlay the founding of the Church of God in Christ. But issues of culture, personality, and class differentiation also fueled the controversy. Lee W. Williams, Sr., a present member and trustee of Mt. Helm Baptist Church at Jackson, Mississippi, says that church archives indicate that Jones was a versatile preacher of holiness but also a self-described extremist.[14] Jones wrote:

> Having reached my decision to follow my convictions and my Lord, I was looked upon as fanatic by some, by others as weak of brain; by yet others as a sharper trying to distinguish myself by being different, by nearly all as a heretic.[15]

14

When the National Baptist Convention met in September 1899, President Elias C. Morris' official message addressed the doctrine of sanctification.[16] On January 23, 1899, the Mississippi Supreme Court ruled that since the land had been given to members of Mt. Helm Baptist Church for a Baptist Church, the name could not be changed.[17] Jones and his followers, numbering several hundred from around Mississippi, were ordered to vacate the property. Jones and his followers in Jackson purchased a lot around the corner from Mt. Helm Baptist Church at the intersection of East Monument and Grayson Streets.

During this period of conflict at Mt. Helm Baptist Church, that year and for several years following, Mason won hundreds of followers in Holmes County with Lexington as the county seat. Mason's local congregation became another strong center for the Church of God in Christ adherents.

A Misunderstood History

With the exception of those written by H. Vinson Synan,[18] histories of the holiness movement (by Timothy Smith, Donald Dayton, and others)[19] have underestimated the place of Jones and Mason in the origins of the holiness churches. Why is this? The denomination that they founded – the Church of God in Christ – arose because of intragroup conflict within the black Baptist community and did not derive from the same roots and racial exclusiveness as did the holiness churches within the white church. The intragroup conflicts within black religion stand outside the understanding of most major white historians.

Moreover, Jones and Mason became increasingly dissatisfied with the Baptists, leading to a crisis in 1899. These events are generally unknown by both white and black historians. They involve ethnocentric issues (the organization and perpetuation of black religious traditions) that until recently were overlooked as insignificant. For that reason, Melvin Dieter, a leading Wesleyan scholar, acknowledges that the history of the holiness movement in the United States and the subsequent pentecostal movement is much more complex than appears on the surface.[20]

Impact of Mason and Jones

The significance of Jones and Mason may be found both in the impact of their personalities on the formation of the Church of God in Christ and their unique spirituality that influenced vast multitudes of black and white working class people in the United States.

Before analyzing the particular spirituality they forged, we must understand the personalities of Jones and Mason. Both were protegés of Elias Camp Morris who, with his colleagues of the Arkansas Baptist Convention, founded the Arkansas Baptist College in 1884.[21] Morris, pastor of Centennial Baptist Church in Helena, Arkansas, became president of the Baptist Educational Convention in 1893.

In September 1895, Morris emerged as the quintessential churchman, able to unite the disparate views and loyalties in the National Baptist Convention. Unanimously elected the first president of the convention, he led it for some twenty-eight years. As president of the Arkansas Baptist State Convention (1882-1895), he inspired, counseled, and nurtured scores of preachers.

Mason turned to Dr. Morris in 1893 after the traumatic breakup of his first marriage. Morris and Arkansas Baptist College president, A. M. Booker, took twenty-six-year-old Mason under their wings. Morris was the father Mason had missed in his young adulthood. Mason also benefited from Morris's mediation and administration skills. From around the nation leaders – both black and white – sought his principled, sagacious, common sense guidance. By observing Morris, Mason developed leadership skills and a pragmatic approach to group interaction.

Jones was more a protegé of the scholarly, creative, and brilliant Charles Lewis Fisher. Educated at what is now the University of Chicago Divinity School, Fisher was the academic dean at Arkansas Baptist College. In 1888, when Jones entered the college, he was immediately attracted to Fisher, a prolific writer. Fisher discerned Jones' literary talent, his penchant for writing prose and poetry, and his oratorical skills. From 1888-92, Fisher honed Jones' skills. Jones became the editor of the *Baptist Vanguard*.

Fisher and Jones were African-American children of the European Enlightenment with its basis in the power of reason. They led the rising black middle class in Mississippi, Tennessee, Arkansas, and Alabama that struggled to convince whites of blacks' intellectual and social equality. They were also admirers of Booker T. Washington. Fisher struggled to exhibit intellectual proficiency. Jones struggled to demonstrate moral virtue.

Jones emerged a cosmopolitan, creative, self-contained leader of unbendable conviction. Jones never intended to leave the Baptist pastorate. He maintained a close relationship with the national Baptist Publishing Board at Nashville, Tennessee, until he died in 1949. He had a strong conviction about holiness as an experience and as a work of God's grace after salvation, however, which offended his Baptist brethren.

Mason emerged an evangelist, preaching in fields and town squares. He was also a pastor, a humble but heartwrenching preacher whose words hit like a hammer.

Attracted to Jones' theology of sanctification, Mason was even more interested in preserving what he believed to be the rich spiritual phenomena resident in Slave Religion. He believed that as blacks clamored for acceptance by whites and assimilation into the American cultural mainstream, they risked losing a spiritual treasure – the power of religious experience.

From 1895-1907, Mason and Jones walked together: the one an urbane intellectual; the other a grassroots prophet. These two personalities strongly influenced the Church of Christ (Holiness) and the Church of God in Christ.

Jones dedicated his life to the moral imperative of a converted life committed to holiness, found in the black church. Mason dedicated his life to preserving the slave cultural tradition also found in the black church.[22] Mason also held suspect the bourgeois nature of many black churches. He had both cultural and scriptural-hermeneutic suspicions about the black church's emulation of white, reason-centered culture and religion.

Why Were They Overlooked?

Mason, the dominant figure in the rise and spread of the Church of God in Christ; Jones, the founder of the Church of Christ (Holiness); and William J. Seymour, the major figure in the watershed Azusa Street revival, are equally significant pentecostal leaders whom major scholars have largely overlooked – even those scholars who have studied Slave Religion and made the black church their major focus.[23]

Why is this? Their neglect results from two fundamental scholarly biases. First, scholars such as Joseph Washington, Sidney Ahlstrom, and Milton Sernett have too often assumed that black religion as a whole is a replica of white evangelicalism.[24] Second, major scholars emphasize elements in black religion that do not serve as expressions of protest. For example, many practical expressions of black religious life are not directly related to socio-political controversy (singing, praying, testifying, evangelism, biblical nurture), and are considered dysfunctional, escapist, or compensatory.

Gayraud Wilmore has indicated that the black holiness-pentecostal expression of black evangelicalism founded by Mason and Seymour "has been one of the most powerful expressions of black religion in the world and is today outstripping the historic black denominations both in physical bodies and spiritual dynamic."

A Rich Heritage

The Mt. Helm Baptist Church, organized as a black Baptist church in 1863, today stands at the corner of Church and Lamar Streets. This site is the headquarters of the Church of Christ (Holiness). The links between the Church of God in Christ and the Church of Christ (Holiness) with the Mt. Helm Baptist Church are significant. The oldest black church in Jackson, it dates from 1835. Mt. Helm is not only the fountainhead of two important denominations but also a repository of the sacred and secular history of the slaves.

In 1844, when the first brick building in Jackson, Mississippi – First Baptist Church – was raised, slaves manufactured the bricks and mortared them into place.[25] Slave labor, the deep commitment of slaves to God, the paradox of mistreatment from and benevolence by white evangelicals, the rise of the black church, and the debates within the black community about caste, class, culture, and creed all share in the heritage of the National Baptist Convention, the Church of Christ (Holiness), and the Church of God in Christ. From a previously enslaved and submerged people robust Baptist, holiness, and pentecostal faiths developed. Millions today subscribe to religious visions rooted in the heritage of ancestors who struggled for identity, integration, and liberation here.

The Church of God in Christ currently celebrates its anniversary based on 1907 as the founding date. Unfortunately, this excludes many who between 1895 and 1907 formulated the culture and tradition that determined the shape of the Church of God in Christ's present ideology, style, and practices.

Tradition is the living faith of our ancestors and the basis for our worldview. In the case of the Church of God in Christ, this tradition should include recorded and oral affirmations of the faith of slaves and the first generation of freedmen and freedwomen. The roots of the Church of God in Christ go back at least thirty years before the Emancipation Proclamation of 1863. Slave narratives, with their heartwrenching descriptions of conversion experiences, provide a rich resource for exploring the beginnings of the Church of God in Christ tradition.[26]

2

THE FORMATIVE YEARS

The National Baptist Convention expelled Jones, Mason, and others in 1899 because of their zeal for Wesleyan perfectionism and their militant defense of slave worship practices the rest of the black church sought to forget. These outcasts chided the Baptist and Methodist churches for neglecting the "spiritual component" in their quest for a more political, social gospel. They understood the radical, prophetic vision of the mainline black churches was essential to break through the ironclad systems of cruelty that oppressed a whole race of people. But attempting to fight the goliath of racism and white supremacy without spiritual sustenance was, they said, to enter the battle without adequate resources.

Mason especially insisted upon the centrality of personal inner transformation *without* shedding distinctive African cultural expressions. Mainline black churches saw adherence to African worldviews and religious folk culture associated with rural life or Slave Religion, which reflected a low cultural standing. Rising middle-class educated blacks seeking assimilation in the majority white culture preferred European worldviews shaped by the Enlightenment.

Shaping Its Mission

The Church of God in Christ forged a mission that was both conservative and radical. While seeking to preserve a black religious and cultural charisma, it critically assessed the black church, white churches, and the majority culture that blacks sought to emulate. Based on black slave tradition and the reading of Scripture from the perspective of poor black people, the Church of God in Christ offered a radical alternative to the majority culture.

Not only did the church contradict the identities and visions of the European worldview, it presented to the masses of disfranchised blacks an identity and vision based upon the despised slave-circle-culture[1] of the black slaves. Mason held that the church's greatest failure would be loss of identity and vision if it blended with the surrounding society.

Because of the pioneering labors of Mason, Jones, and their co-laborers, there exists within the black church cultural distinctions between the "mainstream denominations" and the "Sanctified Church."[2] The founders of the Church of God in Christ maintained their vision and form of worship in the face of derision and ostracism through much of the twentieth century.

Between 1899 and 1907, the fledgling Church of God in Christ progressed, winning hundreds of converts among the poor masses. Jones' prolific writing and hymnology resulted in a hymn book entitled *Jesus Only*. Published by the Baptist Publishing House at Nashville in 1901, it went through several printings. Jones published *Truth* magazine, which became the official organ of the church.[3]

A Powerful Preacher

An evangelist among the grassroots poor, Mason walked from town to town and through the cotton fields of Mississippi, Tennessee, and Arkansas preaching outdoors. Jones said whenever word spread that Elder Mason was coming to town, it was like a holiday. Workers came away from their tasks to hear and be touched by him.

Testimony to Mason's powerful preaching and revolutionary impact upon people of all races, and his vision for the Church of God in Christ, is found in an autobiographical account by James Delk, a white man who was converted and sanctified during an outdoor preaching service at Conway, Arkansas in 1904.

> I first met Senior Bishop Mason at Conway, Arkansas, on the 19th day of November, 1904. I found two or three thousand people standing around a cotton wagon in which Brother Mason stood preaching. The sermon and the songs held the crowd spellbound for something like an hour and a half after I arrived. That day Brother Mason made an impression on me that I have never forgotten and can never forget. Brother Mason attended college very little but has a wide experience with human nature and an understanding of his fellow man such as no other man seems to have.
>
> Brother Mason was born just a short time after the close of the Civil War and had many a hard struggle before and after his conversion. Even after he was saved and sanctified, and was preaching the gospel, he was opposed by many as he was blazing the way for true holiness to be preached and lived in our United States.
>
> Regardless of creed, color, or race, he lived and preached [holiness] until it brought great persecution to him, but he paid very little attention to his persecutors. He became such a power for God that a president of a railroad company was converted under his ministry. I doubt if there has ever been a

minister who has lived since the day of the apostles, who has shown the sweet spirit to all people, regardless of race, creed, or color, or has preached with greater power than Brother Mason.

We read of John and Charles Wesley, founders of Methodism, who were great men: George Fox, Campbell, Roger Williams. I have met and heard William Booth, the founder of the Salvation Army, and Brother Brazil [Bresee], founder of the Nazarene Church, Brother Bell, founder of the Assembly of God, and Rev. Thomason [Tomlinson] of the Church of God. I have heard D. L. Moody preach and was personally acquainted with Aimee Semple McPherson for thirty years and the late Billy Sunday for thirty years. I have heard the Negro educator, Booker T. Washington . . . [who] said, "You measure a man's height from the depths from which he came." But of all the great preachers I have read after, and the great preachers I have met personally, no one has that sweetness and meekness of Jesus like that of our Senior Bishop C. H. Mason.

In 1916, he conducted a great camp meeting for the whites of Nashville, Tennessee, where more than 7,000 attended each night. I have heard some of the highest politicians speak complimentary of Bishop Mason, and I have heard some of the leading white ministers of several different organizations say if Brother Mason was a white man, we would gladly step aside and let him lead our organization.[4]

A life-long Mason follower,[5] Delk founded a Church of God in Christ at Madisonville, Kentucky. Delk called attention to the fact that he, a white man, had been inspired to give complete loyalty to a "colored" man. During Delk's days as a Mason disciple, he was beaten twice by the Ku Klux Klan.

Realigning Black Church Tradition

The wide range between the spiritual orientation of Mason and Jones, and that of the "orthodox" Baptists and Methodists, resulted in a radical realignment of the black church tradition. The Methodists became the primary bearers of the black church's task of educational acculturation. The Baptists became the primary bearers of the black church's social activism and political and economic struggles. The newly formed Sanctified Church became the primary bearers of the black church's emphases on personal piety as an expression of moral integrity and retention of the African [worldview].[6]

Mason and Jones and their colleagues continued to seek a more complete consecration of their lives and a deeper experience with the Lord. Yet their involvement with the major movements and issues of the black church on the one hand and their involvement with the interracial, late nineteenth-century holiness movement on the other made the constituencies of the Church of God in Christ and the Sanctified Church generally a peculiar anomaly.

In the black community, everyone knew the "sanctified people" but could not quite figure them out. Equally significant, the "sanctified" were an enigma to the holiness movement led by whites, who resonated with the Sanctified Church's emphasis on personal piety but shunned its militant defense of ethnic values and black cultural identity.

Forging Their Self-Identity

At a moment in United States history when blacks received constant derision and disrespect, being called "aunt," "uncle," "boy," the mainline black churches insisted on calling their members "Minister," "Miss," or "Mrs." Members of the Church of God in Christ called each other sister or brother and called themselves collectively "Saints."[7] They perceived themselves set apart for the purposes of holiness. These men and women were confident that God "had raised them up" for a special calling.

Regardless of racial oppression, the Saints were responsible to do everything in their power to prevent whites from casting them down. The Saints' sensitivity to nomenclature was a response to the whites' tactic of depersonalization. This strategy of cultural resistance registered their disagreement with the ethic of accommodation that was southern race relations. Accommodation to racism was, in the preaching of the Church of God in Christ, an accommodation to sin.

The "politics of holiness" is essentially a problem of separation and social distance, says Dr. Cheryl Townsend-Gilkes. The Church of God in Christ managed to maintain a distinct identity through mores surrounding dress, schedules (fasting on Tuesday and Friday), and rites of passage. These religious rules not only distinguished the Saints but contained an evaluation and assessment of the behavior of the surrounding culture. By insisting upon holiness, the Saints made a major statement concerning their orientation to the world and to the surrounding culture. Being holy involved some form of rejection of the dominant culture.[8]

Mason's Role in the Pentecostal Movement

The Church of God in Christ forged for itself a significant role in American Christianity. During 1906, Mason and Jones received reports of a widely-heralded revival being held in Los Angeles by Elder William Joseph Seymour, a black brother and the son of slave parents. Seymour's principal biographer indicates that he had become a friend of both Jones and Mason when he traveled to Jackson, Mississippi, in 1905.[9]

In Los Angeles, Mason experienced a radical ideological upheaval, ultimately resulting in a doctrinal reformation of the Church of God in Christ. All three – C. H. Mason, J. A. Jeter, and D. J. Young – experienced pentecostal spirit baptism under the guidance of Seymour on March 19, 1907. Mason wrote of that experience:

> . . . led by the Spirit to go to Los Angeles where the great fire
> of the latter rain of the Holy Ghost had fallen on many. It

26

was in March 1907, when I received Him, Jesus, my Lord in the Holy Ghost.[10]

Little did Mason know he would perform an important and critical task to and for the movement. He appears to have been the only early convert whose church was legally incorporated, who could ordain clergy whose status would be recognized by civil authorities. Clergy who wished to perform marriages and other ministerial functions having legal consequences needed this official recognition. Also, Mason played a crucial role in carrying the revival from its movement phase to its denominational phase. Through Mason's influence:

> Scores of white ministers sought ordination at the hands of Mason. Large numbers of white ministers, therefore, were to obtain ministerial credentials carrying the name of the Church of God in Christ. One group in Alabama and Texas eventually made an agreement with Mason in 1912 to use the name of his church but to issue ministerial credentials signed by their own leaders.[11]

Mason and the Church of God in Christ provided ecclesiastical guidance and development for scores of churches among whites across the United States as a result of pentecostal and holiness revivalism. Moreover, where local congregations of the Church of God in Christ were founded, black and white Saints worked, worshiped, and evangelized together in an interracial, egalitarian fellowship modeled after the interracial fellowship at Azusa Street. This occurred throughout the South including Mississippi, Tennessee, Arkansas, Florida, Louisiana, Alabama, and Georgia at a most racially tense time in the United States.

With the hesitations of Charles Price Jones behind him, Mason freely pursued the new pentecostal emphasis that he had embraced at the Azusa Street revival in Los Angeles. His new partnership with William J. Seymour would have a far-reaching effect on the history of American Christianity.

Sociological Implications

José Comblin, one of the most thoughtful and prolific liberation theologians, has observed:

> Western theology has played within the "Pentecost" event and sought to make everything derive from the "Easter" event. He says that a theology mutilated in this way cannot be effective on the plane of action; without the experience of the Spirit, Jesus could never have moved men and women of His day as He did. If this was true then, we can take it as being true for all times.
>
> Theology has not recognized the need to give equal weight to christology and pneumatology. Throughout the era of Christendom, the church possessed powerful human means and arguments for ensuring the handing on of faith; now, however, invoking a christology is inadequate. Nothing will lead our contemporaries to Jesus the Christ except strong, convincing experience. Not words about Christ, only lived and felt realities, what we call "experience of the Spirit."[12]

Comblin also says that the pentecostal churches flourishing on a popular level today have been much denigrated in a reaction motivated by prejudice against the class of people they serve rather than by versions of its religious character. Elements of great spiritual value in pentecostalism are frequently overlooked, including its insistence upon restoring the balance between christology and the experience of the Holy Spirit.

Pentecostals have been accused of being alienated, other worldly, conservative. In the case of North American white pentecostals, this is true. Among North American black pentecostals and Latin-American base communities, however, this is not true. They display all the signs of the culture of the poor. They are rashly judged by people from the Western, modern ruling cultural classes.[13]

The black church from its inception in the United States has been in part grounded in pneumatological experience. In the black church the transfer of loyalty from the "African spirits" to the "Holy Spirit" was not difficult. Moreover, the black church early on recognized the need to reflect upon the power of the powerless. They realized the need of the power of the Spirit to confront political structures and social and economic systems that perpetuate the miseries of the poor and oppressed.

Fifty years before a widespread attempt to recover the balance between christology and pneumatology was mounted, Seymour and Mason envisioned the transformation of society through the experience of the Holy Spirit. They saw the potential for correcting a theological gap and building a respectable heritage for the poor and oppressed black and white in racist America. Mason and Seymour were not trained theologians, but their initial attempts at Spirit-based theology and practices became the leaven in the dough of Western theological thought.

A Profound Impact

The historic effects of the Mason-Seymour partnership can scarcely be overstated, especially in terms of the impact of the black American Christian insights upon the surrounding white culture. Gayraud Wilmore comments:

> Knowledge of the major black Baptist and Methodist bodies suffers from the general neglect of black church history. But even less is known about black holiness and pentecostal churches and their *distinctive* contributions to the development of black religion in the United States and overseas.

> A few recent studies have shown that these latter communions grew rapidly from the end of Reconstruction through the Depression and made a lasting impression in the black community. There is, moreover, evidence that *the most direct influence of the black church upon white Christianity may have*

come through the black pentecostal and holiness churches, which emerged during that period.

Even if some of these statistics require further research, it is evident that *this remarkable movement, begun by C. H. Mason and W. J. Seymour at the turn of the century, has been one of the most powerful expressions of black religion in the world and is today outstripping the historic black denominations both in physical bodies and spiritual dynamic.*[14]

Sidney Ahlstrom, who credits Seymour with being a most influential black American Christian leader in church history, supports this assessment and also alludes to the place of Mason. Ahlstrom says:

Between 1906 and 1908, at a church on Azusa Street in Los Angeles, occurred the great outpouring of the Spirit from which the twentieth-century revival of pentecostalism flowed. The pastor whose influence spread across the nation and even abroad was William J. Seymour, a Negro.

Seymour thus personifies a process by which black piety exerted its greatest direct influence on American religious history, for the gift of tongues came during those years to black and white alike. Just as pentecostal doctrines and church ways answered to the spiritual and social needs of blacks, so did they to other disinherited or suppressed people all over the world.

In the America of 1908, however, a new religious movement was not likely to remain more than momentarily integrated. Yet certain representative bodies merit mention. Probably largest is the *Church of God in Christ, founded by Charles H. Mason.* Taken as a whole, the black holiness-pentecostal impulse . . . constituted perhaps *the most dynamic and socially functional element in black Protestantism.*[15]

To what degree did the central ideology in holiness pentecostal doctrines (conversion, sanctification, the baptism of the Holy Spirit, vocation) represent ways that poor blacks and whites coped with their harsh environment?[16] It is ironic that in the first decade of the twentieth century, a conscious extension of what Sterling Stuckey has described as slave-circle-culture[17] brought together whites and blacks around biblical teachings.

The Church of God in Christ provided the basis of a rationalized scheme of values and thus became a purposeful subculture. While the radical interracial experiment of 1906-1914 could not withstand the power of American racism, the initial and ultimate impact of that development was profound.

Heritage of African Slave Religion

Pentecostalism is the only denomination of the Christian faith in the United States founded by African-American people. Despite its interracial and ecumenical beginnings, it naturally divided in 1914 from the black Baptists and Methodists because of the tensions between European and African perspectives. While the larger pentecostal movement conflicted with evangelical churches over the introduction of "speaking in tongues," or glossolalia, the Saints also conflicted with other black Christians over whether or not to retain traditional slave religious practices, especially the holy dance, an outgrowth of the ring shout.

Mason was firmly committed to preserving the African spirit cosmology. The ring shout was the flash point of the European-African conflict.

Mason mounted a militant defense of these ecstatic practices, battling to retain and preserve a cultural tradition and expression as much as to preserve a theological perspective on biblical grounds. The ring shout had flourished subterraneously at camp meetings and praise houses throughout black evangelical slave Christianity. Thus, the holy dance, like its predecessor the ring shout, reflected the determination of the children of slaves to preserve both their spiritual autonomy and what they perceived to be elements of ancestral genius. In a tract entitled "Should the Saints Dance?" Mason wrote:

The word of the Lord says: "Let them praise Him in the dance" (Ps. 149:3, also 150:4). "Then shall the virgin rejoice in the dance, both young men and old together" (Jer. 31:13). "When Israel's joy ceased her dance was turned to mourning" (Lam. 5:15). "There is a time of dance or a time of dancing" (Eccl. 3:4). "David danced before the Lord with all his might" (2 Sam. 6:14). "We may sing and dance" (1 Sam. 21:11). "When God builds up his people as they are to be built up, then shall they go forth in the dance" (Jer. 31:4). People may go and dance with the wrong purpose or object in view, as did Israel (Ex. 32:19).[18]

Anthropologist and folklorist Zora Neale Hurston made some pioneering comments about Mason, the Church of God in Christ, and the Sanctified Church in general. She wrote in the early 1920s:

The Saints or the Sanctified Church is a revitalizing element in Negro music and religion. It is putting back into Negro religion those elements which were brought over from Africa and grafted on to Christianity as soon as the Negro came in contact with it, but which are being rooted out as the American Negro approaches white concepts. The people who made up the sanctified groups, while admiring the white brother in many ways, think him ridiculous in church.[19]

Hurston puts her finger on the pulse of the conflict between the black holiness-pentecostal churches and the black mainline denominations: upwardly mobile black people frowned upon the behavior prevalent in most Negro Protestant churches, and universal in the Sanctified Church. The people in the Sanctified Church protested the more highbrow churches' efforts to stop traditional slave practices such as shouting.

The conflict Hurston observed in the 1920s had begun during the Reconstruction and continued for more than a half a century. Despite its lengthy duration, major social scientists were hard pressed to comprehend this conflict.

The basis of the shout's flourishing in the North, says Sterling Stuckey, was laid by the great migrations of blacks from the South from the close of the nineteenth century to the 1950s and later. The implications of this movement were enormous not only for black religion but for American culture and is a subject of great importance that awaits full exploration. We know, says Stuckey, that the ring shout exists in the United States today and retains all the power of expression it held more than a century ago.[20]

In addition to dancing, the use of the drum along with guitars, trumpets, and other instruments was often associated with jazz and blues.[21] The use of these instruments, especially the drums, became a major source of conflict among black religious groups. Baptist and Methodist pastors preached against the use of these instruments. The black holiness-pentecostal churches were the only settings in which these instruments were claimed as part of the sacred worship.[22] The Saints were recognizable in the black communities as they carried their tambourines and Bibles.

The founders of the black holiness-pentecostal churches did not identify their behavior as African. Any suggestions that the Saints behaved like Africans or darkies or slaves was an insult. Charles Parham, witnessing [the holy dance] at the Azusa Street revival, rejected it. He said "it reminded him of a darkie camp meeting."[23] In order to legitimize these modes of worship, [the Saints] argued that such celebration of the presence of the Lord had nothing to do with insistence on any primeval memory or African survival.[24]

David Tucker, in *Black Pastors and Leaders*, details the divergent reactions of middle-class and lower-class blacks to the new pentecostal phenomena of Mason's followers at his Church of God in Christ on Wellington Street in Memphis, Tennessee. While the elite ridiculed Elder Mason's "magic," the masses were spellbound. Many still feared spirits. There was considerable appeal in the all-night services where one could hear unknown languages, witness healings, observe the exorcism of devils, and examine the collection of misshapen potatoes and crooked roots that Elder Mason described as the "mystical wonder of God."[25] Criticized for bringing "magic" into the church, Mason pointed to the ministry of Jesus that was as effective in the twentieth century as it was in the first.[26]

Slave Religious Traditions Forced Underground

A large amount of sociological literature arose during the first half of the twentieth century based upon the tradition that considered African-American culture and personality to be pathological. That literature stressed the inability of African Americans to create adequate coping devices to alleviate the enormous pressures caused by dire conditions. Written mainly by socially mobile, African-American, middle-class scholars (and adopted as true by most misguided white historians such as Tucker), this literature makes sociological judgments about African-American inferiority based on white culture. This literature places African Americans below other racial groups because of values, modes of behavior, or defects acquired from their endurance of political oppression, social degradation, and economic exploitation.[27]

Mason and the Saints rejected this assimilationist African-American ideology. They did not believe acceptance by mainstream American society required the rejection of slave religious culture. They believed the ancestral culture to be rich, vital, and worthy of preservation as blacks moved upward in wealth.

James Baldwin, a son of the black holiness-pentecostal religious tradition, rejected the confinement and constriction of the black pentecostal tradition and revolted against its inhibitions, but also criticized what he called the cold, abstract, lifeless categories of social scientists. For Baldwin, the assimilationalist tradition overlooked the richness and beauty of African-American life.[28] In an instructive scene from his first published fiction, *Go Tell it on the*

Mountain, Baldwin movingly describes a praise service in a Harlem storefront church. He writes:

> While John watched, the Power struck someone, a man or woman; they cried out, a long wordless crying, and, arms outstretched like wings, they began the Shout. Someone moved a chair a little to give them room, the rhythm paused, the singing stopped, only the pounding feet and the clapping hands were heard; then another cry, another dancer; then the tambourines began again; and the cries rose again; and the music swept on again, like fire, or flood, or judgment. Then like a planet rocking in space, the temple rocked with the Power of God. John watched, watched the faces, and the weightless bodies, and listened to the timeless cries.[29]

Ultra-Religious Groups

The black holiness-pentecostal churches, with the Church of God in Christ as the model, were the settings of high religiosity. Solomon Poll calls them an "ultra-religious group,"[30] described as those religious organizations who consider it their primary goal to perpetuate rules, practices, and observances as well as conduct defined by extreme religious dogmas and principles.[31] Poll says that such groups oppose acculturation to prevailing American social patterns with varying degrees of success. In his study of the Hasidim of Williamsburg in Brooklyn, New York, Poll found:

> Resistance to Americanization is such that although there is no physical wall to isolate them, a "strong sociological wall" separates this group from activities that might encroach on its cultural stability. All institutions are such that they are conducive to a Hasidic way of life. The family, the religious organization, the social stratification, the religious leadership, and all other phases of the group's structure are oriented to the preservation of group norms, and only those patterns of behavior that reflect Hasidic values and attitudes are permitted.[32]

Dr. Cheryl Townsend-Gilkes says that the Hasidim is perhaps the most successful ultra-religious group in the United States. Why are these conservative Jews so important? They represent the extreme expression of a tradition that is shared within a wider community. Part of their survival is linked, says Gilkes, to the assistance that they provide for other members of the Jewish community who wish to maintain parts of their tradition while making various adjustments to the problem of assimilation in American life.[33]

The black holiness-pentecostal tradition, says Gilkes, like the Hasidim, is the guardian of the "spark" or the "soul" of the black religious community. Had not the Saints rebelled against the religious consequences of the demands of African-American-Anglo conformity, the quality of African-American religious life would be far different than it is.

True Roots of Pentecostalism

The contemporary renewal of American pentecostalism and charismatic revivalism is, therefore, partly rooted in black culture's rediscovery of African and African-American elements. The "authentic black experience," the genuinely black theology (and pneumatology), for which black theologians of liberation have searched so diligently and so successfully over the past twenty or more years existed in the underground of American [liberation theology].

Long before James Cone wrote *God of the Oppressed*, Charles Mason used that phrase as the official message of the Twelfth Annual Holy Convocation at Memphis, Tennessee. He stressed that God's judgment rested upon the United States because of its treatment of the poor and oppressed. Mason said that God is on the side of the widow, the orphan, and the downtrodden.[34]

White American pentecostalism and neo-pentecostalism, at least since 1914, employed segregationist politics and racist attitudes similar to those of greater North American society. They consciously and unconsciously suppressed their origins and early sources. Black pentecostal churches developed without recognition from "respectable" noncharismatic and charismatic Christianity. They were without access to or proficiency for academic research into their own history. They had no rights to existing theological institutions nor did they have funds to support such study.[35]

Their oral/folk culture of songs, stories, parables, and recounting of visionary hopes were kept in individual memories. They were not a part of modern progressive, conservative, and black evangelical theologies. What was viewed as genuine "pentecostalism" (after social scientists began to reconsider their negative appraisals and assessments) was only a white fundamentalist version of this faith.[36]

James S. Tinney in 1971 became the first American scholar to challenge the prevailing historical, sociological, and cultural judgments. Tinney asks a passionate, rhetorical, ironic question: "Is it not strange that no one has inquired about the origin of the black pentecostal bodies?" Evidently, said Tinney, many assumed that the gift of tongues fell spontaneously and separately on the non-glossolalia black and white churches. Of course this was untrue.[37] Tinney says that acknowledging pentecostalism's black roots as a contribution from the ghetto to the Christian nation at large would have startling implications.[38]

> First, since scholars consider some elements of pentecostalism to resemble closely the early Church, primitive Christianity is not foreign to the experience of American Negroes and hence is not totally a white imposition. Second, while it is true that whites have tended to impose certain aspects of a culturized religion on black churches it is also true that blacks have given to more than a million whites a religious form that is significantly Afro-American. Third, since isolated incidents of glossolalia have appeared and disappeared at regular intervals in church history, it is not unreasonable to

suggest that without the important role of blacks there might be no pentecostal movement of any magnitude today in the United States or the world. Fourth, the ecumenical and interracial factors inherent in pentecostalism may offer mainstream Christianity, both Catholic and Protestant, some direction in building a truly integrated church.[39]

Over the past twenty-five years pentecostalism has mushroomed. Still, its universal impact has not peaked. I am convinced that this is true because "black" stands for all the oppressed, for the "community of the hurt," and "pentecostal" stands for the authentic faith of those who have been genuinely liberated by the Spirit of God. The Church of God in Christ and the black holiness-pentecostal movement that it spawned preserve a rich treasury of slave narrative that contributes a distinctive religious tradition to Christianity. This tradition is available now to all groups of people as they struggle for survival, freedom, and meaning.

H. Richard Niebuhr, in his classic work *The Social Sources of Denominationalism*, provides a framework for self-evaluation to those sect-to-church denominations that have been criticized by the prevailing concepts of the larger society. Niebuhr, a major theologian-ethicist,[40] sought to show how churches can learn to identify, translate, and also transcend their social roots in such a way that they can make a major contribution to the continued vitality of religious faith. Niebuhr best stated the classic ethical dilemma facing a historically, socially determined sect/church. He says:

> Christendom has often achieved apparent success by ignoring the precepts of its founder. The Church as an organization interested in self-preservation and in the gain of power has sometimes found the counsel of the Cross quite as inexpedient as have national economic groups. Given its quest for acceptance by centers of prestige and wealth, the church has all too often allied itself with "power and prestige" rather than the demands of the gospel.[41]

Niebuhr makes a second observation that has direct bearing on the emergence of the Church of God in Christ from seventy-three years of sectarian isolation in 1968. Although the sect represents "the child of an outcast minority," by its very nature, the sectarian type of organization is valid only for one generation. After the first generation, sects tend to compromise with the world and become interested in self-preservation and gaining power.[42]

The early days of the Church of God in Christ, however, received a spiritual empowerment from a revival that began on Azusa Street in Los Angeles. This outpouring of the Holy Spirit profoundly affected Mason and his comrades, changing the face of the denomination.

3

THE ROOTS OF THE
AZUSA STREET REVIVAL

The Azusa Street revival in Los Angeles was not the first place that linked glossolalia to the baptism by the Holy Spirit; however, it is the most definitive event from which all the major pentecostal movements trace their beginnings.[1]

In the past few decades especially, and at the present time, an avalanche of new studies about that event and its implications have been written. For an understanding of the African-American roots and hopes for that revival, the most important study to date remains the 1981 unpublished thesis of Douglas J. Nelson, "For Such a Time as This: The Story of Bishop William J. Seymour."[2] The recent book by Iain MacRobert[3] largely depends heavily on Nelson and supports his thesis.

A few earlier studies, such as the impressive history of the holiness-pentecostal movement by H. Vinson Synan,[4] had shown sensitivity to the factor of racial prejudice in the controversies surrounding the Azusa Street revival from 1906. If historians mentioned this matter, they only discussed the formation of the essentially white Assemblies of God in 1914, composed of ministers who withdrew from the interracial Church of God in Christ with its predominantly black church leadership.

Douglas Nelson went beyond these older studies by offering the first rigorously historical effort to understand William J. Seymour as a "theologian" who demanded that racial equality and love must accompany glossolalia if it was to serve as the sign of the outpouring of the Spirit as on the day of Pentecost. In Nelson's words, "For whites to separate from blacks, reasoning that interracial unity hinders the effective proclamation and expansion of the gospel, is the very essence of sin, a form of self-deception."[5] More bluntly, Nelson asserts, "The simple truth of Seymour's theology means that a separated Christianity is not Christian at all but rather its denial."[6]

In an earlier period of pentecostal histories, William J. Seymour and Charles Parham have often been represented as rival candidates for recognition as the founder of the modern pentecostal movement.

White historical theologians easily found reasons for rejecting both of them. Parham's crude and overt racism, as we shall see, limited his acceptance among black pentecostals. Later charges that he was a homosexual diminished his stature among white pentecostal-holiness groups. Because of their racist outlook on history, white pentecostals hesitated to view Seymour as the founder, so they often accepted the myth that the pentecostal movement had no historical roots or human founders at all.

For example, as late as 1961, we can find the book, *Suddenly . . . From Heaven: A History of the Assemblies of God*, which argued that there were no founders of the pentecostal movement. We now know that Seymour deserves recognition as one, if not the most important, father of modern pentecostalism. At the very least, he ought to be called its first truly original and significant theologian. The Azusa Street revival began among black churches and was sustained far more by black than white leadership.[7]

Seymour's Role at Azusa Street

The revival at Azusa Street finds its roots, initially, in the holiness movement among Christians within black Baptist churches. In conflict with conventional Baptist teaching, the holiness doctrine advocated a second experience of faith after salvation by which one received empowerment to live a life of holiness. The signs of a holy life included adherence to various rules about conduct and behavior that separated the believer from the world. The holiness believers criticized the worldliness of many of their Baptist sisters and brothers.

In the spring of 1905 in Los Angeles, the ministers of the historic Second Baptist Church asked about eight families and Mrs. Julia W. Hutchins, their leader, to no longer attend services because of their holiness views. This group eventually began to meet regularly at the home of a black family, Mr. and Mrs. Richard Asbery, at 214 Bonnie Brae Street. They held effective public services there and eventually leased a mission hall at 9th and Santa Fe.

After joining the primarily black Holiness Association of Southern California, the growing congregation sensed the need for a full-time pastor. Mrs. Neely Terry, a cousin of Mr. and Mrs. Asbery, recommended Seymour whom she had heard preach at his holiness church in Houston, Texas. She stated that Seymour was a godly man who had received the "Holy Spirit baptism," which meant only that he had experienced sanctification as an event of personal transformation distinct from conversion.

In the interim, Seymour had attended Charles Parham's short-term Bible school "for a few weeks at most, and perhaps for only a few days."[8] At that time, Seymour became convinced on biblical grounds that glossolalia, or speaking in tongues, ought to be a sign of the empowerment of the Holy Spirit as seen at Pentecost. Perhaps even then, Seymour also saw in Acts 2 that the evidence of different languages understood by those at Pentecost implied the

43

creation of a multiracial community as an essential complement to glossolalia as a sign of baptism by the Holy Spirit.

Seymour began to serve in 1906 as pastor of this new holiness church in Los Angeles. He openly declared his view that glossolalia represented the most conspicuous biblical sign of baptism by the Holy Spirit, even though he himself had not spoken in tongues. Controversy ensued, and the president of the Holiness Association visited the meetings in order to listen to Seymour's sermons. Afterwards, he expressed strong reservations about this doctrine of glossolalia as a sign of Holy Spirit baptism. As a result, Seymour and those agreeing with him found themselves locked out of the church by Mrs. Hutchins.

Seymour finally reestablished regular meetings back at the Asberys' home on Bonnie Brae Street. Sometime before a 7:30 p.m. service, Seymour anointed Ed Lee, a janitor at a bank, and prayed at his request that he would receive the baptism with the evidence of speaking in tongues. When Lee suddenly began to speak in what seemed to be a new language, he excitedly shouted, "At last, this is that!" (Acts 2:16).

The two men went to the evening service, where an all black congregation shared in the joy of this report. After this testimony at least seven people that evening spoke in tongues. The whole group boldly testified in public about these events, attracting wide attention. The third night of meetings, April 12, Seymour himself spoke in tongues. The little group of interracial black-led holiness believers on Bonnie Brae Street had begun a movement that would catch the attention of the world.[9]

The crowds grew so that the need for a new meeting place became obvious. Some participants, members of the First African Methodist Episcopal Church, the first black church in the Los Angeles area, recalled that the church had formerly used a building at 312 Azusa Street. Originally built as a church, the building had been remodeled for use as a storehouse. It was rundown and located in a poorer, predominately black section of the city. Wooden planks on various supports formed a circle of pews around the central pulpit on the same level.

By April 17 the *Los Angeles Times* sent a reporter to the meetings. The mix of Christians – and even some Jews – as well as the interracial character of the crowds, numbering in the hundreds, startled this outside observer.

Seymour himself saw glossolalia as a sign but not as a proof of Spirit baptism, since the activity of the Spirit must also include evidence of love and communion between all nationalities. He stated in his first newspaper, ". . . multitudes have come. God makes no difference in nationality. Ethiopians, Chinese, Indians, Mexicans, and other nationalities worship together."

Nelson properly observed that whites did not even merit special attention in the meetings.[10] However, many southern whites who attended the meetings later admitted to their "distress" on first encounter with such a common worship with "Negroes."[11] The testimonies of white participants to glossolalia were often accompanied by confessions of a similarly radical change in their attitudes toward black people. But that wedding of glossolalia and multiracial enthusiasm was not shared by all, particularly among some white pentecostal leaders outside of Los Angeles.

Mason's Relation to Azusa Street

The early pentecostal leaders – Seymour, Mason, G. B. Cashwell (white), J. H. King (white), and A. J. Tomlinson (white) – developed supportive relationships with each other. The network of friendships among the leaders of the pentecostal revival linked church groups into a close association. Mason, the quintessential holiness-pentecostal leader, traveled constantly. Attending meetings, ministering to white groups and black groups alike, he was everywhere.

Mason always held in tension and balance the dynamic of holiness, spiritual encounter and spiritual empowerment, and prophetic Christian social consciousness. Mason had gone to the Azusa Street revival very much aroused about the social conditions in the South, especially the lynchings, the maltreatment of Ida B. Wells at the hands of whites in Memphis, Tennessee, the pervasiveness of the deep poverty among blacks and whites, the Ku Klux Klan, blacks' inability to vote, and "the ungodly deeds among the races."[12]

Writing of his experience of seeking the baptism of the Holy Spirit at Azusa Street, Mason says:

> That night the Lord spoke to me that Jesus saw all of this world's wrongs but did not attempt to set it right until God overshadowed Him with the Holy Ghost. And He said that "I was no better than my Lord," and if I wanted Him to baptize me, I would have to let the people's rights and wrongs all alone and look to Him. And I said yes to God.[13]

The Church of God in Christ, through Mason's leadership, held in dynamic tension the holiness of life, spiritual encounter, and prophetic Christian social consciousness. These three dynamics influenced Mason and the Church of God in Christ into the second decade of the twentieth century and the period immediately following World War I.

A White Pentecostal Leader Intrudes

Charles Parham had been convinced that glossolalia was the biblical evidence of Spirit baptism by 1900. One of his students, Agnes Ozman, had been the first among them to speak in tongues on New Year's Eve of that same year. When Seymour wanted to study in Parham's Bible training school in 1905, Parham maintained the common racist policy that would not allow a black man to enroll in a white school. Nevertheless, Parham did allow Seymour to attend some of the day classes, permitting him to sit outside the door.

Seymour became convinced in those classes that glossolalia ought to be a sign of Spirit baptism, subsequent to conversion. Some early scholars distinguish salvation as a baptism by Jesus Christ into the one Spirit, while a pentecostal "Spirit baptism" was by the Holy Spirit unto holiness and an empowerment like that found in Jesus' works of healing and other miracles.

Parham heard rumors from Azusa Street of "white people imitating unintelligent, crude negroisms of the Southland, and blaming it on the Holy Ghost."[14] Upon visiting the Azusa mission in October1906, Parham watched from the back of the building and, then, pushed through the crowds to the center pulpit where he shook Seymour's hand. Seymour invited him to speak from the pulpit, and Parham shocked the congregation by delivering a harshly judgmental criticism of the worship activity of those present. He declared, "God is sick at His stomach" due to the "animism" he perceived in the enthusiastic worship.[15]

Nelson and other white scholars have not fully appreciated that this charge of "animism" is specifically a racist charge that condemns the African roots of American blacks. While Parham could promote glossolalia, sometimes viewed even today as possibly a retention from African religion, he rejected all other forms of worship that developed during the period of slave religion.

Similarly, white evangelicals in this period frequently assumed that much of black church worship was a combination of some Christian ideas with African animistic practices and beliefs. By ignoring their own use of non-Christian customs and practices to the glory of God, these same white Christians rejected African-American forms of worship as inferior or persistently pagan.

Parham expressed openly his disgust at the mix of whites with blacks, and the failure of blacks to recognize their "place."[16] Parham himself later wrote:

> I have seen meetings where all crowded around the altar,
> and laying across one another like hogs, blacks and whites

mingling; this should be enough to bring a blush of shame to devils, let alone equals, and yet all this was charged to the Holy Spirit . . .[17]

In Parham's opinion, Noah's flood was God's wrath partly in response to the intermingling of blacks and whites. He thought whites were the distant and especially elect descendants of the lost tribes of Israel.[18] Parham broke completely with Seymour and started a rival mission at the local Women's Christian Temperance Union building among white pentecostal believers who shared his prejudice. Parham's action seriously undermined the participation of whites in the Azusa Street revival. One might argue that Seymour's dream of a fully integrated pentecostalism had, due to Parham's racism, begun to fall apart less than two years after it began.

More Controversies Surface

Some white participants continued to resist Parham's divisiveness, but other internal conflicts began to threaten harmony with the Azusa Street congregation. Collapse of the dynamic tension of the three basic elements mentioned above – holiness of life, spiritual encounter, and prophetic Christian social consciousness – began in 1908.

Between 1906 and 1908, Seymour achieved his goals with mixed success. On the one hand, he sought to unite denominational leaders into cooperative fellowship with only limited reception. On the other hand, he purchased the building at Azusa Street, sent missionaries around the world, and opened the church's doors to people who came from the United States and other countries.

In the exhilaration of the moment, Seymour declared, "We are on the verge of the greatest miracle the world has ever seen."[19] He could not foresee two major issues that would soon change the entire situation – Seymour's decision to marry Jennie Evans Moore and the controversial preaching of William H. Durham.

Seymour had no way of anticipating that his marriage to Jennie Moore would end his worldwide influence from Azusa Street. A beautiful and intelligent black woman, Jennie Moore listed her nationality as Ethiopian. When she made her interest known and consented to marry Seymour, he wrote a letter to Elder C. H. Mason, later Bishop Mason, requesting personal advice about marriage. With Mason's blessings, Seymour asked Elder Edward Lee to perform a private ceremony with Lee's wife as the witness. The marriage occurred on May 13, 1908.

Soon afterwards, Clara Lum, a white woman and the editor of *The Apostolic Faith,* the official periodical of the Azusa Mission, left Los Angeles and moved to Portland, Oregon. There she joined Frances Crawford, who had formerly been a member at Azusa Street. She continued to publish *The Apostolic Faith* without maintaining a connection to Azusa Street.

The first issue from Portland still had Los Angeles on the main heading but noted the change of address on the second page. Seymour's sermons no longer appeared as had been customary in the past. Clara Lum had taken all twenty-two national and international mailing lists with her. This irreplaceable information, carefully collected over the past four years, prevented the Azusa Street Mission from expressing its voice to its supporters around the world.

Seymour and his wife, in desperation, traveled to Portland and sought to obtain the mailing lists. Lum refused. Without offering any explanation, Lum continued to publish *The Apostolic Faith* on her own until 1909, when it finally ceased to exist.

White clergy began to withdraw and open their own independent missions through California and elsewhere. Nelson and other scholars know these facts but have not been able to explain what lay behind these events. Nelson can only conclude sadly:

> With the passing of the newspaper from Seymour and Azusa Mission, an era ended at Los Angeles. The pentecostal move-

49

ment changed decisively from one of interracial equality characterized by unity to one of white domination separated into divisions.[20]

Fortunately, I had the rare opportunity to converse with C. H. Mason in 1948,[21] specifically about what had actually happened behind the scenes. According to Mason, Seymour told him that Clara Lum had privately made it clear that she fell in love with Seymour and wanted him to propose marriage to her. Seymour had tentatively considered the possibility and discussed the matter in its early stages with Mason who advised him not to even think about the idea.

When Seymour married Jennie Moore a short time later, he tried to do it as discretely as possible in the hopes that Lum would not feel too hurt or rejected since she was important to the life and ministry of the mission. Obviously, Seymour's strategy did not work and he underestimated Clara Lum's revenge. This hidden conflict inflamed racial divisions and misunderstandings.

Despite these disappointments, many white preachers still came to visit. For example, as late as 1910 and 1911, a gifted Canadian preacher, A. W. Frodsham, came to the Azusa Street Mission and reported that the meetings he attended were interracial.[22]

Durham Seizes the Mission

While Seymour was traveling across the country on a preaching mission in 1911, another major controversy began. William H. Durham, a powerful white preacher, tried to take control of the mission.[23] He had formerly been the pastor of The North Avenue Mission in Chicago until his dismissal from that church for some unknown reason. When he moved to Los Angeles, he brought his family and five coworkers who relentlessly supported him and his views.

Durham had visited Azusa Street previously for about a month in 1907. He had a profound religious experience and openly expressed his admiration for Seymour at that time. Now, in Seymour's absence, Durham sought to introduce a major doctrinal position alien to holiness groups, a view popularly called "finished work."

Contrary to the accepted holiness position, Durham argued that sanctification was not a separate experience after salvation. He believed sanctification occurred at conversion since it belonged, according to the New Testament, to the "finished work of Christ on Calvary." Only Spirit baptism, with the sign of speaking in tongues, comes to Christians as a secondary experience after conversion-sanctification.

Durham rejected Wesley's belief that there remains a "residue of sin" after the experience of salvation. Consequently, Durham regarded evidence of an unsanctified life as an indication that conversion itself had not taken place, that one might, in fact, be a counterfeit Christian. His position was really only a variation of the Oberlin theology developed by Charles Finney in the pre-Civil War holiness revivals.[24]

A compelling speaker, Durham attracted large crowds. Soon the mission pulpit seemed captured by this white minister and his team of white associates. Some members of the mission sent word to Seymour that he ought to return at once to restore order.

When Seymour returned to Azusa Street and asked Durham to leave, Durham refused. Consequently, when Durham finally abandoned the pulpit he took about six hundred followers with him. He returned to Chicago with this victory behind him and intended to conduct a two-week retreat for ministers and other church leaders. To everyone's surprise, however, he contracted pulmonary tuberculosis and died shortly after on July 7, 1912.

Repercussions in the Movement

Despite his sudden departure at the age of thirty-nine, Durham had a significant effect on the future of the pentecostal movement.

51

Southern holiness groups were not moved from their doctrinal position. For that reason, a number of major groups defended the standard Wesleyan-holiness view, including the Church of God (Cleveland, Tennessee), the Church of God in Christ (Memphis, Tennessee), and the Pentecostal-Holiness Church (Franklin Springs, Georgia).

Conversely, the "finished work" doctrine did persuade many leaders in the white independent missions across the country. Most of their pastors carried ordination at this time in the Church of God in Christ (Memphis, Tennessee) with C. H. Mason as its overseer.

What was significant about these developments? The dynamic spirit that had given birth to the pentecostal revival – which had been ecumenical, interracial, interclass, and nonsexist – for the first time entered into the heady atmosphere of abstract and rational doctrine. The groundwork was laid for the tragic marriage between a white, racist fundamentalism, with its notional and rational emphasis on "orthodoxy," and pentecostalism as a living liturgy and a spiritual witness within an oral-associative tradition.

Evangelical theology, with its focus on the individual and its social and political conservatism, has acted as a tremendous barrier to the authentic liberation of the fullness of humanity. White American pentecostalism and neo-pentecostalism (at least since 1911) have deceived the Spirit's ingenuity that brought men and women together from all races, social classes, and nations.

These origins of an African-American pentecostalism have gained little recognition despite the fact that Mason and Seymour laid the groundwork. They have not been fully appreciated because most black ministers have not had access to the academic research of this history, nor could one find financial support or even distinctive theological institutions until the rise of the C. H. Mason Seminary in 1970.

The original balanced tension of holiness, spiritual encounter/empowerment, and prophetic Christian social consciousness has been obscured and usually forgotten. Conservative evangelical theologies ignored Afro-American pentecostals. Even many of the major denominations of the black church wrote them off as "cultic."

What eventually came to the forefront as the model of pentecostalism was only the white, conceptual, notional, abstract, fundamentalist rationalization of it. Pentecostalism has been reduced far too often to merely a categorical system of two or three crisis experiences, with historical warrants in various interpretations of Luke's theology found in certain streams of Roman Catholicism, Reformed theology, and in the Wesleyan explanation of holiness.

An End of an Era

The formation of the Assemblies of God in April 1914 greatly influenced the future development of the pentecostal movement. The founding of this new denomination, which inherited the "finished work" doctrine, also represented the end of a notable experiment in interracial church development. The period of doctrinal unity that had existed since 1906 also came to an end. The pentecostal movement split into two camps after 1914 – the "holiness advocates" of the Wesleyan "second work" doctrine and "assembly advocates" of the "finished work" doctrine.

Furthermore, at the very moment they were turning their backs on the pentecostal vision of Seymour and the Azusa Street revival, the Assemblies of God became the leading representatives of a fundamentalistic pentecostal ideology and organization. Glossolalia, rejected by mainline denominations as an aberration and an "enthusiasm" pertaining only to a former dispensation, became for white pentecostals not only a necessity but a virtue. The newly formed Assemblies of God took upon themselves the role of official spokespersons for pentecostalism and misrepresented the message of the initial leaders of the pentecostal revival. At the same time, the Assemblies of God tried to prove their "evangelical" identity by uncritically accepting fundamentalist doctrinal views.

By contrast, *The Apostolic Faith* (volume 1, number 2) offered its own brief catechism and was the original way pentecostals sought to respond to competing ideologies. The catechism appears as the answer to the key question, "What is the real evidence that a man or woman has received the baptism of the Holy Ghost?"

Divine love, which is charity. Charity is the Spirit of Jesus. They will have the fruits of the Spirit (Gal. 5:22,23). This is the real Bible evidence in their daily walk and conversation; the outward manifestations, speaking in tongues and signs following, and the love of God for souls increasing in their souls.

After 1914, glossolalia became, especially in the Assemblies of God and most other white pentecostal denominations, the only distinctive sign of the real presence of the Holy Spirit. Where, as before, pentecostal experience had not been influenced by more abstract doctrinal rationalization, speaking in tongues was highly regarded as a spiritual gift but not as the only sign of the outpouring of the Holy Spirit.

Throughout the twentieth century, white pentecostals more than black pentecostals have been preoccupied with glossolalia. The black church has sought to retain the tension between holiness, spiritual encounter/empowerment, and prophetic Christian social consciousness.

When the Assemblies of God was formed, major southern white holiness-pentecostal leaders refused to attend because of doctrinal differences. Despite doctrinal differences that already existed between the Assemblies and the Church of God in Christ, Mason attended the opening session of the founding meeting of the Assemblies of God as a guest speaker and as an observer.

As the Church of God in Christ and the twentieth-century pentecostal movement entered its second decade, World War I demanded the attention of the entire nation. Racial divisions, doctrinal debates and differences, urbanization, and denominational differentiation became the central issues. Idealistic pentecostal hopes were forced to face historical realities. The watershed Azusa Street revival (1901-1909) became tragically locked behind doors of doctrinal controversy, racism, classism, and sexism. Persons on all sides of these various debates, many defending their positions with vehement acrimony, claimed the blessed pentecostal experience and spoke in tongues.[25]

The Real Message of Azusa Street

Seymour's new egalitarian fellowship, which transcended the walls of nations, color, language, sex, and social class, was destined to break apart. The initial controversy – speaking in tongues – proved to be one of the factors in this collapse of a unified ministry. In spite of the emphasis placed on the tongues doctrine, glossolalia as spoken or sung was not the essence of the message of the Azusa Street revival. At most, these expressions only confirmed the message of an eschatological fellowship and that the kingdoms of this world would ultimately become the kingdom of our Lord and His Christ. As a result, glossolalia served as a sign given to the revival at Azusa Street that the Holy Spirit had indeed come.[26]

Speaking in tongues and singing in glossolalia were not ends in themselves but the beginnings of an eschatological end when Christ, the Lamb of God, would return and God's restoration of the earth would be made complete. Therefore, the goal was always a baptism by the Holy Spirit rather than a show of power by speaking in tongues. The founders recognized that it was possible for someone to speak in tongues, if that was his goal, without receiving the baptism by the Holy Spirit for which it served as a sign. But to those seeking the baptism of the Holy Spirit, the bestowal of tongues was indisputable evidence that they had received the Spirit.

The gift of the Holy Spirit – not the gifts that the Spirit bestows – should be the primary focus of the believer's quest.[27]

In contrast to the black leaders at the Azusa revival, the white leaders who ultimately dominated the revival movement invariably understood the pentecostal distinctive as "speaking in tongues." They overlooked the black church perspective in which speaking in tongues was seen only as the sign of divine power and presence that brings all people together in reconciliation. This reconciliation secured by the Holy Spirit, black leaders often said, is the secret of God's power and plan.

Whites focused on the phenomenology of the pentecostal experience and precipitated a confusion akin to the confusion of the early Corinthian Church. African Americans, by virtue of their tragic sense of history, are perennial "stalkers after meaning." White pentecostals forgot the blacks' search for meaning and placed primary emphasis on the phenomena of speaking in tongues.

A Legacy of the Black Church

Events of the second decade of the Azusa Street revival must be viewed with this difference of perspective in mind to understand the events that followed. For example, many white pentecostals eventually identified Charles Parham (admirer of the Ku Klux Klan) as the founder of modern pentecostalism. The actual historical developments in that period, however, are properly understood only from the perspective of the black church, with William Seymour and Charles Mason being its primary representatives.

Nelson, a white Methodist scholar, has been an exception in his recognition of the spiritual legacy of pentecostalism in the black church. Specifically concerning the Church of God in Christ, Nelson says:

It may be concluded that the Church of God in Christ is justified in likening itself to the scriptural day of Pentecost insofar as both fellowships began with the disappearance of racial and other barriers between believers amid exuberant joy and glossolalic utterance. By contrast, white pentecostals and charismatics invariably understand the pentecostal distinctive to be primarily speaking in unknown tongues, quite overlooking the black perspective which understands tongues to be a mark or a sign of that divine power and presence which brings all people together in reconciliation.[28]

Nelson says that throughout church history there have been numerous instances of glossolalia recorded but none within the context of creating a new community of Christian brotherhood beyond the usual boundaries preventing full fellowship; that is to say, none prior to the arrival of free black American Christian leaders with their insight forged during 400 years of slavery and oppression.

Seymour brought a radical view to the pentecostal revival of the twentieth century. While white pentecostals tended to limit the work of the Holy Spirit to personal piety and charismatic displays, Seymour and Mason brought to the pentecostal revival movement three interdependent dynamics of African-Christian consciousness – holiness, spiritual encounter/empowerment, and prophetic social consciousness, rooted in Slave Religion and preserved in black holiness-pentecostalism. By prophetic social consciousness, I mean a sense that the Holy Spirit not only transforms persons but rearranges relationships and structures.[29]

The interdependence of these three dynamics distinguishes black holiness-pentecostalism from white pentecostal hermeneutics and demonstrates continuity with the black church. These dynamics must be held in continual tension and establish some degree of discontinuity between black holiness-pentecostalism and the black church generally.[30] Three elements give to the black holiness-pentecostal churches the richness in existential meaning that transcended the limitations of white pentecostalism and also transcended the limitations of the black church.

William Turner, a pastor in the United Holy Church of America (black pentecostal), made this point in an unpublished Duke University doctoral dissertation.[31] He says that none of these three dynamic elements can function independently without being seriously deformed. Holiness, at its worst, may be equitable with evangelical piety and become obsessed with personal salvation as an escape from the world. Prophetic social consciousness is likely to be lost if it functions independently. If shorn of spiritual empowerment, it lapses either into anarchy or legalism. Spiritual empowerment as an independent element is the obsession with power in a way that disregards the need for inner transformation verifiable by ethical evidence. Moreover, such empowerment is sought as an attempt to disregard the institutions of society and culture that compromise the objective world.[32] Prophetic social consciousness as an independent element may have no God-centeredness. Instead, it becomes programmatic secularity that relies solely on human analysis, human ingenuity, and human power.[33]

The interrelatedness of holiness, spiritual encounter, and prophetic Christian social consciousness attracted people of all races to the Azusa Street revival. It was an egalitarian, ecumenical, interracial, interclass revival that for about three years defied the prevailing patterns of American life.[34]

The unusual evolution of the Church of God in Christ, one of the major non-white organizational outcomes of the Azusa Street vision, enabled C. H. Mason and his followers to lead an effective assault upon American racism. They were a catalyst and model for the older United Holy Church of America, the Fire Baptized Church of the Americas, the Mount Calvary Holy Church, and a number of other black holiness-pentecostal bodies.[35]

At the Azusa Street revival, whites caught a momentary glimpse of the three interdependent dynamics of the black pentecostal church and embraced them, only to pull back later and rationalize that the social customs of the nation demanded white withdrawal.

The Azusa Street revival also brought a new dynamic into the Church of God in Christ. While visiting Los Angeles, Charles Mason experienced the power of the Holy Ghost in a new way. His transformation enabled him to influence thousands of church members — but not without controversy. Let's look at the spiritual effect of the Azusa Street revival on Mason and the Church of God in Christ.

4

A NEW SPIRITUALITY

During the Azusa Street revival in Los Angeles, C. H. Mason, D. J. Young, and J. A. Jeter had profound encounters with God. Their personally transforming spiritual experiences, occurring in March and April 1907, precipitated a crucial upheaval in the Church of God in Christ.

What Mason, Young, and Jeter saw at Azusa Street was powerful and convincing. Not only was the personal religious experience itself overwhelming, but its social conduct contradicted the majority culture. In the incredible words of Frank Bartleman, "The color line was washed away by the blood."[1] People of all races and nationalities worshiped together in striking unity and equality under the leadership of a black man.

A Dynamic Transformation

Mason received a new vision for the church and a sense of new anointing for ministry. The gift of tongues accompanied other gifts such as interpretation, healing, words of knowledge and wisdom, and exorcism of demons.

Convinced that God was speaking to him in unknown tongues, Mason prayed for the interpretation. He recalled being given images and ideas that had been struggling for expression in his spirit for years. For a number of years he heard "speaking in unknown tongues" following him but did not recognize nor understand what was happening. When he was baptized with the Holy Ghost, the tongues he heard following him were now inside him.

This unusual encounter with the Lord became for him a vehicle of God's deliverance from spiritual and social limitations. He also experienced what he later referred to as a psychological liberation that led to personal growth possibilities for himself and for the poor to whom he was called as a leader. The experience facilitated emotional and psychological healing, growth, and wholeness. At last he had found that central focus for which he had been longing. Of this revolutionary personal experience Mason wrote:

> After five weeks I left Los Angeles, California, for Memphis Tennessee, my home.... I was full of power and when I reached home the Spirit had taken full control of me and everything was new to me. I soon found out the Lord was teaching me and giving me new songs. I asked Him to give me the interpretation of what was spoken in tongues for I did not understand the operation of the Spirit. I wanted the church to understand what the Spirit was saying through me, so they could be edified. The Lord stood me up one day and I began to speak in tongues and interpret the same. He soon gave me all kinds of spiritual utterances.

> The Holy Ghost then began all kinds of drawings and spiritual writings [that were] done without any thought of my mind. "Therefore, behold I send unto you prophets and wise men and scribes and some of them you kill and crucify and some of them shall ye scourge in your synagogues and persecution will be upon them from city to city." I also understood more clearly Matthew 13:52. "Then said he unto them, Therefore every scribe which is instructed unto the kingdom of heaven is like unto a man that is an householder,

which bringeth forth out of his treasure things new and old."
Oh! Glory to His name! How I thank Him for His Word,
that gives light to all who receive and obey it![2]

Mason began to use his spiritual gifts in his public ministry.
He drew large audiences of blacks and whites. Wherever he
preached, hundreds – and at times up to ten thousand – gathered
to hear and receive ministry in outdoor camp meetings. At other
times, the sponsors of his meetings rented the largest halls available. He continues:

> The Spirit through me saved, sanctified and baptized thou-
> sands of souls of all colors and races. Hundreds have been
> healed by my laying on of hands and praying to God to re-
> buke the enemy (the devil). Some of the miracles which
> God performed in healing in obedience to James 5:16 through
> prayer: Tumors have been removed from the bodies of women
> who have been suffering for years. I met an elder who had
> hemorrhages of the lungs. He was a sight to behold. The
> physicians said that it was impossible for him to live. God,
> through prayer, rebuked the bleeding and today he is blessed
> of the Lord and preaching the gospel . . .
>
> God is Almighty, who can hinder Him? My life is conse-
> crated to Him. I am following His example.... I have suffered
> all but death for His name. Naturally man has not been able
> to understand the Spirit working through me. Therefore, I
> have suffered persecution, but God and Him only can ex-
> plain the mysteries being performed by the Spirit.[3]

Mason's new and bold ministry following his pentecostal experience caused great conflict in the Church of God in Christ,
divided the denomination, and eventually thrust him forward as
its undisputed spiritual director and ecclesiastical organizer. From
1896 to 1907, Charles Jones had been the General Overseer. Mason served as Overseer of Tennessee and J. A. Jeter as Overseer of
Arkansas.

The Heart of the Conflict

Mason's new focus and vision for the mission and ministry of the Church of God in Christ precipitated a major crisis for the church. Jones, then the General Overseer, opposed the new scriptural interpretations with which Mason, Young, and Jeter returned. The central issue of the emerging conflict was "speaking in tongues" as the initial evidence of having received the baptism of the Holy Ghost. This issue eventually split the Church of God in Christ.

The events leading up to this crucial doctrinal dispute began when Mason reached Memphis in late July 1907, after conducting a tremendous revival at Portsmouth, Virginia, in which six thousand people were converted between April and July. He was surprised to find that a white brother, Glen Cook, a veteran of the Azusa Street revival, had preceded him to Memphis. Mason knew Cook, who had served as William Seymour's business manager and was on a three-month, cross-country tour to carry the news of what was occurring at Los Angeles. Mason says, "The fire had fallen before my arrival. Brother Cook of California was telling the story and the Lord was sending the rain."

The Saints at Elder Mason's church in Memphis welcomed Glen Cook, who talked of settling there. Mason did not think it best and urged Cook to continue his own evangelistic work. While he welcomed persons of all races, those who came to the Church of God in Christ had to adapt to Mason's determination to keep alive the dynamism of slave religious worship. Whites desired to modify and transform the worship of the black church. Finally, Cook decided against settling with the Saints in Memphis and continued his evangelistic work. (In 1914, Cook became the leading proponent of "Jesus Only" doctrine.)

Mason sought to offer the brethren the vision of the church modeled after the Pentecost experience recorded in Acts 2:1-42. At the Azusa Street revival, he was convinced that classical twentieth-century evangelical dispensationalism was wrong.

64

Dispensationalists held that the outpouring of the Holy Ghost on the day of Pentecost had ushered in a new dispensation, signaled by ecstatic manifestations. For dispensationalists, however, the Jewish rejection of this evidence led to yet another unexpected dispensation know as "the Church Age." The Holy Ghost does not come in the Church Age as at Pentecost. In other words, the outpouring of the Holy Ghost with speaking in tongues pertained only to the dispensation aborted by Jewish disbelief and not to the present Church Age.[4]

Mason accepted the Azusa Street interpretation that the Holy Ghost is to be received and manifested as on the day of Pentecost. He cited speaking in tongues as the initial evidence. Jones, the General Overseer, did not accept Mason's view of speaking in tongues as the initial evidence of the baptism of the Holy Spirit.

A crucial struggle for the future of the Church of God in Christ ensued. Mason led the pentecostal faction. Jones and his followers, however, believed that the Church of God in Christ should reject the new pentecostal doctrine and remain a holiness church as had the Nazarene Church, the Christian Missionary Alliance Church, and the Church of God (Anderson, Indiana).

The Turning Point

At the convocation of August 1907, the brethren searched the Scriptures continuously. At one point they debated nonstop three days and nights. The Jones faction that controlled the convocation insisted that Mason and his pentecostal faction agree that there are other initial evidences of having received the baptism of the Holy Spirit. Mason held firm his position, and the General Assembly withdrew the right hand of fellowship from him. When Mason left the Assembly, about half the ministers and members left with him.[5] Historian H. Vinson Synan says that with the conversion of Mason to the pentecostal position, the pentecostal invasion of the South was complete. In only a few months much of the holiness movement in the South converted to pentecostalism.

65

Mason sent out a letter to the brothers and sisters who believed as he did, requesting that they meet him in Memphis, Tennessee. In September 1907, the Pentecostal Assembly of the Church of God in Christ met and agreed upon two organizational matters. First, they elected Mason as their "Chief Apostle." Second, they agreed to convene a holy convocation from November 25 to December 14 annually.

Nearly all the members of the Church of God in Christ at that time were from the farming areas of the South and needed to harvest their crops and raise sufficient money to make the trip to Memphis. The late fall dates were selected to accommodate the farming and rural constituency. At the first convocation in November 1907, there were three congregations from Tennessee, three from Arkansas, two from Mississippi, two from Oklahoma, and some twelve other leaders who were mostly black, but also included several white preachers from around the country.

For two years following the first Memphis convocation, the Mason and Jones factions engaged in a legal struggle over use of the name and charter of the Church of God in Christ. Attorney R. E. Hart, a leader of the church and Mason's closest advisor, urged the church to seek a court ruling. In 1909 the court of Shelby County, Tennessee, awarded Mason and the pentecostal faction headquartered at Memphis, Tennessee, the right to use the name Church of God in Christ. Forced to reorganize and select a new name, the Jones faction became known as the Church of Christ (Holiness) U.S.A.

Reasons for Rapid Growth

From its base in Memphis, although out of sight of the mainstream of American and African-American social, political, and religious culture, the Church of God in Christ experienced exponential growth. Jones and the church he led, the Church of Christ (Holiness) U.S.A., continued as a distinguished and solid holiness denomination. Yet the Church of God in Christ had greater impact and grew much more rapidly.[6]

Mason's charismatic leadership and organizational genius were stamped indelibly on every aspect of the church's life and witness. Scholars who in recent years have seriously studied Mason's leadership explain the church's growth by the fact that Mason pursued the values of prophetic black Christianity to an extent reached by few other historical figures.

The Church of God in Christ, like the black church generally, accentuated the fallenness of all human beings, and yet was more optimistic than the rest of the black church about the power of God to transform and transcend sinfulness. The Church of God in Christ shared with the black church and the black community a profound sense of the tragic character of life and history, which in the words of Cornel West, "generates a strenuous mood, a call for heroic, courageous moral action and biblically motivated focus on and concern for the wretched of the earth."[7]

Basically a holiness church, the denomination continued to teach an experience and life of holiness as the *teleos* of the Christian life. To this the Church of God in Christ added the necessity of the pentecostal baptism with the Holy Spirit. This baptism requirement brought into the life of the fledgling faith community a dynamism that the community traced back and attributed to the New Testament outpouring of the Holy Spirit recorded in the book of Acts. The watershed Azusa Street revival that launched the twentieth-century pentecostal movement accentuated this belief.

The debate between the Church of God in Christ under Mason's leadership and the Church of Christ (Holiness) U.S.A. under the leadership of Jones resulted from a larger revolution taking place in American Christianity. The pentecostal movement arose as a split in the holiness movement and can be viewed as the logical outcome of the holiness crusade that had vexed American Protestantism for over a half century, and in particular the Methodist Church. It also resulted from the revivalism and social reform that was a major theme in American culture. The Church of Christ (Holiness) U.S.A. followed the more conservative holiness denominations, which included the Church of the Nazarene, the Pilgrim Holiness Church, the Wesleyan Methodist Church, the Christian and Missionary Alliance, the Church of God (Anderson, Indiana) and the Free Methodist Church.

The Church of God in Christ took its position on the radical edge of the new holiness-pentecostal movement along with the Fire-Baptized Church, the Church of God (Cleveland, Tennessee) and the Pentecostal Holiness Church. The key to the amazing spread of the pentecostal movement (especially in the South) was the receptive attitude of holiness leaders such as J. H. King (Pentecostal Holiness), A. J. Tomlinson (Church of God, Cleveland, Tennessee), and C. H. Mason (Church of God in Christ). All three were Armenian in theology and Wesleyan in doctrine.

When the pentecostal revival came, they added a "third experience," the baptism of the Holy Ghost. But their emphasis took them beyond the holiness focus on personal perfection to the focus on power for life and service. In the black community especially, the focus was turned outward from the self to the cries of suffering humanity being dehumanized by an oppressive society.

Releasing God's Power

For Mason and the Church of God in Christ, the pentecostal experience thrust the faith community toward a new spirituality. The Saints in the early years of the Church of God in Christ called it a "spirituality of deliverance." Today, it is called a spirituality of liberation. Mason took Mark 16:15-18 as providing both the basic paradigm of the church and its mission statement. The Church of God in Christ embraced a biblical spirituality that allows God's delivering act in history to penetrate all levels of human existence.

For the black church, freedom is the essence of religion. The Church of God in Christ argued that while this is true, the black church – like the church as a whole – was trapped between Easter and Pentecost. The black church had a high christology without a balancing pneumatology that makes possible the vital release of power.

Modeled after the Azusa Street revival, the Church of God in Christ urged its members to experience what he or she believed to be the essence of vital religion. The human spirit is touched by the divine Holy Spirit from which flows power through the subconscious to the conscious from origins that are cosmic and not merely individual. The experience of the essence of religion – knowing how to release interior powers adequate for life – makes it possible for both the individual and the community to substitute confidence for fear, a sense of security for a life lived on the ragged and vulnerable margins of an oppressive society. It takes a people who thought they had to lift life's maximum load with a minimum of human strength, and transforms them into a people who through the Holy Ghost are put in touch with strength and the death-defying courage needed to lift life's load. This experience, they believed, inevitably affects health, integration of personality, moral drive, character, radiance, and hopefulness.[8]

The prayer tradition of Slave Religion that Mason sought to preserve above all else was and is the essence of life in the Church of God in Christ. This tradition means fulfilling inward conditions of attitude and receptivity and getting appropriate results in heightened insight, self-control, strength, poise, and revolutionary patience.

Mason's success and strength as a leader was based upon his prophetic thought and action that kept alive essential elements of a tradition bequeathed to blacks from the past. Mason was revolutionary – departing from the mainstream of both black and white evangelicalism. He projected a vision and inspired a practice that

69

would fundamentally transform the prevailing status quo in light of the best of the African tradition – a tradition African Americans were more anxious to forget than to remember for the sake of acceptance and assimilation.

The Church of God in Christ took root as the first and major denomination to spring from the interracial, ecumenical, inter-religious Azusa Street revival. At the same time, it was, ironically, the kind of expression of Slave Religion that most black Americans thought hindered the progress of the race because of its strong defense of the ecstatic tradition.

Not Confined to Race

The most noted feature of the Church of God in Christ was Mason's concern for all people, especially poor blacks and whites. He also displayed unusual ability to attract those of other races and religions. A number of Jewish people joined the church. Mason's very first organizational meeting was described as follows:

> These were a group of black and white men working together under a black leader. The Holy Ghost fell on Azusa Street on a mixed congregation . . . proving the thing God tried to show to Peter, that He no respecter of persons, no racial God, but a God of every nation. Bless His name.[9]

The Church of God in Christ saw a link between religious practice and racial identity. A variety of organizational arrangements resulted from the interracial ideal of the Azusa Street revival. The white brothers and sisters who formed the Assemblies of God had been part of the Church of God in Christ from 1907 to 1914,[10] during which time Bishop Mason ordained some 350 white ministers who later withdrew from the Church of God in Christ to form the Assemblies of God. According to white scholars, they left because the larger society, especially in the South, refused to modify its worship pattern to accommodate whites. Moreover, whites became restive when they could not assume the prevailing leadership role.[11]

Charles Harrison Mason is looked upon as a race-transcending prophet – someone who never forgot the significance of race but refused to be confined to race. Such a prophet never understands black people solely as victims. He recognizes that part of the plight of blacks and whites alike, but blacks especially, is to be continually plagued by racism. Mason stood within the African-American prophetic tradition that links the African-American religious experience and its prophetic critique of race, gender, and class.

In 1914, the Assemblies of God organized as a white denomination separated from the Church of God in Christ. In the second week in April of that year, Mason traveled to Hot Springs, Arkansas, to attend the organizing meeting of the Assemblies of God. He preached on Thursday night, illustrating the wonders of God by holding up an unusually shaped sweet potato. He sang his spontaneous, improvisation of spiritual songs that Daniel Payne in 1879 called "corn-field ditties." With him were the "Saints Industrial," singers from Lexington, Mississippi. Mason bid the white leaders a warm farewell and gave them leave to void their Church of God in Christ credentials in order to switch to those of their new denomination.

While the whites gradually began to withdraw from the Church of God in Christ, the denomination saw the growth of holy convocations. These gatherings brought church members together from many different states to experience prayer, preaching, worship, and testimonies – a time set apart to solidify their identity as a people. Let's look at the development of the holy convocation, a season of refreshing that still impacts members of the Church of God in Christ today.

5

THE HOLY CONVOCATION

The half-decade from 1908-1914 marked Seymour's watershed pentecostal revival and significant changes in the identity of the Church of God in Christ. "Speaking in tongues," or glossolalia, crossed all boundaries of race, class, and sex and proved too radical a departure from the norm for white believers. Moreover, the vision and style of the Negro "circle culture," with its vigor and echoes of Africa that Mason and his colleagues sought to preserve, had a profound influence on the pentecostal revival. However, it also puzzled black and white mainline American Christianity.[1]

The reorganized Church of God in Christ, unlike many denominations, was created not so much by existing congregations coming together from the grass roots to form a national denomination, as by the efforts of one charismatic and visionary leader.[2]

Both Mason and Seymour had the quality of personality that would give to another person the gift of reconciliation. From the beginning, that was the very essence of the holiness pentecostal experience – not speaking in tongues. Mason and Seymour, as spiritual directors, introduced harmony in individuals and communities, encouraged them, and became a source of empowerment to masses of people.

Mason may have also been bequeathed the reconciliation gifts of E. C. Morris, his mentor, who was the first president of the National Baptist Convention U.S.A.[3] He developed his doctrinal and church government differences with Charles Jones and had a personal pentecostal experience under the ministry of William Seymour. These gifts and experiences helped Mason attract the masses to a yearly gathering called a holy convocation.

History of the Convocation

The annual holy convocation united elements of the annual revival (popular among black Christians in the middle and late slave period in the United States) and the holiness camp meeting (popularized by the National Holiness Association in the late nineteenth century and later, by the pentecostal Azusa Street revival of 1906-1908).[4]

From 1907 through 1960 – fifty-three years – Charles Mason did everything within his power to capture and perpetuate the same atmosphere that he appreciated so deeply at the Azusa Street revival of 1906-1909 and also to preserve the spiritual-cultural idiom of his slave forebears. Through the personal charisma of Mason, the Church of God in Christ was structured fluidly. The leaders, on the one hand, desired to defer to the leading of the Spirit and wanted to avoid the weaknesses of the Azusa revival. On the other hand, leaders in the Church of God in Christ did not want to emulate the frustrating contentions that seemed to be built into the Baptist conventions.

Moreover, Mason and the early leaders carefully based their vision, structure, and gatherings on what they contended were biblical models. They also desired to be experientially relevant. Mason and his colleagues found their biblical model in a description

74

of the agrarian economy of ancient Israel. They discerned in that economy a similarity to their farm life. The following verses shaped the way they organized denominational gatherings:

> Speak unto the children of Israel, and say unto them, Concerning the feasts of the Lord, which ye shall proclaim to be holy convocations, even these are my feasts . . . an holy convocation; ye shall do no work therein: it is the sabbath of the Lord in all your dwellings. These are the feasts of the Lord, even holy convocations, which ye shall proclaim in their seasons (Leviticus 23:2-4).

> Gather my saints together unto me; those that have made a covenant with me by sacrifice (Psalm 50:5).

Their strong African base and their marginal life in the United States motivated the early black holiness-pentecostal founding fathers and mothers to link the spiritual and the temporal.[5] The unique spirituality gave the Saints their own sense of reality. The gatherings were designed to ground the Saints in their unique identity. In racist America the poor and oppressed needed another sense of reality, not an escape from their historical marginalized existence but a transcendent sense that informed and gave meaning to the present. The convocation became a strengthening, transforming experience. At Memphis, Tennessee, headquarters for the Church of God in Christ, members of the church and the black community at large gathered with the Saints.

A Sacred Time

William Turner, theology professor at Duke University Divinity School, in his enlightening doctoral dissertation on the history of the United Holy Church of America, says the convocation was for the Saints, as for ancient Israel, a "sacred time." The opening moment, like a threshold, stood at the juncture between the profane time measured by calendars and clocks and "real time" that gives life meaning.[6]

It was Jubilee, a time to put aside the routine, the social, political, and economic pressures, and to convene. Held annually from November 25 to December 14, the convocation allowed the farmer-preachers and evangelists to harvest their crops and save a few dollars to travel to Memphis. From across the country, the preachers, evangelists, missionaries, and auxiliary leaders of the Church of God in Christ would come together and travel to Memphis. They hastened to be there for the three-day, three-night fast. Dr. Turner, in a 1983 interview with Bishop J. T. Bowen, heard this description of the convocation:[7]

> The institution of convocation required its observance with feasting and no laborious work (Lev. 23:4-8). The "ingathering" of convocation was a repeat of the return of God's scattered people who came from the East, the West, the North, and the South to Zion.
>
> Bishop Fisher cited this meaning in his message to the 1936 Quadrennial Convocation by quoting from Zephaniah 2:1 and Psalm 50:5: "Gather yourselves together, yea, gather together, O nation not desired.... Gather my saints together unto me; those that have made a covenant with me by sacrifice!"[8]
>
> The very name given to the session is bound with its manifold meaning; for the name "convocation" was deliberately chosen instead of other names such as conference, convention, general assembly, or camp meeting. These mothers and fathers, being simplistic in their approach to God and the Scriptures, saw where the Israelites were instructed, "Ye shall have a holy convocation." Work normally associated with conferences and conventions was incorporated, but not in such a way that the focus on prayer, praise, preaching, and refreshing would be lost.

For the black holiness-pentecostal people generally, whether the Church of God in Christ, the United Holy Church, the Fire-Baptized, Mt. Calvary Holiness, or others, the convocation began and ended the "sacred year." Turner observes that this Jubilee time belonged to neither the year that was ending nor the year that was beginning. He called it an "interlude" that contained the potential of a *kairos* moment.[9]

Those *kairos* moments contained an experience of ultimate reality that affirmed significance and value for a people otherwise degraded because they were black, poor, followers of a "holiness" doctrine, and scorned even by the larger black church world, not to mention mainline white Christianity and the secular world at large.[10]

The convocation provided an opportunity to fellowship with a large number of Saints from around the country, giving one a sense of renewed determination. Delegates heard testimonies of victory and blessing that inspired faith and courage to sustain them when they returned home to the "battlefields." Those who often felt small, forsaken, and helpless gained a renewed sense of worth. The sacred time[11] charged one with life, vigor, vitality, vision, and purpose sufficient for another year of service for Christ and His church. The experience of convocation reminded each participant that he or she was a part of something greater, grander, and mightier than what the member experienced on a day to day basis.

The Convocation Program

From its inception at Memphis, Tennessee, under the strong and charismatic leadership of Charles Mason, the Annual Holy Convocation of the Church of God in Christ began with seventy-two hours, three days and nights of fasting and prayer in the Temple. The three-day fast was a "gesture away from the living space being left behind and the ritual act indicating that the Saints had arrived at their destination."

There were no lengthy treatises on the purpose of the convocation. But the Saints knew what they were about. Mason and the fathers and mothers (the state overseers and state mothers) who led delegations from various parts of the country to the convocation at Memphis carefully stressed the dependence of the Saints individually and the church collectively on God more than upon human structures.

Mason merited his reputation as a most prayerful saint, remaining on his knees nine hours at a time.[12] Mason as Chief Apostle and General Overseer led the prayer. He taught that during the cruel days of oppression the slaves had no institution but the "Invisible Institution." Poor black slaves built their lives around their dependence upon God, rising before day to pray. Mason's annual messages stressed that blacks and the nation as a whole had strayed from dependence upon God, instead putting ultimate trust in intellectual and scientific progress.

The convocation was twenty-one days of nonstop prayer, Bible teaching, testimonies, preaching, singing, laying before the Lord, listening for a word from the Lord, miracles of healing, midnight to morning evangelistic services, and pentecostal celebration.[13] Until recently, historians have called the convocation a ritual of magical trappings of the past.[14] Sociologists have short-sightedly said that when people have been subjected to a life of misery and persecution, they tend to demand passionate religion.[15] Black folk religion, they have said, rather than searching for political and secular solutions to oppression, escapes from the troubles of this world by dwelling on the rewards of the next.

In the rituals of the convocations, the Saints were involved in an act of remembrance that was more than simple inner reflection. Just as in Israel, where each successive generation witnessed in faith to a reality that could be encountered by observing tradition, so the Saints, envisioning themselves the new Israel of God, encountered the God of Israel through rituals commemorating specific historical moments.

To the casual or intellectual/scientific observer, the gathering of black people with their investment of emotional intensity in religious celebration might appear an escapist ritual in response to oppression or social marginality. To the initiated, however, the convocation had a far more significant purpose than the mere en-gendering of enthusiasm. Convocation was the means for translat-ing the manifestation of the sacred that had given rise and distinc-tion to this "holy people."[16] In the convocation, the ritual – the prayer, the praise, the testimony, the "frenzy" (to use DuBois' term for shouting), and above all the preaching – were fragments of origi-nal events that called out a people separated unto God.

Fired by Zeal

The purpose of the convocation was to preserve through rep-etition and reenforcement the essence of the original events. Ma-son deliberately tried to preserve and maintain an experience or series of experiences. As it was with Mason and his co-laborers, so it was with H. L. Fisher and the leaders of the United Holy Church of America and W. E. Fuller of the Fire-Baptized Church in America. These leaders, in articulating the purpose of convocation, repeated specifically Zephaniah 2:1, "Gather yourselves together, yea, gather together, O nation not desired" and Psalm 50:5, "Gather my saints together unto me; those that have made a covenant with me by sacrifice."

Convocation provided a time for the members to hear the stories of the mothers and fathers and the meaning of being a "holy people." Why was this important? Leaders wanted successive gen-erations to experience God by the Holy Spirit and gain a sense of being *called out* and *called to* service. Convocation provided the sacred time and space whereby those in attendance could be in-spired by the narratives and fired by the original zeal. As they caught the meaning of the original vision, they returned to their places with a mighty increase of strength by the Holy Spirit in the inner man (Ephesians 3:16). It gave concreteness to the deepest longing for an alternative to the world of trials, and an empowerment to engage the world of trials.[17]

In black holiness-pentecostalism, each individual is expected to experience a personal baptism of the Holy Spirit. Both the community and the individual have charisma (gifts of the Spirit) that have to be nurtured. In this process, the convocation is a movement toward organic wholeness. The convocation gave to the new member of the Church of God in Christ a directed retreat setting in which he or she could resolve the "Who am I?" question through a felt resonance with the denomination's story.

As the Church of God in Christ spread from one state to another and overseas to Europe, Africa, and Asia, the convocation at Memphis became the model for state convocations. State convocations[18] became the bases for building the organizational integrity of the church. Convocations of the Church of God in Christ have become the primary settings for transacting ecclesiastical operations.

Convocation leaders attempt to create community, to preserve the integrity of the church as a viable and value-disseminating moral agency. They attempt to reconcile the church and the larger community, particularly the African-American community. They finally seek to bridge the chasm between the rapidly expanding secular underclass and the upwardly mobile middle class in the African-American community.

Today, the Annual Holy Convocation at Memphis, with its 40,000 to 50,000 delegates pouring some 25 million dollars into that city's economy, is by far the largest annual convocation gathering during the year. The church's 110 jurisdictional convocations draw from 1,000 to 10,000 persons, profoundly impacting many cities.[19]

Earlier this century, the U.S. population gradually began to shift from rural to urban centers. This transition also impacted the Church of God in Christ, challenging it to meet the different needs of city dwellers. Let's look at the spread of the denomination in urban areas.

6

MOVING INTO THE CITY

R evolutionary changes occurred in the United States during the formative years of the Church of God in Christ (1895-1914). The country rapidly moved from a rural/agricultural economy to an industrial/urban one.[1] The transition began in the mid-nineteenth century with its first great thrust for blacks occurring in the years immediately following the Civil War.

In 1850, less than 13 percent of all Americans lived in cities, and only nine of these cities contained more than 50,000 people. In the 1880 census, 25 percent lived in the cities. By 1920, over half of all Americans lived in urban clusters. At mid-twentieth century, 60 percent of Americans made their homes in the city.

America, 1890-1920, was not only the locus of a clash between the South and the North, between black and white, but also between two cultures – one static, individualistic, agricultural; the other, dynamic, collectivistic, urban. Booker T. Washington, whose Atlanta Exposition Speech of 1895 thrust him forth as the new spokesperson for black America, was shrewd enough to sense this clash in the American psyche and urged newly freed blacks to exploit it. W. E. B. DuBois decried the price that Washington was willing to pay for such a vision and eloquently denounced his accommodationism.

In the South, black Americans lived under terrible cruelty. C. Eric Lincoln best depicts their perilous existence. He says:

> Floods, crop failures, boll weevils, and night-riding Klansman all served to hasten the Negro's exodus from the South. One hundred Negroes were lynched during the first year of the twentieth century. By the outbreak of World War I, in 1914, the number lynched stood at 1,100. When the war was over, the practice was resumed; Twenty-eight Negroes were burned alive between 1918 and 1921. Scores of others were dispatched by equally cruel methods.[2]

In the Mississippi Delta, where the Church of God in Christ was founded, the lynch mob and flaming cross symbolized the enforcers of hate-filled white supremacy. In his characteristic vivid and picturesque language, Lincoln says that in the last sixteen years of the nineteenth century, 2,600 human beings were sacrificed to the rope and fagot. And from 1900 to the outbreak of World War I in 1914, "seventy-eight black men and women graced the magnolias or popped and sputtered in the bonfires before the altar of white supremacy."[3] Small wonder southern blacks should largely ignore Washington's accommodationist challenge to "cast down your buckets where you are."[4] Blacks left the South for the North and West in increasing numbers.

Between 1910 and 1920, net migration of Negroes from the South was 454,000; between 1920-1930, about 750,000; from 1930-1940, 347,000; between 1940-1950, 1.2 million; and between 1950-1960, 1.5 million.[5]

Fleeing from intensifying racial violence in the South, Negroes searched for more and better employment opportunities, and, during the Great Depression of the 1930s, the availability of public welfare (then called Home Relief). By 1965, 75 percent of the black population lived in cities – and half of it in the northern cities. By 1980, New York had the largest black population of any city (1.7 million), followed by Chicago (1.2 million), Detroit (758,939), Philadelphia (638,878), and Los Angeles (505,210).[6]

Beginning in 1970, blacks led a gradual reverse migration to the South and sunshine states of the Southwest. Studies indicate that during the 1970s the South gained more than 259,000 black reverse migrants.[7] The causes for this reverse migration are complex. A new South emerged with the civil rights movement led by Martin Luther King, Jr. The relocation of industry from the North to escape high taxes and strong labor unions made available increased employment opportunities in the South. Besides this, drugs, crime, and depressing living conditions in the northern and western urban ghettoes undermined the northern dream of black people.

Impact on the Church

Scholars Lincoln, Mamiya, Franklin, and Turner give a detailed accounting of the massive migration of black Americans and the multifaceted meanings of that fascinating drama for black life – particularly its meanings for the black church. Franklin reminded us that the urbanization of black Christianity was not altogether a twentieth-century phenomenon, although it did not assume massive proportion and increased velocity until the period following the first World War. He points out that during the late eighteenth century independent black churches were founded by free blacks in northern cities.

Richard Allen and Absolom Jones, for instance, established the African Methodist Episcopal Church and the black Episcopal churches in 1794 and 1796, respectively. Following the Civil War, many blacks went to the urban areas of the South, seeking the protection of union troops. Many left the plantations to assert their freedom and to nourish their sense of personhood that for so long had been crushed.[8]

The twentieth century, however, opened a new chapter in black urban migration, similar to the massive European immigration that occurred in the same period. The black church, like the Catholic church, and to a lesser degree the mainline Protestant churches, faced the challenge of resettling and reorienting hundreds of thousands of newcomers.[9]

What is the significance of the massive migration of Negroes to the urban centers of the South, North, and West? The Church of God in Christ experienced rapid expansion and explosive growth in the cities.

Mission Churches Begin

Between 1900-1961, C. H. Mason watched the Church of God in Christ evolve into a national, largely urban, African-American denomination.[10] From its fountainhead in the region of the southern Mississippi River, Mason's co-laborers – men and women – traveled to the northern industrial cities to evangelize the migrating masses.

Between 1912-1914, Bishop Mason sent from Mississippi, Tennessee, and Arkansas a large number of preachers and female missionaries. To Texas, he sent Elder E. M. Page; to Kansas, he sent D. J. Young; to Missouri, he sent V. M. Barker and D. Bostic; to Illinois, he sent Lillian Brooks Coffey and soon thereafter Elder W. M. Roberts; to Ohio, he sent Mack E. Jonas; to New York, he sent Mother Maydie Payton and her husband, Elder Charles Payton; to California, he sent Elder E. R. Driver; to Michigan, he sent Mother Mary Johnson and her husband, Elder William G. Johnson.

To the emerging southern cities, he also sent trusted co-laborers who were materially poor but spiritually rich. He sent Elders Henry and Feltus to Louisiana; Elders O. T. Jones and Arthur Jones to Oklahoma; Elder S. T. Samuel to North Carolina, and A. J. Reed to Virginia. All these leaders had strong talents, natural abilities, and force of character and personality. They were fiercely loyal to Mason.

Leaders with the talents and force of character that Mason possessed frequently tend to overpower or override others; they tend to gather around them, those persons whose gifts do not overshadow theirs. Not so with Mason. He viewed himself as a spiritual catalyst.

Mason attracted strong and gifted men and women. He fired them up, sent them out, and turned them loose to proclaim the gospel of an unconsenting conscience to the majority culture on the basis of Scripture. Mother Mary Magnum Johnson's personal reflections, written in the 1930s, give us insight into typical Church of God in Christ mission churches during the urban migrations. She wrote the following letter for her husband:

> We left Memphis, Tennessee, March 16, 1914 for Detroit, Michigan. We began work among the colored people. God gave me to rent a mission for Him. I paid my last eighteen dollars for it. I did not have money to pay the man for moving, so I helped him to load the things, and I left trusting in the Lord to give me the money to pay him. So on my way to the mission, the streets gave me enough money to pay him. Then we had nothing to eat. I borrowed twenty-five cents to buy supper and gave it to my wife. She asked me, "What are you going to do?" I replied, "I will do without." My wife then said, "I know it is the Lord, who makes you willing to suffer, praise His Name." She had one dollar which I did not know she had, so she gave it to me. I bought food for us both, and we were glad and happy that the Lord counted us worthy to suffer for His Name that other souls might be saved.[11]

Mother Johnson recounts how the white Evening Light Saints[12] worked with them to establish the Church of God in Christ in Michigan. On street corners in Detroit and Pontiac and other cities, they held evangelistic rallies to which blacks and whites responded. Mother Johnson recounts how Bishop Mason constantly traveled to visit them to encourage and oversee the spread of the work. She also recounts that as the Assemblies of God and other white pentecostal denominations began their work in Michigan, the white Saints gradually withdrew.

The founding of the Church of God in Christ in Michigan reflected a similar pattern of development in numerous northern and western cities – New York, Newark, Baltimore, Chicago, St. Louis, Kansas City, Denver, Las Vegas, Los Angeles, and San Francisco.

Explosive Growth

Many studies of black urban churches during the period from 1915 to 1950 indicate that the black church as a whole experienced phenomenal growth, not only in the membership rolls of the older, established mainline churches but also in the founding of numerous new churches, often started in rented storefronts in the poorer sections of the city.[13] In their study, Mays and Nicholson reported that a comparison of the figures given in the *Federal Census of Religious Bodies* of five northern cities (Chicago, Detroit, Cincinnati, Philadelphia, and Baltimore) showed a 151 percent increase in the number of black Baptist churches and a 200 percent increase in Baptist membership between 1916-1926; the AME churches in these cities showed an increase of 124 percent for churches and 85 percent for members.[14]

Lincoln and Mamiya assert that the phenomenal growth in church membership and the rise of new urban churches and storefronts did not represent a major spiritual revival bringing in new converts, but the growth represented a transfer of membership from rural to urban ones.

About 10 percent, mainly the upper class in black Chicago, were attracted to the predominantly white denominations such as the Episcopal, Congregational, or Presbyterian churches. The middle class were usually Baptist or Methodist and occasionally Roman Catholic.

The membership of the Sanctified churches (holiness and pentecostal storefronts) were persons of low status.[15] The Church of God in Christ was viewed as one of a plethora of aberrational religious groups that competed for the souls of the lower-class black masses.

Los Angeles and Eddie R. Driver, Sr.

The ethnohistory of Saints Home Church of Los Angeles, the first Church of God in Christ to be established in the western part of the United States, provides a clear example of the dynamics that transformed the church into a rapidly growing urban denomination.

In 1914, Charles Mason urged Elder Eddie R. Driver, Sr. of Memphis, Tennessee, one of his best and most formally-trained preachers, to answer the call of some praying mothers who had migrated from Texas to Los Angeles. Mothers Millie Crawford, Martha Armstrong, Rosie Tucker, Thomas, Catley, Emma Cotton, and Mattie Cummings had written. Several of these mothers – Cotton, Cummings, and Catley _ were veterans of the Azusa Street revival. They gathered a host of saints who were left wandering when the Azusa Street revival ended. They were of various racial and ethnic groups – blacks, whites, Mexicans, Filipino. Through Elder Page, whom Mason had sent to pioneer the work in Texas and Oklahoma, these Saints learned of Mason, Driver, and the Church of God in Christ. The late Bishop Samuel Crouch said of Driver's migration to California:

In 1914, when he was on his way out here to California, I was in Dallas at the time, and I remember he came down from Memphis, en route to California, and he stopped in the city because he didn't have his fare; so there was a sister there named Florence Drake and she gave him $100 so he could have his fare.[16]

When Driver arrived in Los Angeles, he was amazed by the mixed congregation of people attending the services at the Apostolic Mission at 14th and Woodson Streets. Being from Mississippi and Tennessee, he was not accustomed to all races worshiping together in equality and apparently without regard to color or nationality. Yet he had preached in many churches other than the black church.

Driver himself was of mixed ancestry and could easily, but for his strong sense of black culture, been mistaken for Mexican or Filipino. Driver was a powerful preacher and a sharp-tongued man whom God used mightily. Souls were saved and bodies were healed. The Church of God in Christ, unknown before his coming, became established. He was an organizer, a civil rights activist, and a businessman.

Born in 1869 in Nesbit, Mississippi, Driver graduated from LeMoyne Normal School in Memphis, Tennessee, and returned to his hometown to teach school. He married Annie Smith in 1890 and returned to LeMoyne to study law. In 1892, he was permitted to practice general and corporation law in Memphis, Tennessee. In 1893, he accepted the call to preach. He was licensed and became a pastor in 1894. He pastored Salem Baptist Church of Memphis, Tennessee, until 1896. He was deeply affected by the powerful ministry of Charles H. Mason and the brethren of the "sanctified movement." Because he accepted Mason's views, the Baptist Church dismissed him. He became chairman of the Council of Elders of the Church of God in Christ. He wrote the original Articles of Incorporation for the organization and filed them in Washington, D.C.[17]

At Los Angeles in 1914, the congregation outgrew the Apostolic Mission and asked Driver to pastor them. The mission moved to larger quarters at 15th and Santa Fe Streets. The Saints rented the building, which had been a Methodist Church. News of the church spread through Los Angeles, a cosmopolitan, religiously

Bishop C. H. Mason Meets with Older Overseers - Mason Temple, Memphis, Tennessee. Just after 1945
Front Row (left to right): Overseer J. H. Boone, Overseer Charles Pleas, Bishop C. H. Mason, Overseer W. M. Roberts, Overseer S. M. Crouch
Back Row (left to right): Overseer Taylor, Overseer C. E. Bennett, Overseer J. S. Bailey, Overseer A. B. McKewan, Overseer V. M. Barker

Bishop C. H. Mason receives Proclamation from the Mayor on Civic Night of Convocation - Mason Temple, Memphis, Tennessee. 1949 or 1950
Left to right: Bishop O. T. Jones, Sr.; Bishop Charles Pleas; Bishop A. B. McKewan; The Honorable Wyeth Chandler, Mayor of Memphis; Robert (Bob) Mason, Bishop
C. H. Mason's oldest son; Bishop C. H. Mason; Bishop C. E. Bennett; Mother Lillian Brooks-Coffey; Bishop J. O. Patterson; J. Burns, Assistant to the Mayor

The Dedication of the COGIC Publishing House - Memphis, Tennessee. About 1951

Front Row (left to right): Bishop Cornelius Range, Bishop O. M. Kelly, Bishop J. O. Patterson, Bishop U. E. Miller, Bishop J. S. Bailey, Bishop C. H. Mason, Bishop A. B. McEwan, Bishop O. T. Jones, Sr., Bishop S. M. Crouch, Bishop Wyoming Wells, Bishop F. D. Washington. Back Row (left to right): Bishop L. H. Ford, Bishop C. L. Anderson, Sr., Bishop John White, Bishop C. E. Bennett, Bishop R. E. Ranger, Bishop J. Neaul Haynes, Bishop B. S. Lyle, Bishop David D. C. Love, Unknown, Bishop T. D. Inglehart, Bishop A. M. Cohen

91

Members of the Building Committee that was responsible for the building of Mason Temple - U. E. Miller Hall at Mason Temple, Memphis, Tennessee. 1945
Seated (left to right): Overseer U. E. Miller, General Secretary of the Church and Architect of Mason Temple; Overseer W. G. Shipman, Chairman, Pastors and Elders Council
Standing (left to right): Overseer A. B. McKewan; Elder James Delk; Elder Morris; Bishop C. H. Mason; Overseer C. C. Cox; Bishop R. F. Williams, Chairman, Building
Committee; Mother Lillian Brooks-Coffey; Overseer Wyoming Wells; Bishop O. T. Jones, Sr.; Superintendent L. C. Patrick; Overseer Howard Dell, Unknown

The Pastors and Elders Council - The U. E. Miller Hall at Mason Temple, Memphis, Tennessee. 1949
Seated (left to right): Bishop J. Howard Dell, Secretary, Pastors and Elders Council; Bishop Pickens, Vice Chairman, Pastors and Elders Council Standing (left to right):
Bishop J. O. Patterson; Bishop C. H. Mason; Officer Pelmo Berkley, Memphis Police; Officer Ben Whitney, Memphis Police; Bishop W. G. Shipman, Chairman,
Pastors and Elders Council; Officer R. J. Turner, Memphis Police; Officer Joel Jobent, Memphis Police; Unseen; Bishop L. O. Swingler; Bishop A. B. McKewan

93

Women's Day, 67th Annual Convocation
Mason Temple, Memphis, Tennessee. 1974
Standing at podium: Mother Annie Lee Bailey, International Supervisor,
Women's Department, Church of God in Christ

Remembering Bishop L. H. Ford
St. Paul Church of God in Christ, Chicago, Illinois. April 1995
Left to right: Bishop Chandler D. Owens, Presiding Bishop, Church of God in Christ
Reverend Dr. Clay Evans, Bishop Ithiel C. Clemmons

President Bill Clinton with the General Board and Board of Directors of the Church of God in Christ International Women's Convention, New Orleans, Louisiana. Thursday, May 30, 1996

experimental city. Rumors much like those about the Azusa Street revival circulated and drew curious visitors.

In 1915, Driver sent for his family to come from Memphis. He had established a strong church that, after much debate, was incorporated as The Saints Home Church of the Church of God in Christ. Its trustee board and various auxiliaries were fully integrated with blacks, caucasians, Mexicans, and Filipinos. The mother of the church, a Mother Hubert, was caucasian according to Louis Driver, the son of Eddie, who succeeded his father as pastor of Saints Home Church.

Convocation in Los Angeles (1916)

In the summer of 1916, Mason was invited to hold a thirty-day convocation. The first Church of God in Christ convocation on the West Coast was held under a large tent across the street from Saints Home Church's first building. Elder O. T. Jones, a young preacher of twenty-three from Fort Smith, Arkansas, accompanied Mason to Los Angeles. This convocation drew hundreds of all races. The joyful, upbeat, celebrative worship of the Church of God in Christ, its continuous evangelistic preaching that went on night and day, and the reports of miraculous healings attracted hundreds of people.

During the 1916 convocation, Mason appointed Elder Eddie Robert Driver, Sr. as state overseer and his wife, Sister Annie Driver, as state mother.[18] This appointment was the beginning of the urban outreach of the Church of God in Christ throughout the western states of the United States. The convocation became an annual event.

Why is the convocation of June 1916 important? It set the pattern for the urban organization of the Church of God in Christ.

From Interracial to Black Constituency

From 1918-1922, the Church of God in Christ in Los Angeles slowly became predominantly black. Why did this transition occur? Sister Aimee Semple McPherson had often worshiped at Saints Home Church before launching her own ministry. When she organized the Foursquare Group in the Glendale section of the city and began to build Angelus Temple, many of the whites who were part of the Church of God in Christ began to follow her.[19] Slowly the white Saints left the Church of God in Christ. By the time Angelus Temple was completed, its outreach through radio attracted a major portion of the white members of the Church of God in Christ. McPherson and Driver remained friends, exchanged pulpits, and at times held fellowship services.

Eyewitnesses report that Driver was quite blunt about civil rights. One eyewitness reported:

> White people began to leave, because he [E. R. Driver] would talk so bad about them. He stood up and said a lot of civil rights things about white people, much like the Black Power people say today . . . ! "A white man don't mind if you marry his daughter, but he don't want me to marry his wife's daughter!" And after a while, it began to dawn on the whites what he was saying, and he drove them away. People began to leave there.[20]

Although the ethnic makeup of the church was changed, some of the caucasian officers, such as Deacon Saterwhite and other members, remained at Saints Home Church until they died.

Meeting the Urban Challenge

Observers unacquainted with historical development of the Church of God in Christ have often held the notion that the church's emphasis on personal experience of the Holy Spirit caused it to withdraw into revivalistic Christianity and defensive political and social accommodationism. The church was viewed within black Christianity as a politically passive sect.

But the record shows that preachers sent by Mason from the rural ministries in Mississippi, Tennessee, Arkansas, and Louisiana to the urban centers of the South and North were successful in meeting the overwhelming urban challenge. Strong charismatic leaders, they shared Mason's vision of cultural nonconformity, which included not simply the preservation of the best features of Slave Religion but also a commitment to replicating the nonracist early church and creating a just society. William Roberts in Chicago (1914), E. M. Page in Dallas (1913), C. C. Fredrick in Pittsburgh (1916), R. F. Williams in Atlanta and Birmingham, Mark E. Jonas in Cleveland, S. P. Nesbitt in Jacksonville, A. M. Cohen in Miami, and Frank Clemmons in New York (1923) were strong leaders who established congregations that unified people of various backgrounds under great stresses of religious criticism, political powerlessness, and economic deprivation.

We could frame the overwhelming urban challenge in the form of several questions, says Robert Franklin of Chandler Divinity School:

> Could a premodern, intimate, southern Christianity flourish in a secular, impersonal northern culture? Was compromise necessary and permissible? What responses could be offered when religion as the social cement of family and community life began to weaken under the peculiar urban strains of individualism, impersonal competitiveness, materialism, unemployment, organized political conflict, and institutionalized racism? To that list of centripetal urban pulls there must also be added now the underworld of drugs, guns, and crime.[21]

The phenomenal growth of the Church of God in Christ in the urban areas of the United States, the upward mobility of its membership through its rigorous moral codes, and its contemporary influence on mainline black Christianity makes the affirmative response to the above questions obvious. The Church of God in Christ experienced dramatic growth for two reasons:

1. The oral culture of African-American religion received a far greater opportunity for free expression than in the mainline churches.

2. While the language of "soul winning" resembled the terms employed by white fundamentalist churches, the Church of God in Christ wed evangelism to home mission work in its own unique manner. The church mothers and missionaries went into the ghettoes, tenement houses, and public housing projects to care for children, to pray for the sick, to teach homemaking skills. They were unashamed to have street worship services, to approach and talk to gangs of roving, idle youth.

Like Driver and Saints Home Church, these leaders established a tradition of meeting the urgent social needs of people experiencing the traumas of great social dislocation. They nurtured and empowered the large migrating masses by proclaiming the reality of serving a present God who would bring power and joy into the life of a person who had been regenerated and filled with the Spirit. No particular social status was necessary to become a believer or member. These elements resulted in the tremendous growth of the Church of God in Christ, especially in the cities.

Women were very instrumental as the Church of God in Christ moved into urban areas. Two church mothers spearheaded much of the women's ministry in the early days of the denomination. Let's look at the forces that influenced women's work and the dynamic lives of these female leaders.

7

MOTHERS ROBERSON AND COFFEY – PIONEERS OF WOMEN'S WORK: 1911-1964

Adrienne M. Israel [1]

In 1911, only four years after its incorporation as a pentecostal denomination, the Church of God in Christ established a women's department that transformed women's work. What other denominations had relegated to a secondary auxiliary status became an essential force at the center of church growth and sustenance.

In the early years, from 1911 to 1945, women helped establish new churches and stabilized essential areas of church work. Their labor sustained the denomination through its formative years as a struggling maverick group composed primarily of poor southern farmers, farm workers, washerwomen, and maids.

By forming a unique church structure reminiscent of sociopolitical systems developed by their West African ancestors and transformed by slave societies, the denomination harnessed the spiritual fervor, mental acumen, physical energy, and economic potential of its female members while maintaining male authority. As a result, the church cultivated female leadership without alienating the men, took advantage of women's abilities to "plant" new congregations without authorizing them to preach or pastor, and established an auxiliary structure that sustained basic pentecostal-holiness doctrine through periods of strife among the church's male leaders.

The Church of God in Christ was founded during a crucial stage in African-American history: the first decade of the twentieth century when black women organized independent clubs to promote their image and interests, established schools and colleges, staged protests against lynching and white mob violence, and joined white women to press for social reform, including temperance and woman's suffrage. By 1911, black political leaders were openly challenging what had become a traditional black loyalty to the Republican Party.

Given the entrenchment of segregation and near total loss of black political influence, black leaders sought an alternative to the patient, accomodationist approach of Booker T. Washington. Upwardly mobile black church leaders had stressed conformity to white religious norms as a key to black success. But the leadership of the Church of God in Christ opposed mainstream religious ideas and many of the social aspirations of the small, but influential, black middle class.

A Minority Voice

The Church of God in Christ was a minority voice in black religion, both in terms of its ideas and sheer numbers. In 1906, a year before the denomination's first national convocation, the vast majority of all black church members were either Baptist or Methodist with Baptists clearly dominating African-American religious life. Numerically, Methodists came in a distant second.

In 1906, about one-third of all African Americans claimed church membership: 3.6 million out of a total population of 9.8 million;[2] 3.2 million belonged to independent black denominations. The rest were Roman Catholics, Presbyterians, and members of the predominately white Northern Baptist Convention, most of whom worshiped in separate black congregations under white ecclesiastical control.

Of the 3.2 million members of independent black denominations, 2.2 million belonged to the National Baptist Convention. Another 50,000 were Primitive and Freewill Baptists. The African Methodist Episcopal (AME) churches had less than a half million members, the AME Zion churches about 180,000 and the Colored Methodist Episcopal (CME) another 170,000.[3] The tiny minority of new holiness denominations had a combined total of only about 5,000 members.[4]

The Role of Women

After it adopted the pentecostal teaching on tongues (glossolalia), the Church of God in Christ began to attract spiritual seekers from the dominant church groups. As Baptist and Methodist women began to join the denomination in large numbers, their work needed structure. Bishop C. H. Mason organized women's work within the context of important historical forces as well as his own determination to preserve the spiritual heritage of his slave parents.

One of the prevailing historical forces at the turn of the century was the role of women in the nineteenth century holiness revival and its pentecostal offspring. Both movements encouraged public leadership roles for women in ministry. During this era women spoke in public as preachers and evangelists and pastored churches at a rate unequaled since.

Women evangelists were common at holiness camp meetings in the late nineteenth century. The pentecostal movement, ushered in at the 1906 Azusa Street revival in Los Angeles, created a brief but intense period of religious leadership and public ministry for women. An estimated 3,000 female clergy served Christian congregations at the turn of the century.[5]

Although their numbers declined sharply after 1920, when the Church of God in Christ was laying its organizational base, mainline Protestant churches had yielded to women's demands for recognition by creating the deaconess position and women's auxiliaries such as home and foreign mission departments.

In the first half of the nineteenth century male holiness preachers, especially Presbyterian and Methodist ministers, had encouraged women to testify in public about their experiencing "entire sanctification and heart purity."[6] These public testimonies led to women being allowed to conduct Bible readings in which they expounded on a passage of Scripture in a manner nearly indistinguishable from a sermon. Bible readings led to public preaching, and by the turn of the century, women spoke regularly in newly founded holiness churches. Some were ordained to preach and pastor.[7] This egalitarianism carried over into the pentecostal movement whose early leaders were as often female as they were male.

The Self-Help Movement

A second historical force that influenced the formation of women's ministry in the denomination was the black self-help movement. When compromise ended the Reconstruction era, the federal government yielded to former confederates by phasing out legal protection and compensatory aid for freed slaves. This left black southerners to suffer the exploitation of an economy that fixed their wages below the poverty level and a society that suppressed their aspirations through white vigilante terrorism. The federal government continued limited support for black education. Northern philanthropists contributed money to black schools, but the former slaves were shut out of most economic and political opportunities.

Their leaders grasped education as the key to upward mobility from poverty and ignorance. They also determined to protect black women from sexual assault and exploitation. Black communities concentrated on educating women, and the newly educated women embraced the slogan "lifting as we climb" to express their aim to achieve personal success and help others do the same. This zeal to "improve the race" through education survived into the early twentieth century despite escalating anti-black mob violence and the tightening grip of racial segregation. A growing corps of black women educators participated in community affairs and helped establish direction for black organizations, including the church.

Women's Suffrage

A third force that formed the context in which women's ministry developed was the women's suffrage movement. Suffrage activists often belonged initially to temperance groups, the largest of which was the Woman's Christian Temperance Union (WCTU), the first national women's organization controlled by women.

Black women participated in the WCTU from its inception. Many of them later joined and supported suffrage even though white women suffrage leaders refused to denounce white mob lynching of black men accused of raping white women. The fervor of suffrage rhetoric extended to African-American communities where men were more likely to support women's rights than were their white male counterparts.

These three historical forces — the holiness and pentecostal revivals, the black self-help movement, and woman's suffrage — helped produce a climate conducive to black women's emerging as prominent leaders in the early years of the Church of God in Christ. Because they fail to completely explain the character of the women's ministry, however, we must also look to the denomination's founder.

Mason's Influence

C. H. Mason's resolve to preserve elements of slave religion may have been the determining factor in the formation of women's ministry. The slave heritage included two essential elements that Mason carried over into the denomination:

1. The principle of spiritual equality, which allowed women free expression of their spiritual gifts.

2. The ideal of shared social responsibility in which women worked side by side with men in community life as well as in the fields.

Slave tradition allowed women to wield authority in spiritual and civil matters, but preserved ultimate authority for a male leader: the father in the slave home and the male pastor in the slave church. The slave heritage derived from a joining of slavery's necessities and selected customs inherited from Africa and transformed by years of fusion. In many areas of West Africa women commonly functioned as priestesses and diviners, and pre-Christian, non-Muslims often worshiped female gods.

After converting to Christianity, American slaves reflected the strict patriarchal values of white mainline Protestant churches to which their masters belonged. Although white Christians may have restricted women from expressing themselves in church, black slaves did not.

West African Roots

As C. Eric Lincoln noted in his epic study of black religion in North America, "The African strain in their African-American heritage . . . made possible prominent roles in religion for women both in Africa and on American plantations."[8]

In addition to their prominence in spiritual matters among many of the West African societies, women wielded authority over specific areas of life set apart as their domain, such as farming, marketing, trading, or household and family affairs.[9] To institutionalize their power they formed solidarity groups from which they gained a strong "psychological sense of self-esteem." As a result,

African women "were bound to other women through a complex set of associations; that sense of belonging provided the base from which they carried on their day-to-day affairs."[10]

Some West African societies insured women political power that transcended their domain by developing what anthropologists have called a "dual-sex" system. Women's councils not only governed women's affairs but their representatives also voiced women's interests at each level of government from the village to the king's court.

Some societies even crowned two rulers, a male and a female, who lived separately and were never man and wife. These societies have two separately selected leaders; the male heads the overall community while the female heads women's affairs, yet "the entire population pays homage to both monarchs."[11] The dual-sex system involved women in society as office holders, religious leaders, and political advisors. Women participated in community life as a collective pressure group, "interceded with the supernatural on the community's behalf, and shouldered significant responsibility for the general welfare."[12]

Although the dual-sex system gave prominence to women in community affairs, they remained, as a group, subservient to their husbands. Nevertheless, villages sometimes selected outstanding individual women to lead them as chiefs, and some African queens ruled in their own right as heads of empires.[13]

A Rich Heritage

The structure that the Church of God in Christ developed to involve women in the work of the ministry strikingly resembles the West African model in principle and form. Given the continuous influx of slaves into the southern states until the outbreak of the Civil War, African ideas and customs continuously affected slave communities whose members preserved, revised, and transformed them to suit the demands of their new hostile environment.[14]

Slave culture often conflicted with the values and practices of the dominant whites. Labeled a deviant, inferior subculture, slave culture allowed women a social equality at odds with contemporary American values. Slave women worked in the fields with men and returned to their cabins at night to cook and care for the children. They tended small family gardens and sold crafts when they could. The prayer life of Christian slave women rivaled the reputations of male slave preachers for evidence of spiritual power. Many came to slave women late at night for the comfort and support they needed to survive.

C. H. Mason's parents were slaves, and his mother was one of those women known for her power with God in prayer. As an adult, Mason committed himself to preserving the slaves' religious heritage, including their worship styles and reliance on prayer. Implicit in the slaves' religious heritage was the freedom of women to use their spiritual gifts.

Refusing to Conform

Largely conducted out of the sight and hearing of whites, the services of the underground or invisible slave church significantly differed from those held by slaves in the open. The visible black church conformed more to white norms. The invisible church did not.

After emancipation the formerly invisible slave churches began merging into the already established black churches that were pastored by free blacks and ex-slaves. These visible churches were offshoots of mainline white denominations. Free and ex-slave Christians developing their own churches immediately after the Civil War "often accepted into the rules, beliefs, hierarchy, structure, and patriarchal conventions of their white counterparts from whose churches they were now separated."[15]

In contrast to this drive to conform, C. H. Mason stood with those who refused to accept dominant white religious values, including the strict patriarchy of their church structures. Mason decided that the free expression of women's spiritual gifts and the harnessing of their organizational skills were essential to the welfare of black churches and to the preservation of the power that had been evidenced in slave religion.

While he structured into the church a position of authority for women, he restricted their influence by preserving the office of pastor and title of preacher for men. Women expounding on Scripture were said to be teaching — not preaching — and they were allowed to speak only from a secondary lectern, not from the pulpit.

Women's ministry heads remained subject to male authority at three levels: in the local church the church mother would head the women's department and be under the authority of the pastor; at the state level the state mother or state supervisor served under the authority of the state bishop; and at the national level, the national supervisor remained under the authority of the presiding bishop, an office created after Bishop Mason died in 1961.

Functioning in the ambivalent position of shared, but secondary, authority, this system closely resembled the dual sex system that operated in some West African societies. The Church of God in Christ established separate spheres of ministry and power for male and female, allowing the two genders to work "together and in harness"[16] in spiritual warfare. This continually engaged the dynamic of the early slave church. At the same time it preserved the male dominance that conformed the denomination to biblical imperatives and met the psychic needs of an oppressed people.

Mother Roberson — An Early Leader

In 1911, upon the recommendation of Lillian Brooks who later became Lillian Brooks-Coffey, Bishop Mason appointed Lizzie

Woods over the Women's Work, the original name for what became the Women's Department. Woods later remarried and took her husband's name, Roberson. She is hereafter referred to as Mother Roberson.

The denomination gave the title "mother" to the heads of women's work in their churches and to senior women in general. In the original structure of the Church of God in Christ, the church mother acted in the pastor's stead whenever he was absent from the church. Thus all members were bound to respect the authority of the church mother.

Mother Roberson's background illustrates the convergence of spiritual ferment and the striving of her race and gender. She was born April 5, 1860, in Phillips County, Arkansas, where she, her mother, and siblings were freed from slavery with the millions emancipated after the Civil War. Her father died during the war, leaving her mother to raise five small children.

Like other former slaves, her mother wanted a better life for her children and sent them to school for an education. As an eight-year-old child, Mother Roberson began reading the Bible to adults in the community. When she was fifteen, her mother died, leaving her to fend for herself and her siblings.[17]

Accounts of her life differ as to when she married, but a recent biographical sketch by a church historian indicates that her first husband was named Holt. While married to him she gave birth to her only child, Ida Florence Holt. When her first husband died, she married a Mr. Woods, who also apparently died during their marriage.[18] Current research has not confirmed this detail.[19]

Sanctification and Spirit Baptism

Mother Roberson joined a Baptist church in Pine Bluff, Arkansas. Yearning for spiritual growth, she was drawn to the doctrine of sanctification as taught by the holiness revival that Methodists had launched but had been taken up by all denominations.

According to Mother Roberson's account, in 1885 a white Baptist Bible teacher, Miss Joanna P. Moore, began a publication called *Hope*. Mother Roberson recalled, "The women of almost every denomination in the Southland began to read this little paper and to organize Bible bands in their churches."

A native of Pennsylvania, Moore had begun missionary work among freed black people in the South during the Civil War. The first woman appointed by the American Baptist Home Mission Society (ABHMS), Moore settled on an island in the Mississippi River near Memphis in 1863. There she worked with 1,100 black women and children who had fled to the union army for refuge from slavery. In 1864, she moved to Helena, Arkansas, and after the war, between 1868 and 1877, lived in the New Orleans area.[20]

In 1885, Moore began publishing *Hope* in Plaquemine, Louisiana. It contained Sunday school lessons, guides for Bible bands, and instructions on child-rearing and family devotions.[21] Forced to leave Louisiana because she taught "among Negroes,"[22] Moore opened a school for women in Little Rock, Arkansas in 1891 and continued publishing her magazine.

In 1901, Mother Roberson read *Hope* in the Bible band of her church in Pine Bluff, Arkansas. Besides Sunday school lessons and instructions on home management, *Hope* also contained teachings on holiness, which Mother Roberson avidly read.

"I studied this paper until the Lord sanctified me," Mother Roberson recalled. She testified in church that she had received the experience of sanctification.[23] Then she began promoting holiness as a Bible teacher and gained a reputation as an "organizer able to inspire and direct."[24]

She and Moore apparently became friends. Mother Roberson reported Moore's direct influence on her decision to stop working as a washerwoman and enter full-time mission work. She recalled:

> Sister Moore said that she saw something in me that touched her. She begged the Lord to take my hands out of the wash tubs and fill them with good books and Bibles, that I might go from house to house and teach God's Word to people that were lost sheep, that didn't know the way.[25]

Moore convinced the Baptist Missionary Society to send Mother Roberson to school at the Baptist Academy in Dermott, Arkansas.[26] After she completed her education, she went to work there as a matron. According to one account, Bishop Mason met Mother Roberson at a meeting he conducted at the college. According to another account, she met him at one of his revivals in the area. Mother Roberson recalled:

> I received the baptism of the Holy Ghost through Bishop C. H. Mason. I had to leave the school on account of the baptism of the Holy Ghost. When they put me out, Bishop Mason picked me up and said the Lord sent him to that school to pray out a mother to put over the women in the Church of God in Christ.[27]

Having heard about her abilities and spiritual fervor before they met, Bishop Mason told Mother Roberson, then Mrs. Woods, about his experience at the Azusa Street revival in Los Angeles, and showed her supporting scriptures. Through his witness she received the baptism of the Holy Ghost.

Overseer of Women's Work

After being forced to leave her job and the Baptist church, Mother Roberson attended a Church of God in Christ convention in Pine Bluff, Arkansas, where she met Lillian Brooks. Despite her relative youth, Brooks had already become a leading evangelist for the denomination and had conducted numerous revivals.[28]

Mother Roberson then left Arkansas for Tennessee where she worked for a time with Elder D. Hart in Trenton and Jackson. At the 1911 national convocation in Memphis, Bishop Mason appointed her overseer of women's work.

When she assumed office, women's activities in the Church of God in Christ were uncoordinated and scattered. Bishop Mason had been searching for a mature woman to organize and harness the potential of the women who were joining the denomination in large numbers, many of them leaving older, established Baptist and Methodist churches that had begun to tighten restrictions on women and limit their roles.[29]

The women who joined the denomination's ranks were mainly poor and working class, as were the majority of black women in the early twentieth century. For them Jesus was a Savior who identified with those at the bottom of society and who "empowers the weak."[30] Poor black Christian women in general held this view of Jesus.

The women in the denomination drew additional strength from the church's emphasis on Acts 1:8. The power of the Holy Ghost fired their ministries through the imperative to witness and to become agents of change. For them Jesus was a spiritual and social liberator, allowing them to exercise authority on the spiritual ground of the church. This stood in stark contrast to their subservience as poorly paid washerwomen, maids, cooks, and field hands.

Fusing the ambitions of a rising middle class, the aspirations of the poor, and the evangelistic vigor of the early church, women under Mother Roberson's leadership founded churches, organized Bible studies, prayer groups, and mission work.

After she accepted the appointment as overseer, Mother Roberson began observing women's activities in the churches. She found two strong areas of women's work: prayer and Bible study conducted by two separate groups. She combined the two to form the prayer and Bible band, the foundation for teaching a uniform doctrine and establishing regular prayer in the churches.[31]

"I was to evangelize and systemize the work among the women,"[32] Mother Roberson recalled. "I was to appoint from among the group of missionaries a state supervisor endorsed by the state overseer; such office is known as state mother.

"The duty of the state supervisor is to organize and systematize the work throughout her territory. She shall organize prayer and Bible bands, home and foreign mission bands, sunshine bands, sewing circles, and the such like; she shall be subject to the overseer with whom she may work."

The state mother also collected funds from each auxiliary and brought those funds to the annual convocation in Memphis.[33] Indicative of the financial power of the women organized under her authority, Mother Roberson is said to have presented Bishop Mason with the initial funds to open the denomination's first bank account.[34]

Partners in Ministry

While traveling to various churches, she met and married her third husband, Elder Roberson. The two became an evangelistic team, traveling throughout the Midwest to establish churches. Lacking financial backing, they often traveled by foot or wagon and often faced open, violent hostility to pentecostal-holiness doctrine.[35]

Soon after their marriage she and her husband settled in Omaha, Nebraska, where, with help from two church women, Lucinda Bostic and Nancy Gamble, they established the first Church of God in Christ in the state.[36] The pentecostal-holiness movement had enjoyed its greatest success in the Midwest and the South at the turn of the century.

The mainly white Fire Baptized Holiness Church, whose members spoke in unknown tongues before the Azusa Street revival of 1906, was based in the Midwest. Organized in 1895, the

Fire Baptized Holiness Association had wielded considerable influence from Texas to Nebraska in the latter years of the nineteenth century. C. F. Parham, the pentecostal leader whose teachings influenced Elder William J. Seymour, the primary figure in the Azusa Street revival, had begun his work in Kansas.[37]

Although the Church of God in Christ grew from southern roots, many of its early pioneers, like the pioneers of modern pentecostalism in general, migrated to the Midwest and the West. When the Robersons left Arkansas for Omaha, they were riding the crest of a small black migration west that had begun in the 1880s.

By 1910, black Nebraskans were a tiny minority; Nebraska ranked thirty-third among the forty-eight states for the number of blacks in its total population. Eighty-five percent of the nation's blacks lived in thirteen southern states, the majority in Georgia, Mississippi, Alabama, and South Carolina.

In the region where the Church of God in Christ established its first congregations — Mississippi, Arkansas, and Tennessee — black people were a substantial portion of the population. Over a million lived in Mississippi and nearly a half-million in both Tennessee and Arkansas.[38] Even after the post-war migration of blacks from the South, Nebraska's African-American population remained relatively small. In 1930, over 200,000 people lived in Omaha. Eleven thousand of them, about five per cent, were African Americans.[39]

The Robersons were pioneers, representing both a racial and religious minority in their new home state. When they began proclaiming the pentecostal message, mainline church leaders — including many holiness leaders — severely criticized the doctrine on tongues. Hostility led to violence, and the Robersons suffered verbal and physical attacks.

On the Move

Despite hardships and risks, Mother Roberson usually traveled without her husband. She took extensive journeys doing missionary work while he remained in Omaha pastoring the church. Her daughter, Ida, and other young church women accompanied her on the mission field where she trained them to become church leaders, including state mothers.[40] Lillian Brooks-Coffey, a young evangelist who would succeed Mother Roberson as national supervisor of women, frequently accompanied her on these trips.

Mother Roberson traveled continually. At age sixty-five, she visited churches in forty cities, covering eighteen states in less than a year. Everywhere she went she led prayer meetings, taught church doctrine, and helped new churches establish themselves. She organized auxiliaries, ferreted out trouble in local churches, and advised congregations on matters of doctrine and behavior.

Mother Roberson described the extensive travel she undertook at age sixty-five in her annual report for 1925. She began her visits in Arkansas, where she spent over a week at Geridge School, established by Elder Justus Bowe. One of the industrial schools founded by the Church of God in Christ in the early part of the century, Geridge combined secular and religious education with prayer meetings being held on the school grounds.

She went from Geridge to Little Rock, then back home to Nebraska at the end of January to spend time with her husband. She left home in March for Kansas City, Missouri, then went on to Kansas City, Kansas and other small towns in the state.

From Kansas she traveled to Oklahoma, spending time in Tulsa and Hot Springs. From there she traveled to Memphis. Then she attended the state convocation in Union City, Tennessee, and in May she went to St. Louis.

After returning to Kansas City, she headed west to Denver. A stint into California took her to Oakland, San Francisco, and

Los Angeles. After traveling to Phoenix, she went north to Minneapolis and St. Paul, Minnesota. She returned to Omaha for five days, then left again for Dallas, Oklahoma City, Topeka, Wichita, Kansas City, and St. Louis. She continued on to Mound City, Illinois, and Henderson, Kentucky. Her journeys also took her to Milwaukee, Chicago, Detroit, and Buffalo.

After spending a night in Philadelphia, she went to Norfolk, Virginia. She returned to Washington, D.C., and then went on to Trenton, New Jersey. She remained a night in Harrisburg, Pennsylvania, then went west to Pittsburgh, Cleveland, Toledo, and Detroit. She also stopped in Ypsilanti, Michigan, and Gary, Indiana. After returning to Chicago, she headed for Decatur, Illinois. She also visited St. Louis before returning home again for eleven days. Then she left for Little Rock to attend her brother's funeral and stopped at Brinkly, Arkansas, where she rested before that year's holy convocation in Memphis.[41]

This demanding pace illustrates the commitment and the independence of early church women as well as their husbands' apparent acceptance of prominent roles for women in the church. Mother Roberson established the principle that the church mother's role is to undergird the pastor, establish a strong women's department, and teach the women "things that women should know," including modest dress, prayer, and respect for the pastor's authority.[42] She helped to enforce a strict code of behavior for women that prohibited them from wearing shoes that exposed heels or toes. In addition to forbidding dresses that exposed their knees, the code also banned jewelry and feathers.[43]

Finishing Her Work

As Mother Roberson reached her final years, she spent her time and energy raising funds to help build the national headquarters in Memphis. With the help of her national assistant supervisor, Mother Coffey, she launched a campaign that utilized the state structure she had so carefully built in over thirty years of travel.

In 1942, she issued a letter to the state mothers, the heads of the women's departments in every state, delineating the exact amount they were to collect from the women of the church. The contributions to build the "tabernacle" were in addition to the regular amounts the women donated each year to help their pastors raise the "national report" that supported the headquarters. This national report was due for the November convocation in Memphis. The special drive to build the new headquarters was due in April.

The letter read in part: "Our Senior Bishop, Elder C. H. Mason, again calls the women of this Church for Special Help to complete our National Tabernacle. Therefore we are calling every official and every woman who is a member of the Church of God in Christ to this Loyality (sic) Call.... Please daughters, do not be slowthful (sic), this must be done, and we can do it."[44]

When Mother Roberson attended the national convocation in 1945, the funds had been raised to build the new headquarters and purchase a neon sign for the entrance. Mother Roberson died while taking a nap during the convocation. An octogenarian, she had led the women's work for thirty-four years, establishing and solidifying the foundations upon which later women's leaders would build.

Although women in the denomination have gained renown for their collective financial strength and spiritual gifts, the basis from which these outward contributions have developed may lay more in the structure that the pioneers created — the prayer and Bible band, sunshine band, and other auxiliaries, and the principles of female leadership they preserved from slave tradition — than from historical and sociological factors that influenced American culture at the beginning of the twentieth century.

Lillian Brooks-Coffey

Born in Memphis in 1896,[45] Lillian Brooks-Coffey was converted under the ministry of Bishop Mason. In 1903, at age seven,
she joined the Church of God in Christ along with her grand-
mother. According to Mother Coffey's account, hostile opposition
from the rest of her family, who were active in Baptist churches,
forced her to leave home. "These were days of great ridicule against
holiness,"[46] she recalled, and as a result she often lived in the homes
of members of the Church of God in Christ and spent her summers
with Bishop Mason and his wife. She said:

> As I grew he [Bishop Mason] carried me into Lexington [Mis-
> sissippi] every summer to help Sister Mason with the babies....
> I was happy to take my vacation in their home. As I grew
> older . . . I traveled on the road with Brother Mason and
> older sisters. I sang and read the Bible as he preached, as we
> always did in those days.... He was loving and tender with
> me and seldom scolded me because I always tried to please
> him in everything. When my parents died, he became my
> earthly father.[47]

When Mother Coffey was sixteen, her mother died. She
moved briefly to Chicago to live with relatives but returned to
Memphis to care for her sick father, who also died shortly thereafter. She went back to Chicago to live with an aunt and went to
work as a hotel maid.

In her early twenties she met and married Samuel Coffey, an
interior decorator. After she had given birth to their two daughters, they separated, possibly because her husband was not a member of the Church of God in Christ, was impatient with her church
activities, or not as committed to spreading the holiness message.
They never reconciled. In addition to raising their two daughters,
she also raised a younger brother and sister in her charge.[48]

As a young evangelist Mother Coffey organized a prayer band
that became the first Church of God in Christ in Chicago. "There

was no church in Chicago, so I rented a place, started a mission, and sent for a preacher to come," she recalled.[49] Bishop Mason appointed Elder Isaiah Roberts to pastor the first Church of God in Christ in Chicago, which was located on the South Side at 40th and State Streets. Mother Coffey developed an evangelistic team that organized other churches in Illinois, Indiana, Wisconsin, and Minnesota.[50] At age twenty-nine, she was appointed state supervisor of women for Michigan, which then had about 400 women in the denomination's churches.[51]

She also worked as Bishop Mason's secretary and assisted the denomination's financial secretary, Jessie Strickland, until she assumed the office herself.[52] When Mother Roberson died and Bishop Mason appointed her national supervisor of women, Mother Coffey began to expand the influence of the Women's Department by organizing the first International Women's Convention, which convened in Los Angeles in 1951.

Traveling an estimated 100,000 miles each year in the early 1960s, she had charge over 89 state supervisors. The Women's Department had grown substantially along with the rest of the Church of God in Christ. Their five-day conventions raised about $35,000 and attracted attention from national political leaders.[53] Mother Coffey was also active in the National Council of Negro Women and was an associate of renowned educator and political activist, Mary McLeod Bethune, thus giving women of the denomination additional national influence and visibility. She expanded missions and schools, then operated by the Women's Department, to Haiti, Jamaica, Nassau, Hawaii, Bahamas, London, and Liberia and organized women "to distribute food and clothing overseas and Bibles, tracts, and candy at home."[54]

After the death of Bishop Mason in 1961, and as church membership grew, the accepted balance between male and female authority seems to have become strained. Mother Coffey complained in an interview that she could not get exact figures from male authorities on the numbers of women members and she had not been able to accomplish her organizational goals. She noted:

> I'm supposed to reach every woman and to organize them in one or another of our groups, but this has never been accomplished. The men don't want women to have too much influence. The big thing is the church and they have that all, but it's hard to make them see it.[55]

After suffering a series of strokes, Mother Coffey died June 9, 1964.

During the subsequent political turmoil that sent the denomination to court over governance and control, the Women's Department stayed cohesive and helped preserve continuity by maintaining organized prayer and Bible study, community outreach, and financial support — the legacy of the pioneering decades under the leadership of Mothers Roberson and Coffey.

Mother Lillian Brooks-Coffey was succeeded by Mother Annie Lee Bailey (1894-1975) of Detroit, Michigan, as leader of the Women's Department. She served from 1964-1975. She was succeeded by her assistant, Mother Mattie McGlothen (1897-1994) of Richmond, Virginia, who served from 1975 until her death in May 1994. Mother Emma Frances Crouch, an educator, organizer, and missionary, took the reins of leadership as the Women's Department heads into the next century.

8

THE CHURCH OF GOD IN
CHRIST – FACING CHANGE
AND CHALLENGE

The Church of God in Christ, celebrating its first 100 years, is both awed and challenged by the covenant that God made with its founder, Bishop Charles Harrison Mason, in March 1897. While Mason was walking and praying on a street in Little Rock, Arkansas, God said to him, "If you take this name, the Church of God in Christ (1 Thess. 2:14), there will never be a building large enough to house the people whom I will send to you."

As it reflects upon its journey over the past century, the Church of God in Christ stands in awe of God's faithfulness and realizes that its incredible growth — both in numbers and influence — is because of God's covenant with its founder.

This book has chronicled the life of C. H. Mason and the roots of the Church of God in Christ. Why is it important to look into our history? Edmund Burke said, "We can only know who we are if we know from whence we have come." Abraham Lincoln expressed a similar thought: "Only as we know from whence we are can we perceive wither we are tending."

The immense contribution of the Church of God in Christ to the black church, the holiness movement, pentecostalism, and American Christianity is worthy of serious, if belated, examination by scholars familiar with its history and doctrine. As a major American denomination, the Church of God in Christ has helped to shape gospel music, black worship, and African-American spirituality, as well as helped to define black pentecostalism in the United States. Moreover, in the twentieth century, the denomination has played a major role in the urbanization of black Christianity.

An increasing number of scholars recognize the Church of God in Christ as a major, but neglected, influence within American Christianity. This belated recognition is due in part to the original research that has been done, and is presently being done, by a growing group of excellent holiness-pentecostal scholars. Since the 1970s, they have made the history, theology, and ethics of a group of some fifty African-American denominations called the Sanctified Church Movement the focus of their inquiry.[1]

Almost all the recent encyclopedias of American religion have included entries on the Church of God in Christ,[2] Bishop Mason, and other leaders of the denomination. Many scholars have become aware of the historical significance and the growing influence of the Women's Department because of the ground-breaking scholarship of Professor Cheryl Townsend-Gilkes who built on the 1975 historical work of the late Lucille Cornelius, a Church of God in Christ missionary from northern California.

Until 1970, black holiness and pentecostal churches developed freely and without serious recognition. They had little access to academic research of their history, financial resources, or theological institutions. Because they embodied their oral culture in songs, stories, and parables, their visionary hopes of liberation and reconciliation were preserved. Unfortunately, however, modern progressive and evangelical theologies ignored them. As a result, what scholars declared genuine pentecostalism was only the white conceptual, abstract, doctrinaire, fundamentalist rationalization of it. Even African-American scholars viewed the Sanctified Church Movement as simply a conglomeration of store-front churches, termed sects and cults, and thereby not to be taken seriously.[3]

This has changed, thanks to the work of inside analysts of the black holiness-pentecostal movement. In the 1970s and early 1980s, capable scholars, such as Drs. Bennie Goodwin, Leonard Lovett, Donald Wheelock, Sherry DuPree, Robert Franklin, Cheryl Townsend-Gilkes, and William C. Turner, broke new ground with their analyses of the history, theology, and ethics of the Sanctified Church Movement generally and the Church of God in Christ in particular.

The 1990s marked the emergence of a younger generation of excellent ministers and scholars — historians, theologians, and ethicists such as David Daniels, Alonzo Johnson, Thomasina Neely, Cheryl J. Sanders, Adrienne Israel, Odie Tolbert, Philip Boyer, and others who are producing ever deepening insight into the life and thought of the saints.

Because of the visionary leadership of persons who succeeded Bishop Mason, we stand poised on the threshold of the twenty-first century with the possibility and challenge for greater ministry to and on behalf of the poor and oppressed. The need to bring together these younger researchers and the institutional leaders, groomed by the late Bishop Patterson, has never been more urgent.

Transitions: The O. T. Jones, Sr. Era (1962-1968)

When Bishop C. H. Mason died on November 17, 1961, Bishop O. T. Jones, Sr. eulogized him on November 25, using this verse: "For David, after he had served his own generation by the will of God, fell on sleep, and was laid unto his fathers, and saw corruption" (Acts 13:36).

Bishop O. T. Jones, Sr. was the last surviving of the first five bishops appointed by Mason (1933-1934). He had trained youth since 1915, developed the Young People's Willing Workers (YPWW), and founded the International Youth Congress. Jones, a theologian, put the experiences of the saints into words. As a partner with Bishop Mason, he had helped to codify the doctrines and disciplines of the denomination.

In 1961, his own physical powers had begun to wane. Yet, in November 1962, as the church's senior bishop, he was called upon to lead the denomination through a difficult transition. He did so amid great tumult. Always an advocate for a trained clergy, Bishop Jones, Sr. laid the foundation for the church's participation in the Interdenominational Theological Center (ITC), a cooperative venture in theological education by the black church. In 1965, he invited Dr. Harry V. Richardson, one of the pioneers of ITC, to come to Memphis, Tennessee to put ITC's vision before the leaders of the denomination. Dr. Richardson did that, but the implementation of the vision had to await the church's passing through its time of transition.

Mason lived and led the Church of God in Christ longer than the founder of any major denomination in modern history (1897-1961) and left his indelible imprint on its life and thought. Following his death the church struggled to transcend the ordeals of transition. Bishop Jones, Sr. led the church during a difficult period. Some historians erroneously described the period between 1961 and 1968 as "the wilderness wanderings,"[4] referring to the dispute concerning Mason's successor. Despite inevitable differences of opinion, however, through much prayer and with the assistance of the Chancery Court of Shelby County, Tennessee, the Church of God in Christ rose above the challenges of change.

In January 1968, the denomination convened a constitutional convention to restructure the church. In November 1968, the church elected its first General Board, then elected Bishop James

Oglethorpe Patterson, Sr., Bishop Mason's son-in-law, as presiding bishop, with Bishops John Seth Bailey and Samuel M. Crouch first and second assistants.

The Patterson Era (1968-1989)

Patterson's leadership was long and decisive. Re-elected in five subsequent quadrennial elections, he served as presiding bishop for twenty-one years. During this period, partially because of Patterson's leadership, the church grew into national and international prominence as a leading Christian denomination. Perhaps nothing symbolized this fact more than the April 3, 1968 message that Martin Luther King, Jr. gave at Mason Temple, the headquarters for the denomination. This was King's historic "Mountaintop Speech," his final sermon to America generally and to the African-American community in particular. No one could have predicted that he would deliver his last message at Mason Temple while leading a march on behalf of the Memphis sanitation workers. Bishop Patterson, along with many other local leaders, was heavily involved in the strike, and many of the sanitation workers belonged to the Church of God in Christ.

Professor Alonzo Johnson, pastor in the denomination and faculty member in the Department of Religion at the University of South Carolina, has observed that Dr. King's last public rally at Mason Temple represented the broader shift taking place in the church during this period. In the 1970s and 1980s, the focus changed from its more insular, morally rigorous, holiness identity to a more internationally recognized pentecostal identity. The Church of God in Christ entered the mainstream with the broadening of ministry, worship styles, and leadership models. This included bringing a younger, new generation of ministers into positions as pastors, bishops, and other leadership capacities. By the mid-1980s, the Church of God in Christ was being touted as the second largest African-American denomination with a membership totaling some four million persons.

Ecumenism

More significantly, during the 1970s and 1980s, the denomination became more intentionally ecumenical. The Church of God in Christ took the lead among pentecostals as an ecumenical church in dialogue with non-fundamentalist denominations. Some of our most prominent pastors and congregations took leadership roles in such ecumenical organizations as the National Association of Evangelicals, the Congress of National Black Churches, the Pentecostal World Conference, and the North American Congress on the Holy Spirit and World Evangelism. Many ministers and lay persons also involved themselves in a host of local ecumenical activities.

Central to this ecumenical thrust was its establishment of the C. H. Mason Seminary in 1970 as a member of the Interdenominational Theological Center at Atlanta, Georgia. For many years Mason Seminary was the only pentecostal seminary in the nation fully accredited by the Association of Theological Schools. As a participant in the ITC, the Church of God in Christ became both an educational force and an ecumenical leader within the African-American community. While Saints Academy had long affirmed the late Bishop Mason's and the denomination's commitment to the educational process, Mason Seminary represented a major commitment to graduate school education and to the idea of a trained clergy and laity.

The establishment of the C. H. Mason Seminary paralleled the rise of a generation of theologians beginning with Ozro Thurston Jones, Jr.; Leonard Lovett, dean of C. H. Mason Seminary from 1970-1975; Dr. Oliver J. Haney, dean of C. H. Mason Seminary since 1975; Bennie Goodwin; Donald Wheelock; Robert M. Franklin; Dorothy Exumé; this author; and others.

Growth and Expansion

Another significant development of the 1970s was the creation of the United National Auxiliaries Convention (UNAC), the first effort to merge the auxiliaries of the denomination under one umbrella. The national staff expanded, including staff for the publishing house and the bookstore. Two prized projects of this era, Saints Center, the proposed international headquarters of the denomination, and All-Saints University did not materialize, but the centralization of the organizational and fiscal affairs of the church did occur.

Also during this era (1974-1975), the church expanded to include ministries to the military, prisons, and hospitals. This author had the opportunity to negotiate with the Pentagon's Armed Forces Chaplain's Board, the Prison Fellowship, and the College of Chaplains to endorse chaplains for all the black pentecostal denominations. Male and female military chaplains have served not only the military but also the Church of God in Christ by establishing jurisdictions in Europe, Africa, and Asia. For over twenty-one years, the denomination has launched the chaplaincy careers of scores of men and women in all branches of the armed forces, in prisons, hospitals, and on college and university campuses.

The Women's Department

The most effective department within the Church of God in Christ has been the Women's Department. Although the most prominent names associated with the development of the denomination are male, members are aware of the pivotal role played by such women as Mother Lizzie Roberson (Robinson), Mother Emma Crouch, and Dr. Arenia C. Mallory, former president of Saints Industrial and Literary School that became Saints Junior College, Lexington, Mississippi. Cheryl Townsend-Gilkes, in her impressive work on the Church of God in Christ, says:

Mason recruited educated women to work in the building of the denomination and the educational ministries. These women developed a "women's work" that became known as the "women's department." It was the women who were migrating to the cities who carried the movement to urban areas, preaching revivals, "digging out" new works, and then writing home for a pastor.[5]

Under the leadership of Mother Lillian Brooks-Coffey (1897-1964), Annie Lee Bailey (1894-1975), Mattie McGlothen (1897-1994), and Emma Frances Crouch, the Women's Department has grown in stature as the leading and most well-organized department in the church. It consistently runs the most effective convention, drawing together some twenty to twenty-five thousand delegates, and contributes significantly to international ministry initiatives. Moreover, this department has helped to nurture and groom new generations of female leaders at the local and national levels.

The impact of Dr. Arenia C. Mallory (1926-1977) upon an entire generation of post-World War II church leaders is a powerful and impressive story. One of her prized pupils was Louis Henry Ford, a young man from Clarksdale, Mississippi, who became presiding bishop of the denomination in 1990.[6]

The Ford Era (1990-1995)

Upon the death of Bishop J. O. Patterson, Bishop L. H. Ford, the first assistant presiding bishop, served as interim leader and in 1990 was elected the second presiding bishop, fourth leader in the church's history. Spanning the Mason, Jones, and Patterson eras, Bishop Ford had served the church as pastor and bishop in Chicago, Illinois, and on the national level as the director of public relations. He knew the church like few contemporaries and longed for the church he discovered as a lad in Mississippi. From his first day in office, he unapologetically proclaimed his restorationist vision.[7] He wanted to take the church back to its holiness-pentecostal, less structured, liturgical roots. Believing this was the Mason style of ministry, he wanted to return the church to this vision. He embodied what he viewed as the "golden years" of the Church of God in Christ.

His restorationist vision also centered on the denomination's symbolic institutions, particularly the national properties such as Mason Temple and Saints Junior College. Alonzo Johnson says that Bishop Ford affirmed these institutions as having been the prime jewels of Bishop Mason's ministry. During his brief tenure of five years, Bishop Ford undertook the refurbishing of Mason Temple and the Mason Residence and building a four million dollar Deborah Mason Patterson All-Purpose Facility on the campus of Saints Junior College in Lexington, Mississippi.

His first priority became the resurrection of an almost defunct school. At the Lexington campus, not only was a new building erected, but a new president, Dr. Goldie Wells, was appointed along with supporting staff. These valued treasures in their history gained a new mission and focus.

Bishop Ford's vision, however, was not exclusively restorationist or preservationist.

Professor Robert Michael Franklin, Bishop Ford's assistant pastor at St. Paul Church of God in Christ in Chicago for many years, gives us an in depth view of Bishop Ford's illustrious career. Dr. Franklin says in his latest work, "Every organization has a person who places it on the map in a memorable way. Through Malcolm X, the Nation of Islam moved from the margin to the center of the Civil Rights movement.[8] Similarly, Bishop L. H. Ford placed the Church of God in Christ firmly in the public square at the intersection of religion and politics."[9]

A protegé of the late black Southside Chicago Democratic Congressman William Dawson, Bishop Ford was also a member of the late Chicago Mayor Richard J. Daley, Sr.'s inner circle. He was

a competent, consummate member of Chicago's political establishment, part of its ruling elite, as well as being the leading Church
of God in Christ pastor in the area. For him, ministry and politics
were not mutually exclusive. Bishop Ford was a progressive, popu-
list preacher known for his street meetings, tent revivals, Christ-
mas days spent with prisoners, and distribution of food to the needy
through a network of over thirty churches. He was recognized on
the Southside, as was Rev. Cobbs of First Church of Deliverance,
as the people's preacher.

More than any other leader before him, Bishop Ford raised
the political profile of the Church of God in Christ and provided a
concrete model of what Dr. Franklin calls political urban ministry.
He referred to Jesus' time in Palestine as an example of a holy man
who was not afraid of the "city realities." He quoted Bishop Mason's
favorite passage — 1 Timothy 2:1,2 — in which the apostle Paul
admonished the saints to pray for those in political authority. Says
Franklin, Ford dismissed the world-rejecting theology of an earlier
era[10] as a heretical, selfish escape from serious public engagement.[11]
He felt that the saints had insulated themselves and were inclined
to ignore social and political realities far too long.

Although thought by some in his church to be less than pru-
dent in his political involvement, Bishop Ford's astute public theology put him on the cutting edge of garnering resources for the
poor and oppressed. He led the church to feed the hungry, clothe
the naked, visit prisoners, open the doors for employment, and support the NAACP, the Urban League, and scores of organizations
whose visions coincided with that of the Church of God in Christ.
Franklin asserts that those visions included humanizing the violent, individualistic, materialistic, cold, inner city where most African Americans live.

Upon becoming the presiding bishop, he led a delegation of
the denomination's bishops to visit with then Governor William
(Bill) Clinton at Little Rock, Arkansas, during the Holy Ghost

Conference in that city in 1991. He also invited Governor Clinton to the Memphis Convocation. In November 1991, presidential candidate Clinton visited the 84th Annual Holy Convocation, asking Bishop Ford's and the church's blessing and help in his bid for the presidency of the United States.

In April 1993, President Clinton returned to Mason Temple to thank Bishop Ford and the church for their support. Through his friendship with President Clinton, Bishop Ford was able to harness resources for a spillway in Holmes County, Mississippi, to correct a serious flooding problem that the residents had endured through this century. Ford broadened the black pentecostal tradition's view of ministry from direct acts of charity to infusing the arena of public policy with a humanizing moral perspective.[12]

The Current Era (1995-present)

Bishop Ford died suddenly on March 31, 1995, three years into his first full term as presiding bishop. Ten years earlier he had been near death, but had experienced a miraculous healing and regained his full strength. In exactly five years (April 5, 1990-April 5, 1995), he had completed his divinely appointed assignment, was called home to glory, eulogized by the saints, and laid to rest with his fathers and mothers.

His unexpected, untimely death precipitated a generational shift in the leadership of the church. In November 1995, the General Assembly selected Bishop Chandler David Owens, Bishop Ford's first assistant presiding bishop, as the fifth leader of the denomination.

Bishop Owens brought to the office of presiding bishop a more collegial leadership style. Bishop Ford's leadership style, characterized as authoritarian and aggressive, was thought by some to be more suited to behind the scenes, heavy political action than diplomatic public governance.[13]

The General Assembly selected eleven other General Board members: Bishop Cleveland Landis Anderson of Detroit, Michigan, first assistant presiding bishop; J. Neaul Haynes of Dallas, Texas, second assistant; Philip Aquila Brooks of Detroit, Michigan, secretary; Ozro Thurston Jones, Jr. of Philadelphia, Pennsylvania; Charles Edward Blake of Los Angeles, California; Roy Lawrence Haley Winbush of Lafayette, Louisiana; Leroy Robert Anderson of Buffalo, New York, assistant secretary; Bishop Ithiel Conrad Clemmons of New York City; Gilbert Earl Patterson of Memphis, Tennessee; Levi Edward Willis of Norfolk, Virginia; Samuel Lee Green, Jr. of Newport News, Virginia; Wilbur Wyatt Hamilton of Seaside, California, general secretary; Frank Otha White of Hempstead, New York, financial secretary; and Bishop Samuel Leon Lowe of Memphis, Tennessee, treasurer. This new generation of leaders now faces the awesome challenge of bringing the church into ministry in the twenty-first century.

These men must face this central question: How can we in a market-driven, market-dominated culture keep from being consumed by an exclusive preoccupation with "getting and spending" and refocus on our core identity and vocation?

In the words of Cheryl J. Sanders, we are a faith community with a dual heritage. Our roots are anchored in the evangelical imperatives of holiness and unity associated with the nineteenth century egalitarian, holiness movement and in the fires of Azusa Street, which set the pentecostal revival ablaze in the twentieth century as a global, multicultural phenomenon. That faith community — the Church of God in Christ — is challenged to sustain a socially conscious and profoundly spiritual Christian witness.[14]

In July 1995, Bishop Owens called the leadership to dialogue with him regarding the vision, mission, and priorities of the Church of God in Christ as it approaches the year 2000. The General Board had been primarily focused on Bishop Ford's restorationist vision and priorities until his unexpected death. In January 1996, Bishop

Owens, together with the General Board, launched Vision 2000 and Beyond.

The present General Board and the Board of Bishops, who lead some 150 jurisdictions, are composed of strong, successful leaders. They are builders, organizers, communicators, and administrators who are committed to the renewal of the church and the redemption of our society. These leaders are conscious that this church is not summoned to be an echo of the culture, to admire its economics, to embrace its psychology, or to certify its morality. To be a faithful church, we are not called to replicate the things of another generation but to confront the dangers peculiar to this generation.

We are conscious of the dialectic of being "in the world but not of the world."[15] This means, as professor Walter Brueggemann points out, that while we are a faith community that continues to seek order, security, and prosperity, at the same time we face the harder, more demanding human issues of justice and humaneness. As we seek academic excellence and financial well-being through our educational and fiscal programs, we also embrace the more demanding challenges of passionate commitment in a sea of apathy and community in culture of individualism. We want to be a church that continues to seek growth, influence, and respectability, but we also seek the more demanding evangelical questions of faithfulness, renewal, and information.[16]

As a historian and believer, I believe that an account of our historical journey helps us to better focus upon the *heilsqeschete* — the unfolding of God's providential purpose within the warp and woof of secular events. In the midst of human events, salvation history occurs. The historical journey is essential to renewal. It is a prophetic concern to return to the root, the original covenant, as the prophets of Israel were constantly saying to the religious establishment of their day.

Among the projects set in motion in Vision 2000 and Beyond, the one that has really caught fire is the Regional Pastors'

Church Growth Conferences. Black pentecostals are now able to concentrate on techniques of growth rather than on issues of survival. This indicates an economic and social class shift has occurred, which is both a cause to celebrate and also a challenge to fulfill Vision 2000 and Beyond.

Our Focus on the Future

The Church of God in Christ has at least three major objectives as it looks toward a second century of witness and work. These objectives are as follows:

1. To reach every person and culture it can, by every possible means that it can, in every possible way that it can for Jesus Christ. The denomination believes and proclaims that Jesus Christ, the wisdom and power of God, can heal mankind's divisions and alienation.

2. To teach those who come to Jesus Christ through its proclamation of the gospel the length and breadth and height and depths of God's love in Christ Jesus. The Church of God in Christ contends that it is about more than partaking of another form of stimulation in an already over-stimulated society.

3. To equip God's people for ministry in and to a world in transition. The denomination realizes it is a prophetic minority within post-Constantinian Christendom, that its particular message of God's truth and life is proclaimed amid the resurgent conflict of Muslims, Jews, Christians, and secularists. What it means to be Christian at the end of the second millennium is important to the denomination.

Other scholars have put forth several helpful and studied proposals that the Church of God in Christ would do well to consider as it focuses on the future. Biblical scholar Walter Brueggemann's insightful, prolific exegetical Old Testament work speaks directly to the denomination as a covenant people. In his books, *Living*

Toward a Vision, Hope Within History, and *Hopeful Imagination: Prophetic Voices in Exile,*[17] he holds up a distant mirror — ancient Israel — and helps us to see ourselves, a marginal people in American culture — all too often a people for whom these Egyptian and Babylonian cultures are too much with us. Black and white holiness-pentecostal scholars are finding Brueggemann's theological, ethical, ecclesial, social, and economic insights immensely helpful.

Cheryl J. Sanders, in her excellent study of the Sanctified Church tradition, puts forth several cogent proposals for the renewal of holiness-pentecostal ecclesiology, ethics, spirituality, and biblical reflection. She finds in Brueggemann's exegetical work on Jeremiah, Ezekiel, and I and II Isaiah, a key to understanding the exilic consciousness of the African-American diasporic people in America. She argues that exile is a more effective theme for the church's mission than liberation. A church with an exile identity, she argues, is an alternative community formed by a coherent set of values that are at odds with the surrounding culture.[18] Her analysis helps us to think clearly about twenty-first century ministry.

In his 1995 Azusa lectures at Regent University, respected Harvard theologian Harvey Cox admitted that the metaphor of Pentecost, with its central experience of the Holy Spirit's bringing people together, is more suited for the global situation at the close of the twentieth century than the liberationist Exodus metaphor.[19] Like theologian J. Deotis Roberts, I believe that liberation and reconciliation have to be the dual focus of the black church.

I also believe the vision of the Church of God in Christ must address new challenges for all black churches. In 1964, with the inner city riots, there arose in the African-American community a schism between middle-class African Americans and the disadvantaged class. Our communities were invaded by crack-cocaine — a drug that has drowned us in a sea of meaninglessness and despair. Beside this host of pathologies, due in part to political and economic dislocations, a "health and wealth" gospel arose that paralleled televangelism.

The Church of God in Christ has succeeded as a vehicle for upward mobility. The saints taught its constituents to work hard; not to drink, smoke, or do drugs; and not to break up their families through separation and divorce. Over nine decades the saints have been upwardly mobile — educating their children, buying property, and building houses of worship.

The saints are challenged now, says Sanders, to decide whether the goal of ministry is spiritual formation or socialization to the middle class. Hans Baer and Merrill Singer identified within the black holiness-pentecostal movement a growing shift away from traditional concerns with spiritual salvation to acceptance of bourgeois values of temporal success and material acquisition.[20] When I hear the criticism of the expanding black middle class that are becoming members of black holiness-pentecostal churches, I'm dubious. Yet pentecostalism's climb up the social strata hides subtle temptations.

The greatest temptations of evangelicalism in our time, says Walter Brueggemann, are the same as those that Moses warned against in his final address to Israel in the book of Deuteronomy: amnesia and assimilation. Walter Hollenweger has written "The Pentecostal Elites and the Pentecostal Poor," an essay to pentecostals that sounds much like Moses' valedictory. His essay on the global expansion of pentecostalism is highly critical of people who are upwardly mobile and exclusive in their religion. They reject the basic principles that made it possible for racial, social, and linguistic barriers to be broken down. We dare not, after nine decades of explosive growth among the disinherited, repeat the same mistakes of mainstream churches. "We cut ourselves off from our own poor people in the interest of a streamlined theology, of an efficient organization, and facade of unity."[21]

The Rev. W. H. Amos was a pioneer of the then Colored Methodist Episcopal Church (CME), which is now the Christian Methodist Episcopal Church (CME). Bishop Mason's oldest daughter, Alice, married Rev. Amos' son, who became a venerable and beloved bishop of the CME Church. Rev. Amos said to Bishop Mason, "Brother Mason, I hope that you sanctified folks don't make the same mistake we Methodist folk are making. We have become elite and we're dying."[22]

Evangelist/Missionary Elsie Shaw, Bishop Mason's protegé and heir to his prayer ministry, often says, "Come on, saints! Bishop Mason taught us that what God offered us we ought to have sense enough and faith enough to receive and use to His glory." I contend that God has a covenant with the Church of God in Christ that is both a blessing and a responsibility.

Professor Robert Franklin, from whose writings we have gleaned some insight into the denomination's life and work, shares the challenge of Vision 2000 and Beyond. He observes:

> The [Church of God in Christ] story reminds us that black people who migrated to the cities were economically poor but spiritually rich. It was precisely this alternative culture and community that reinforced their sense of dignity, creativity, and collective power in the midst of racism, classism, sexism, and other forms of oppression. Urban ministry in the future must take seriously how human selves may be affirmed and sustained amidst the assaults of impersonalism, individualism, and materialism. The [Church of God in Christ] story is a story of humanizing modern city life through spiritual renewal, economic empowerment, cultural preservation, collective resistance, and existential celebration.[23]

By remembering the spiritual vitality of its founder, Bishop C. H. Mason, and the church's goal to remain a vibrant witness in the next century, the Church of God in Christ will continue to influence many lives and transform our inner cities.

EPILOGUE

I set out to chronicle the history of the Church of God in Christ primarily because so little of it was in print. Not until scholars such as James Cone, James M. Washington, and James A. Forbes emerged on the theological scene did the Church of God in Christ receive much needed academic credibility. Far too long has the denomination been ignored as solely an irrelevant group sanctified, rural, and marginal people whose storefront buildings were seen as unimpressive and their pastoral leadership seemed filled only with inspiration and speaking in tongues. Clearly, the time has come for the denomination to assert itself as a church that is not only equipped to meet the challenges of the twentieth century, but a major group within the black church that has made a significant contribution historically to the life of African-American Christianity.

The work of Mason, Seymour, and Jones confirm that some solid theological underpinnings belong to the origins of the Church of God in Christ. Their prophetic preaching and sense of mission reached whites as well as blacks. Early in its history, these founders understood the creative tensions between blacks and whites and sought to provide a sound biblical foundation for its membership that enabled it to survive during the period of racial segregation in the United States. The fact that white clergy sought the counsel and advice of Mason and Jones – and followed their leadership for a considerable period of time – attests to the genius of these men. The church always taught the significance of sisters and brothers sitting together to work on the social issues of the day.

The legacy of the founders is still apparent in the memories and traditions of the present leaders. Although Bible study and prayer meetings and emphasis on glossalia continue to be prominent in the Church of God in Christ congregations, churches are finding new ways of meeting the challenges of a decadent society and participating in various efforts to bring the church and the needs of the community together. Mason and Seymour demonstrated early on that inspiration and feelings prove to be essential to one's wholeness and well-being. But they also understood the value of networking, facilitation, and negotiation with regard to the racial conflicts of that era. In summary, the founding spirituality and vision remains a vital force in the lives of ministers and congregations of the Church of God in Christ today.

APPENDIX A

A PRAYER AND A VISION OF BISHOP C. H. MASON

This is from the book *Conversations with God* by James Melvin Washington, Ph.D., HarperCollins Publishers. The author wrote: "This is a transcription of Mason's unusual form of extemporaneous, exhortative, and prophetic public prayers. In order to preserve the intentionally mystical quality of his style, I chose to conserve this transcription with its obvious lapses in grammar and syntax."

An Exhortative Invocation

Father, Thou openeth the gates of wonders, making us enjoy the gift of the Christ, His word standing. When the wicked comes against us, the power of Thy word is for us.

Open the gates of Thy wisdom for us and rebuke the power of the wicked against us. In the glory of Thy council we stand. The Christ of Thy work has made us stand.

We see the door of Thy mystery. Let the poor confess their sins and see the glory of Thy resurrection. Thy goodness and greatness is among the daughters. Fill these with the fullness of Christ. Bless us with light and prudence in the power of the Holy Ghost. The presence of God is with us and the blood prevails. Anoint us so we will in Thy pity come to Thee.

Bless those who have died to sin fighting in the spirit.

We enjoy saying the Lord gives us the living bread.

Look to God, be faithful to God and say no more, "I can't." God comes in you to do. Humble yourselves that Christ may be your portion.

Speaking from a sign of God, a cleaver. The day of the Lord never comes till the signs of the Lord appear. Man in God's hand is a sign. Thou art my battle axe, my weapon of war. God's wonders coming, doing a strange work. Ministers of God preaching the word out of season and in season. Not using swords imposing God's little lambs.

God standing a wonder in man. Who can hinder God? His wonders are telling. We delight to see Jesus in signs. Confirming us out from snares, Jesus, great God at hand, His word telling about His ways bring us out from the mystery of evil. Watching for His wonders; telling God, I believe.

Scriptures are signs of the only Christ, the glory of God. From the Scriptures Jesus spoke to the minds of the people, and they looked at Him and marveled. Jesus showing forth the wisdom of God. Jesus the sign spoken against. Jesus, a sign overturning the evil time; gathers the nation with His understanding and binds His children together as one. Jesus, the wonder among nations, having done the work He came to do. Earth owned Him. When His soul was offered, His glory was upon Him. He was a Prince and a Son to rule. He obtained favor of the Father, but evil hearts abused Him. Through unbelief He cried out mercy for them who knew not what they did. The world looked on Him in a wonder. The sign of God's longsuffering. The sun, in obedience, acknowledged the Son of

God's love and veiled His face. Darkness formed over the mountains, the earth trembled and said it is the Son of God. The veil in the temple parted itself from top to bottom. The mystery of God's greatness. Saints of God on earth. God's signs and wonders, witness of His glory and return. Jesus Christ, persecuted, led to the cross, crucified and said not a word. Even so shall the children who were baptized in the glory of His death, be persecuted, tarred and feathered, imprisoned, lied on, and killed. Signs that their redemption draweth nigh. Hated of all men for My name's sake. The children of God hated because they enjoy wisdom from on high. Hating them because they love their enemies and pray for them that despitefully use them.

These signs shall follow believers. The people receiving the Holy Ghost have something which the world cannot understand. The Comforter proceeding from the Father going on in us, and through us. Earth testify to the shortage of the Church, knowing nothing of the greatness of God. All praise to God. Having found the faith baptized in Him, I'm telling the story of Him. He is God for you. He is God to you. He is your thrilling life, the only help now we know. Pouring upon us the help of His power and love. Accept Him in might, saying God is right. Ask the Lord for help the more. Looking for God to guide the soul.

A Vision at the Great Azusa Prayer Meetings (1907)

The first day in the meeting I sat to myself, away from those that went with me. I began to thank God in my heart for all things, for when I heard some speak in tongues, I knew it was right though I did not understand it. Nevertheless, it was sweet to me. I also thanked God for Elder [William] Seymour who came and preached a wonderful sermon. His words were sweet and powerful and it seems that I hear them now while writing. When he closed his sermon, he said, "All of those that want to be sanctified or baptized with the Holy Ghost, go to the upper room; and all those that want to be justified come to the altar." I said that is the place for me, for it may be that I am not converted and if not, God knows it and can convert me . . ."

Glory! The second night of prayer, I saw a vision. I saw myself standing alone and had a dry roll of paper in my mouth trying to swallow it. Looking up towards the heavens, there appeared a man at my side. I turned my eyes at once, then I awoke and the interpretation came. God had me swallowing the whole book and if I did not turn my eyes to anyone but God and Him only, He would baptize me. I said "yes" to Him, and at once in the morrning when I arose, I cound hear a voice in me saying, "I see . . ."

I got a place at the altar and began to thank God. After that, I said Lord if I could only baptize myself, I would do so; for I wanted the baptism so bad that I did not know what to do. I said, Lord, You will have to do the work for me; so I turned it over into His hands.... Then, I began to seek for the baptism of the Holy Ghost according to Acts 2:44 which readeth thus: "Then they that gladly received His word were baptized." Then I saw that I had a right to be glad and not sad.

The enemy sad to me, there may be something wrong with you. Then a voice spoke to me saying, if there is anything wrong with you Christ will find it and take it away and will marry you.... Some said, "Let us sing." I arose and the first song that came to me was "He brought me out of the Miry Clay." The Spirit came upon the saints and upon me.... Then I gave up for the Lord to have His way within me. So there came a wave of Glory into me and all of my being was filled with the the Glory of the Lord. So when He had gotten me straight on my feet, there came a light which enveloped my entire being above the brightness of the sun. When I opened my mouth to say "Glory," a flame touched my tongue which ran down to me. My language changed and no word could I speak in my own tongue. Oh! I was filled with the Glory of the Lord. My soul was then satisfied.

146

APPENDIX B

100 COGIC CONGREGATIONAL SONGS AND CHORUSES[1]

In 1956, after much concern over the "Rock and Roll" type of gospel singing that had invaded our church, the Lord spoke to my heart to compile a list of the songs that were sung in our church in years gone by, and call the list "Down Memory Lane." This list of songs was used for a "Songspiration" service, and many of the Saints enjoyed them

These songs have a message. They not only thrill our hearts, but inspire us to go to higher heights and deeper depths in Him.

It is our endeavor to bring these songs back to your memory by publishing this book of heartfelt, soul searching songs.

Thelma L. Williams, Compiler

This book is dedicated to my beloved pastor and his wife, Bishop and Mrs. J. O. Patterson, and our mother, Mrs. Carrie Williams, because of their love for the old time Holy Ghost songs.

Earline Nelson, Compiler

HE'S SWEET, I KNOW

I can't forget when I was sad
Head hanging down (and) soul feeling bad
All I could say (was) Lord take my heart
Jesus heard and saved me (and) gave me a start

Chorus

He's sweet, I know. He's sweet, I know
Dark clouds may rise and strong winds may blow
I'll tell the world wherever I go
I have found a Savior. He's sweet, I know

Sometimes I'm tired by Satan's snare
My burdens seem so hard to bear
I'm talked about whatever I do
But I know a Savior (and) He'll take me through

SWEETER AS THE YEARS GO BY

Sweeter as the years go by
Sweeter as the years go by
Richer, fuller, deeper
Jesus' love is sweeter
Sweeter as the years go by

THE LORD FOLLOWED ME

I went to the meeting one night, and the Lord followed me
My heart was not right, but the Lord followed me
I tried to run away. I said I could not stay
I refused to let them pray, but the Lord followed me

Chorus

I am glad He followed me. I know He followed me
I am glad He condescended and followed me
My life was very sad. My heart was very bad

But now I am so glad that the Lord followed me
I tried to think I wasn't bad, but the Lord followed me
Their shouting made me mad, but the Lord followed me
I thought I knew it all, but my pride took a fall
On His name I had to call as the Lord followed me

I didn't like the way they did, but the Lord followed me
When the preacher looked at me, my meanness he seemed to see
Then I told it publicly, that the Lord followed me

I SHALL SURELY RISE

When the Holy One on high shall give command
He the all wise King of the skies
Calls the dead of every nation and every land
Then I shall rise, surely shall rise

Chorus

When He comes bright'ning the skies
Jesus the King
When the dead everywhere rise
Praises to sing,
Then O death my soul shall cry
Where is thy sting?
I shall meet Him in the skies
Jesus the King
Then over land and sea, shall ring the mighty sound
Seas give up your dead, and graves be empty found

Past the long night, come the daylight
Then I shall rise, surely shall rise
In that day, shall soon awake to meet their doom

Sinner be wise. Open your eyes
Whenever He comes, I know he'll take
   me home
Then I shall rise, surely shall rise

I MEAN TO CONQUER

I am going to run the race with patience
I am going to stay on the battle field
Jesus gave me grace to conquer
And I got on my breast plate, sword and
   shield

Chorus

I mean to conquer. I mean to conquer
I mean to conquer every day
Jesus gave me grace to conquer
I mean to conquer every day

He turned my sorrow into praises
And my weeping into song
Turns my moaning into dancing
And I feel like going on

SO GLAD I'M HERE

So glad I'm here
So glad I'm here
So glad I'm here
I'm here in Jesus' name

I CAN TELL THE WORLD ABOUT THIS

Chorus

I can tell the world about this
I can tell the nations I'm blessed
Tell them what Jesus has done
Tell them that the Comforter has come
And He brought joy, great joy to my soul

My Lord, He told Moses what to do
He did, my Lord. O yes, He did
To go lead the children of Israel through
Yes He did, my Lord. O yes, He did
And He brought joy, joy, joy to my soul

My Lord done just what He said
Yes, He did, my Lord. O yes, He did
He healed the sick and then He raised
   the dead
Yes He did, my Lord. O yes, He did
And He brought joy, joy, joy to my soul

My Lord, He rose up in the air
Yes He did, my Lord. O yes He did
And He called poor sinners from every-
   where
Yes He did, my Lord. O yes He did
And He brought joy, joy, my to my soul

OH, THE JOY THAT COMES TO ME

When my Savior found me
Put His arms around me
Whispered peace and made me free
How He walked beside me
To protect and guide me
Oh, the joy that came to me

Chorus

Oh, the joy that came to me
When I knew that I was free
When my Savior found me
Placed His arms around me
Oh, the joy that came to me

When I know the story
Of the life in glory
When I heard of
And how He pleaded
Just for what I needed
Oh, the joy that came to me

When the supernatural
Of life eternal,
In the home beyond the sea
That awaits the lowly
Faithful, pure and holy
Oh, the joy that came to me

149

THERE IS SOMETHING MIGHTY SWEET ABOUT THE LORD

There is something mighty sweet about
the Lord
There is something mighty sweet about
the Lord
Oh eyes haven't seen it and the ears
haven't heard it
There is something mighty sweet about
the Lord

THE DAY OF THE LORD HAS COME

Blow ye the trumpet of Zion
Sound aloud the holy command
Let the earth's inhabitants tremble
For the day of the Lord is at hand

Chorus

Oh! What a weeping and wailing
From among the sinful throng
Men are dying, nations falling
For the day of the Lord has come

The judgment of God against the wicked
Everywhere we can plainly see
But God's strong arm of deliverance
Give peace to the blood washed re-
deemed

It is a day of distress and trouble
Such as never was known in the land
For men shall be crying for mercy
Oh! Who shall be able to stand

LET'S GO

When the spies returned from Canaan
Land
Where milk and honey flowed
Some said, "We can never possess the
land"
But others said, "Let's go"

Chorus

Let's go
Let's go to the land where the milk and
honey flow
Let's go. Let's go
Where the grapes of Eschoel grow
Let's go
We can possess the land, I know,
With a bounding heart, We'll make a
start
Come along. All aboard. Let's go

When Moses came to the great Red Sea
How to cross he did not know
But the Lord just raised the waters up
high
And the angel said, "Let's Go"

It was the same when Joshua took his
place
And stopped the Jordan's flow
They marched around Jericho's wall
After Joshua said, "Let's go"

And some glad morning bright and calm
From this world of sin and woe
The Lord will come and take us home
Amen, dear Lord. Let's go

And those who are sleeping in the grave
Will hear the trumpet blow
And say, while coming from the grave
"To one and all: Let's go"

OH I WANT TO SEE HIM

As I journey through this land, singing
as I go
Pointing souls to, to the crimson flow
Many arrows pierce my soul, from with-
out and within
But my Lord leads me on through. Him
I must win

Chorus

Oh, I want to see Him and look upon his face
There to sing forever of His saving grace
On the streets of glory let me lift my voice
Cares of past, home at last, ever to rejoice

When in service for my Lord, dark may be the night
But I'll cling more close to Him. He will give me light
Satan's snares may vex my soul, turn my thoughts aside
But my Lord goes ahead and leads whatever betides.

I WILL NEVER GIVE UP THE GOAL

I am so glad He is in my heart
I know some day I'll get my part
I know He'll bless me and then He'll test
To see if I will give up the goal

Chorus

I will never give up the goal
I'll press along with courage bold
I'll look to Jesus who died to save me
His love is yet untold
While the storm is raging high
I know my Savior will be nigh
There to protect me and always bless me
If I never give up the goal

I know this world is full of shame
But there is power in His name
His grace can guide me. His love can hide me
If I never give up the goal

Jesus told me long ago
That I could live forever more

If I'd obey Him and always praise Him
And don't ever give up the goal

WITNESS

I've never been to heaven, but I've been told
My soul is a witness for the Lord
The gates are pearl and the streets are gold
My soul is a witness for the Lord
For all that He has done for me
My soul is a witness for the Lord
And for his grace so rich and free
My soul is a witness for the Lord
He keeps me every day and hour
My soul is a witness for the Lord
Right now I feel His cleansing power
My soul is a witness for the Lord

Chorus

I'm a witness, witness, witness, witness
My soul is a witness for the Lord
I'm a witness, witness, witness, witness
My soul is a witness for the Lord

I CAN'T FEEL AT HOME ANYMORE

This world is not my home
I'm just passing
My treasures and my hopes are all laid
Where many friends and kindred are gone on before
I can't feel at home in this world anymore

Chorus

O Lord, You know that I have no friend like You
If heaven's not my home, Lord, what shall I do?
Lord's gonna beckon me from heaven's welcome door
And I can't feel at home in this world anymore

Over in Beulah land is no dying there
The saints are shouting victory, singing
    everywhere
I hear voices of them whom I have
    known before
And I can't feel at home in this world
    anymore

Heaven's expecting me and that's one
    thing I know
I fixed it up with Jesus a long time ago
I know He'll take me in though I am
    weak and poor
And I can't feel at home in this world
    any more

I'm S - A - V - E - D

Some people wonder why we say
I'm S - A - V - E - D
I'm S - A - V - E - D
I'm F - R - double - E
They want to know why we don't go
To the D - A - N - C - E
The answer's easy to be had
We are S - A - V - E - D

Chorus

It's G - L - O - R - Y to know
I'm S - A - V - E - D
I'm H - A - P - P - Y to tell
I'm F - R- double - E
I once was B - O - U - N - D
With the chains of S - I - N
It's V - l - C - T - O - R - Y
To know I've Christ within

IS EVERYBODY HAPPY?

Down in the valley where the violets
    grow
I met a man who was meek and low
He's a friend that will never fail
A solid rock that will never quail
The devil is a liar from the world's begin
He says that we can't live free from sin

But I've been redeemed from the raging
    foe
And I don't have to sin no more

Chorus

Is everyone happy? Is everybody glad?
I don't want to see you looking wearied
I don't want to see you looking sad
I want to see you keep a'smiling
As if Jesus was at the door
Keep on a'shouting hallelujah
Until we meet on the other shore

Thou art fair, my beloved one. Thou art
    fair
Unto Thee whom can I compare?
Thou art unto me as a banner of love
Shining and gleaming as the stars above
Teach me the way that I shall go
That I may never walk in sin no more
For if I walk as I've once before
To me it's woe, woe, woe

On the hill called Calvary I can see
Where Jesus suffered and died for me
He walked the seashore of Galilee
There was never such a man as He
The world would have never been rec-
    onciled
If Jesus had never suffered, bled and died
He's a friend and a friend indeed
Over this whole, wide world

DIG A LITTLE DEEPER IN GOD'S LOVE

Nearer to Thee, I want to be
I want to dig a little deeper in the store-
    house of God's love
I want to shine, with love sublime
I want to dig a little deeper in the store-
    house of God's love

Chorus

I want to dig a little deeper, yes dig a
little deeper
I want to dig a little deeper in the store-
house of God's love
I want to talk like Jesus would
Walk like a Christian should
I want to dig a little deeper in the store-
house of God's love

I want to do what's always true
I want to dig a little deeper in the store-
house of God's love
Each passing hour, I want more power
I want to dig a little deeper in the store-
house of God's love

THIS IS THE REASON

This is the reason I'm happy at last
Facing the beautiful goal
Fearing no longer the future or past
Jesus abides in my soul

Chorus

This is the reason. This is the reason
I'm so happy and whole
Sweetly I'm singing. Joy-bells are ring-
ing
Jesus abides in my soul

Pleasures are powerless to lead me astray
Out of His blessed control
Cheering and guiding me day by day
Jesus abides in my soul

This is the reason that I shall rejoice
While countless ages shall roll
Praising His goodness with heart and
with voices
Jesus abides in my soul

HEAVENLY SUNSHINE

When my heart is bowed in sorrow, and
it seems all help is gone

Jesus whispers, "Do not falter. I will not
leave you alone"
Then somehow among trials, how it is I
cannot see
Still I hear a voice from heaven, gently
saying, follow me

Chorus

There is sunshine in the shadow
There is sunshine in the rain
There is sunshine in our sorrows
When our hearts are filled with pain
There is sunshine when we are burdened
There is sunshine when we pray
There is sunshine, heavenly sunshine
Blessed sunshine, all the way

Sometimes my friends do forsake me, and
I'm tempted to despair
Then I think of my dear Savior, to lay
His head He had nowhere
Oh it pays to follow Jesus, just to learn
of Him each day
And I'll guarantee, my brother, you'll
have sunshine all the way

Chorus

Let me recommend Him to you
I have found no better friend
He is One Who'll not deceive you
But stay with you to the end
If you would have peace and comfort
Let His banner be unfurled
For He lifted that rugged cross
And His name can save the world

MOVE UP THE KING'S HIGHWAY

All up the way the host is tramping,
tramping
While Satan's band around is camping,
camping
Make no delay, if you would win the day
Christians, move, move, move up the
King's highway

Chorus

Let us move, move, move up the King's
highway
As we tramp, tramp, tramp, let us sing
and pray
Christians close up the ranks to gain today
Let us move, move, move up the King's
highway

Saints gone before us all are resting, rest-
ing
Satan today our faith is testing, testing
Work while you may, but Jesus' word said
obey today
Christians move, move, move up the
King's highway

IF I WERE YOU
I'D MAKE A CHANGE

If I were you, I'd make a change
If I were you, I'd make a change
If I were you, I'd make a change
Oh my friends, don't you hear God call-
ing, "Make a change"

Backsliding girl, why don't you make a
change
Backsliding girl, why don't you make a
change
Backsliding girl, why don't you make a
change
Oh my friends, don't you hear God calling, "Make a change"

WHOSOEVER WILL
LET HIM COME

Whosoever will let him come, let him
come
Whosoever will let him come to Christ
and live
Whosoever will let him come, let him
come
And drink of the water of life

I heard the voice of Jesus say
"Come unto Me and rest
Lie down, thy wearied one, lie down
Thy head upon My breast"

HEAVEN ON MY MIND

I am glad I found a Savior. He guides me
every day
I have left this sinful world behind
And at morning noon or midnight
You can always hear me say (children)
I've got heaven on my mind

Chorus

(Children) I've got heaven on my mind
And it keeps me singing all the time
As I walk the narrow way, you can al-
ways hear me say
(Children) I've got heaven on my mind

I've got no time for folly, no time to waste
away
I am working for my Master all the time
And Satan tried to stop me, these are
the words I say
Satan, I've got heaven on my mind

I am walking in the light
I am going where the sun always shines
There's a place called heaven, And Jesus
is the light
(Children) I've got heaven on my mind

MOUNTAIN RAILROAD

Life is like a mountain railroad
With an engineer that's brave
We must make the run successful
From the cradle to the grave
Watch the curve that fills the tunnel
Never falter, never fail
Keep your hand upon the throttle
And your eye upon the rail

Chorus
Precious Savior, Thou wilt guide us
Till we reach the blissful shore
Where the angels wait to join us
In Thy praise forevermore

You will roll up grades of trials
You will cross the bridge of strife
See that Christ is your conductor
On this lightning train of life
Always mindful of obstructions
Do your duty, never fail
Keep your hand upon the throttle
And your eye upon the rail

You will often find obstructions
Look for storms of wind and rain
On a hill or curve or trestle
They will almost ditch your train
Put your trust alone in Jesus
Never falter, never fail
Keep your hand upon the throttle
And your eye upon the rail

As you roll across the trestle
Spanning Jordan's dwelling tide
You behold the Union Depot
Into which your train must glide
There you'll meet the Superintendent
God the Father, God the Son
With a hearty, joyous plaudit
Weary pilgrims, welcome home

JESUS
Jesus, when troubles burden me down
Jesus, I know your love's all around
Jesus, oh precious King
When darkness gathers, and friends for-
sake me
I know You'll never let me down
I know You'll answer what'er betide me
You're a jewel I have found
Jesus, on You I always call
Jesus, You're life. You're my all in all,

Jesus, oh Precious King
Jesus, You suffered and died on the cross
Jesus, You bought me with such a great
cost
Jesus, oh precious King
A friend in trouble and always willing
to lift a fallen soul in need
You're ever ready and always listening
for a sinner's earnest plea
Jesus, Your name the sweetest I know
Jesus, I'll tell it wherever I go
Jesus, oh precious King

THE LORD WILL MAKE A WAY YES, HE WILL
I know the Lord will make a way
Yes, He will
I know the Lord will make a way
Yes, He will
Though you may not have a friend
He'll go with you to the end
I know the Lord will make a way
Yes, He will

Chorus
Yes, He will. Yes, He will. Yes, He will.
 I know He will. I know the Lord will
 make a way. Yes, He will
He will make a way for you and He will
 lead you safely through
I know the Lord will make a way. Yes,
 He will

I have a Savior I can tell my troubles to
When I'm burdened and I don't know
 what to do
I go to Him in secret prayer
I can leave my burdens there
I know the Lord will make a way. Yes,
 He will

Chorus
Yes, He will. Yes, He will
Yes, He will. I know He will

155

I know the Lord will make a way. Yes, He will

When through storms you're tossed about

I know the Lord can bring you out

I know the Lord will make a way. Yes, He will

He holds the wealth of the world in His hands

All the silver and gold He commands

All my needs to Him are known

And He never forsakes His own

I know the Lord will make a way. Yes, He will

Chorus

Yes, He will. Yes, He will

Yes, He will. I know He will

I know the Lord will make a way. Yes He will

When burdens press you down

Almost level to the ground

I know the Lord will make a way. Yes, He will

I am trusting in His promise everyday

For He promised to go with me all the way

And though Satan's hosts assail

I know Jesus can never fail

I know the Lord can make a way. Yes, He will

Chorus

Yes, He will. Yes, He will

Yes, He will. I know He will

I know the Lord will make a way. Yes, He will

Though obstructions block the way

Just fall on your knees and pray

I know the Lord will make a way. Yes, He will

THAT'S ALL I NEED TO KNOW

If I were hungry without bread or meat

If I were naked, no shoes on my feet

I would never doubt Him

My Lord knows and sees

For the Lord is my shepherd

He'll supply all my needs

Chorus

The Lord is my shepherd, that's all I need to know

The Lord is my shepherd, He'll protect wherever I go

On the land, on the sea, any time, anywhere

The Lord is my shepherd, that's all I need to know

If you but ask Him a door, He'll open wide

If you but trust Him, I'm sure He'll provide

You must never doubt it, the wonders of God's grace

For the Lord is your shepherd, He'll provide and make a way

Yes, I love the Lord Who saves and sanctifies

I'm walking daily by His side

Yes, I will follow Jesus all the time

For the Lord is my shepherd, praise God He's mighty fine

LEAVING ALL TO FOLLOW JESUS

I'm leaving all to follow Jesus

I'm turning all the world away

I'm stepping out upon His promise

And all I have is His today

MUST BE JESUS' LOVE DIVINE

I have something, something within me

Makes me know that I'm His child

I have something, something within me
That keeps me meek and keeps me mild
I have something, something within me
Brings me love and peace sublime
I have something, something within me
Must be Jesus' love divine

Chorus
Must be Jesus' love divine
Moving in this heart of mine
Must be Jesus' love divine
Keeps me singing all the time
For when I'm tempted to despair
Something within gives me cheer
I have something, something within me
Must be Jesus' love divine

I have something, something within me
What it is I cannot say
I have something, something within me
Guides my feet along the way
I have something, something within me
Keep me on the firing line
I have something, something within me
Must be Jesus' love divine

I have something, something within me
Keeps my hands from doing wrong
I have something, something within me
Keeps me from all hurt and harm
I have something, something within me
I have something, something within me
Greater joy I cannot find
I have something, something within me
Must be Jesus' love divine

ALL THE WAY
Use me, Lord, in Thy service
Draw me nearer every day
I am willing, Lord, to run all the way
If I falter while I'm trying, don't be angry. Let me stay
I will be willing, Lord, to run all the way

Chorus
All the way, all the way
I'll be willing, Lord, to run all the way
If I falter while I'm trying, don't be angry. Let me stay
I'll be willing, Lord, to run all the way

Pained by heartaches, scorned by loved ones
A little sunshine now and then
There are mountains in my life so hard to climb
But I promise I'll keep climbing
If you will only let me in
I'll be willing to run all the way

Wasted days are now behind me
My evening sun is sinking fast
Every moment brings me nearer to the end
I will hurry in Thy service
If You will only let me in
I'll be willing, Lord, to run all the way

When I've done my last service
And there's nothing I can do
Just a weary, tired pilgrim, sad and lonely
Only linger ever near me
While I near my home, sweet home
I'll be willing, Lord, to run all the way

THE LORD IS MY SHEPHERD WHAT COULD I DO?
He's my bread. He's my water. He's my life. He's my everything
He's my comfort, whatever years may bring
He's my rock, mighty tower
He's my strength, all my power
What could I do if it weren't for the Lord?

Chorus
What could I do? What could I do?
What could I do? What could I do?

157

What could I do without the comfort of
His word?
What could I see? What could I say?
What could I feel well? How could I pray?
What could I do if it wasn't for the Lord?

He's my doctor. He's my lawyer
He's my teacher. He's my friend indeed
He's everything it takes to fill my needs
Keeps me young, keeps me strong
Keeps me right when I'm wrong
What could I do if it wasn't for the Lord?

I'M GOING TO LIVE THE LIFE I SING ABOUT IN MY SONG

Every day, everywhere on the busy thor-
oughfare
Folks may watch me. Some may spot me
Say I'm foolish, but I don't care
I can't sing one thing and then live an-
other
Be a saint by day and a devil under cover
I'm going to live the life I sing about in
my song

Chorus

I'm going to live the life I sing about in
my song
I'm going to stand for right and always
shun the wrong
In the crowd or if I'm alone
On the streets or in my home
I'm going to live the life I sing about in
my song

If at day, if at night, I must always walk
in the light
Some mistake me, underrate me, because
I want to do what's right
I can't go to church and shout all day
Sunday
Go get drunk and raise sand on Monday
I've got to live the life I sing about in my
song

ONE DAY

One day when heaven was filled with
its praises
One day when sin was a black as could
be
Jesus came forth to be born of a virgin
Lived among men, my Redeemer is He

Chorus

Living He loved me. Dying He saved me
Buried He carried my sins far away
Rising He justified, freed me forever
One day He's coming back, glorious day

One day they led Him, up Calvary's
mountain
One day they nailed Him for me on the
tree
Wonderful Counselor, they had ac-
claimed Him
Lived, loved, and labored, my teacher is
He

THE LORD WILL MAKE A WAY SOMEHOW

Like a ship that's tossed and driven
Battered by the angry sea
When the storms of life are raging
And the fury falls on me
I wonder what I have done
That makes this race so hard to run
Then I say to my soul, "Take courage
The Lord will make a way somehow"

Chorus

The Lord will make a way somehow
When beneath the Cross I bow
He will take away each sorrow
Let Him have your burdens now
When the load bears down so heavy
The weight is shown upon my brow
There's sweet relief in knowing
O, the Lord will make a way somehow

Try to do my best in service
Try to live the best I can
When I choose to do the right thing
Evil's present on every hand
I look around and wonder why
That good fortune pass me by
Then I say to my soul, "Be patient
The Lord will make a way somehow"

Often there's misunderstanding
Out of all the good I do
I go to friends for consolation
And find them complaining too
So many nights I toss in pain
Wondering what the day will bring
But I say to my heart, "Don't worry
The Lord will make a way somehow"

THE ROYAL TELEPHONE
Central's never busy, always on the line
You may hear from heaven almost any
time
'Tis a royal service, free for one and all
When you get in trouble, give this royal
line a call

Chorus
Telephone to glory, O what joy divine!
I can feel the current moving on the line
Built by God the Father for His loving
own
You may talk to Jesus through this royal
telephone

There will be no charges, telephone is
free
It was built for service, just for you and
me
There will be no waiting on this royal
line
Telephone to glory always answers just
in time

LET'S GO BACK
In this modernistic day, we have strayed
too far away
From our camp meeting and praying
ground
Where we would fast and pray all day
and let God have His way
Back there on that old praying ground

Chorus
Oh! Let's go back. Let's go back to our
Father's praying ground
God is not pleased. Let's go back on
bended knee
Too far away we have strayed
Just now and then a soul is saved
Let's go back to our Father's praying
ground

Through the country they would ride
With their children by their side
Traveling through some cold and rain,
just the same
Going to the house of the Lord, where
they would bow in one accord
Singing come ye that love the Lord in
Jesus' name

Though the preacher could hardly read
What he said, sinners took heed
And would steal away somewhere and
bow down
Sometimes by an old tree
One would cry out, "He spake peace to
me
Just before, at my old praying ground"

I SHALL WEAR A CROWN
Watch ye, therefore, you know not the
day
When the Lord shall call your soul away
If you labor, striving for the right
You shall wear a golden crown

Chorus
I shall wear a crown
When the trumpet sound
I shall wear a crown
Oh, I shall wear a golden crown

Be not like the foolish virgins then
For He's coming, and you know not
when
Have your lamps all trimmed and burn-
ing bright
And you shall wear a golden crown

Though the host of hell your soul assail
Naught of these against your soul pre-
vail
Never faint nor lay your armour down
And you shall wear a golden crown

I'M GOING BACK TO JESUS
I'm going back to Jesus, I can no longer
wander
My heart I turned to Jesus. I cannot
grieve Him longer
I miss the sweet communion, the peace
of heavenly union
My heart is turned to Jesus and I must
go

Chorus
I'm going back to Jesus (repeat)
I'm going where the living waters flow
I can hear my Savior calling. Repentance
tears are falling
My heart is turned back to Jesus and I
must go

I'm traveling back to Jesus. My steps are
slow and feeble
I pray that the Lord will help me and
keep me from all evil
And should my strength forsake me, dear
Jesus come and take me
My heart is turned to Jesus, I must go

160

HE IS A BRIGHT AND MORNING STAR
Who is this coming from Eden
With His garments dyed from Bozah?
'Tis Jesus Christ of Nazareth
I am His and He is mine

Chorus
He is the Lion of the Tribe of Judah
He is the Root and Offspring of David
He is the Lily of the Valley
He is the Bright and Morning Star

He is the fairest of ten thousand
He is altogether lovely
He is the sweetest rose in Sharon
He is the Bright and Morning Star

Return unto thy God, O Israel
Who healeth all of thy diseases
Who forgiveth thy transgressions
And remembereth them no more!

COME UNTO ME
Hear the blessed Savior calling the oppressed
"All ye heavy laden, come to Me and
rest
Come, no longer tarry, I your load will
bear
Bring your heavy burden, bring Me every care

Chorus
Come unto Me, and I will give you rest
Take My yoke upon you, hear Me and
be blessed
I am meek and lowly, come and trust My
might
Come, My yoke is easy and My burden's
light"

Are you disappointed, wand'ring here
and there?

Dragging chains of doubt, and loaded down with care?
Do untold feelings struggle in your breast
Bring your cares to Jesus, He will give you rest

Have you cares of business, cares of pressing debt?
Cares of social life or cares of hope unmet?
Hear the tender Shepherd, "Come to me and rest"
Come right on to Jesus. He will give you rest

LIFT UP A STANDARD

Now when Daniel found out
That the writing was signed
He went to his room in his own set time
He fell on his knees and began to pray
In the spirit I could hear him say
"I'm going to lift up a standard for the King

Chorus

I'm going to lift up a standard for the King,
I'm going to lift up a standard for the King,
I'm going to lift up a standard for the King,
All over this world I'm going to stand"

When the king had signed the wicked decree
Daniel was found down on his knees
"I'm going to pray three times a day
And look to Jesus to open the way
I'm going to lift up a standard for the King"

When Daniel was caught by the wicked men
They cast poor Daniel in the lion's den

Daniel went down feeling no fear
Just because he knew his God would hear
"I'm going to lift up a standard for the King"

The King was in trouble all night long
He felt that he treated poor Daniel wrong
He went down early in the morning to see
"King the God I serve has delivered me"

HE'S GOT THE WHOLE WORLD IN HIS HAND

Just come on with your money
Don't be afraid to give
He's got the whole world in His hand
He sure will let you live

Chorus

He's got the whole world in His hand
He's got the whole world in His hand
He's got the whole world in His hand
He's got the world in His hand

He just asks for a dime of a dollar
He'll bless you if you will
But in the free-will offering
He'll take whatever you give

The Holy Ghost is a teacher
Indeed He will make you wise
If you listen to His teachings
He will teach you to pay your tithes

Some say I give to the cripple
Some say I give to the blind
But when you get through giving
You owe the Lord that dime

I AM OUT ON THE BATTLEFIELD

I was alone and idle. I was a sinner too
I heard a voice from Heaven saying,
"There is work to do"

I took the Master's hand. Joined the
Christian band
Now I am out on the battlefield for my
Lord

I left my friends and kindred. I am bound
for the promised land
The grace of God upon me, the Bible in
my hand
In distant land I've trod crying, "Sinner
come to God"
I am out on the battlefield for my Lord

I lost my flag in battle. The staff is in my
hand
I'll take it to Jesus over in the glory land
And then the sun will shine in this little
soul of mine
I am out on the battlefield for my Lord

Chorus
I am out on the battlefield for my Lord
Yes, I am out on the battlefield for my
Lord
And I promised Him that I would serve
Him till I die
I am out on the battlefield for my Lord

GOD RODE IN A WINDSTORM
God sent Jonah to Nineveh land
To preach the gospel to the heathen men
If Nineveh don't repent in forty days
I'll make away with their wicked ways

Chorus
God rode, in a windstorm
God rode, in a windstorm
God rode, in a windstorm
Troubled everybody's mind

Jonah went down to the seashore
Made up his mind which way to go
Boarded the ship. Paid his fare
God got angry with Jonah right there

Ship got wrecked. Came untied
Captain on board got troubled in mind
Searched the ship down in the deep
Found old Jonah lying fast asleep

Wake up stranger, tell me your name
My name's Jonah and I'm fleeing from
my king
All of this trouble's just on account of
me
If you'll throw me over board your ship'll
sail free

I'D GIVE UP ALL MY SINS
TO SERVE THE LORD
When I sought the Lord I heard His
blessed word
I just gave up everything to follow Him
I heard him in a song. I gave up every
wrong
I just gave up everything to follow Him
My broken heart was mended
My life in Him was blended
And now I recommend my Savior as a
friend
I'd give up all my sins and seek the Lord

Oh sinner if I were you, I tell you what I
would do
I'd give up all my sins and seek the Lord
I'd heed his tender voice. His way I'd
make my choice
I'd give up all my sins and serve the Lord
It's great to follow Jesus
He can always please me
He'll dry your tears away turn darkness
into day
I'd give up all my sins to serve the Lord

This world is not your home, no matter
where you roam
Someday you've got to answer to the
Lord

162

It may be soon or late. Why do you hesi-
tate?
I'd give up all my sins and serve the Lord
Should he call today or tomorrow
Would there be joy or sorrow?
Right now is the time,to seek and serve
the Lord
If you're turned away, there will be no
time to pray

LIVING ON STRAIGHT STREET
I used to live in Broadway
Right next door to the liar's house
My number was self-righteousness
And a very little guide of mouth
But I moved, now living on Straight
Street

Chorus
I have moved, living on Straight Street
I moved, living on Straight Street
I have moved off Broadway
I am living on straight Street

On day my heart got troubled
About my dwelling place
I sought the Lord for His saving grace
And He told me to leave that place so I
moved

Before I moved over here
Let me tell you how it was with me
Old Satan had me bound to sin. I had
no liberty
Until I moved, living on Straight Street

My heart got faint and worried
My own way I got tired
I wanted to be saved and sanctified, so I
moved
Now I am living on Straight Street

When I lived on Broadway
Adulterers were my pals

We ran together hand in hand
Till I got my feet all snared
Then I moved, I'm living on Straight
Street

ALL ALONE
On Mt. Olive's sacred brow
Jesus spent the night in prayer
He is the pattern for us all, all alone
If we could only steal away
In some portion of the day
We will find it always pays to be alone

There are days to fast and pray
For the pilgrim in this way
There are days I like to be with Christ
alone
We can tell Him all our grief
He will give us quick relief
There are days I like to be with Christ
alone

Chorus
There are days I like to be alone with
Christ the Lord
I can tell Him all my troubles, all alone
There are days I like to be all alone with
Christ the Lord
I can tell Him all my troubles, all alone

BRING BACK THOSE
HAPPY DAYS
When we used to meet on the street
It was Glory! Hallelujah! Praise the Lord
We would greet each other with a holy
kiss
Lord, bring back those happy days

Chorus
Lord, bring back those happy days
Lord, bring back those happy days
When the love of God was found in ev-
ery heart
Lord bring back those happy days

When we use to pray for the sick
And the Lord sometimes would raise the
dead
We were kind to the widows, and we
were good to the poor
Lord, bring back those happy days

THERE'S A HIGHWAY
TO HEAVEN
My way gets brighter
My load gets lighter
Walking up the King's highway
There's joy in knowing
With Him I'm going
Walking up the King's highway

Chorus
It's a highway to Heaven
None can walk up there but the pure in
heart
It's a highway to Heaven
I am walking up the King's highway

Don't have to worry
Don't have to hurry
Walking up the King's highway
Christ walks beside me
Angels to guide me
Walking up the King's highway

If you're not walking
Start while I'm talking
Walking up the King's highway
There'll be a blessing
You'll be possessing
Walking up the King's highway

JUST A LITTLE WHILE
Soon this life will be over. Our pilgrim-
age will end
Soon we'll take our heavenly journey, be
at home again with friends
Heavenly gates are standing open waiting for our entrance

Some day we're going over, all the beau-
ties there to share

Chorus
Just a little while to stay, just a little while
to wait
Just a little while to labor, in the path
that's always straight
Just a little more of troubles in this low
and sinful state
Then we'll enter Heaven's portals sweep-
ing through the pearly gate
Soon well see the light of morning, then
the new day will begin
Soon well hear the Father calling,
"Come, my children enter in"
Then well hear the choir angels singing
out the victory song
And our troubles will be ended, and well
live heavens throng

CAUGHT UP TO MEET HIM
One day I'm going where Jesus is
One day I'm going where Jesus is
One day I'm going where Jesus is
I'll be caught up to meet Him in the air

Chorus
I'll be caught up to meet Him
Caught up to meet Him
Where joy, happiness, and peace abide
There we'll meet in glory and we'll tell
the story
Pressing onward to glorious day

Jesus, He saved my soul one day
Jesus, He saved my soul one day
Jesus, He saved my soul one day
I'll be caught up to meet Him in the air

Oh bye - bye and by I'm going for a
chariot ride
Oh bye - bye and bye I'm going for a
chariot ride

164

Oh bye - bye and bye I'm going for a chariot ride
I'll be caught up to meet Him in the air

FARTHER ALONG

Tempted and tried, we are oft made to wonder
How it could be true all the day long
While there are others living about us
Never molested though in the wrong

Chorus

Farther along we'll know all about it
Farther along we'll understand why
Cheer up, my brother, live in the sunshine
We'll understand it all bye and bye

When death has come and taken our love ones
It leaves our home so lonely and drear
Then we will wonder how others prosper
Living so wicked year after year

When we see Jesus coming in glory
When He comes from His home in the sly
Then we shall meet Him in the bright morning
We'll understand it all bye and bye

Faithful till death, said our loving Master
Just a few more days to labor and wait
Toils of the road will then seem as nothing
As we sweep through the beautiful gate

THE GOSPEL SHIP

I have good news to bring
And that is why I sing
And my joy with you I share
I'm going to take a trip

In that old Gospel ship
And go sailing through the air
O, I can scarcely wait
I know I won't be late
For I'll spend my time in prayer
And when my ship comes in
I'll leave this world of sin
And go sailing through the air

Chorus

I'm going to take a trip
In that old Gospel ship
And I'm going far beyond the sky
I'm going to shout and sing
Until the heaven rings
When I bid this world good bye
I'm going to take a ride
Right by my Savior's side
And I will not have to care
I'll leave my burdens here
Just every sigh and fear
And go sailing through the air

If you're ashamed of me
You had not ought to be
Yes you better have a care
If too much fault you find
You'll sure be left behind
While I go traveling through the air
Joshua, Samuel and Ruth
Who love the Gospel truth
I shall see when I get there
O, won't that all be grand
To join that holy band
And go traveling through the air

HE'S ABLE TO CARRY YOU THROUGH

He's able to carry you through
No matter what the world may do
Try Jesus, for He satisfies
He's waiting just to hear you cry
Trust Him in everything you do

For He will bear the load for you
He's able, able, able, able, able, to carry
   you through

I met Him when I was young
This race had just begun
Sometimes the hills are hard to climb
I found in Him a peace of mind
Though' tempted in this sinful land
He took me and held my hand
He's able, able, able, able, able, to carry
   you through

THERE IS POWER IN THE BLOOD

Would you be free from your burden of
   sin?
There's power in the blood, power in the
   blood
Would you o'er evil victory win?
There's wonderful power in the blood

Chorus

There is power, power, wonder working
   power
In the blood of the lamb
There is power, power, wonder working
   power
In the precious blood of the lamb

Would you be free from your passion and
   pride?
There's power in the blood, power in the
   blood
Come for a cleansing to Calvary's tide
There's wonderful power in the blood

Would you be whiter, much whiter than
   snow?
There's power in the blood, power in the
   blood
Sin stains are lost in its life giving flow
There's wonderful power in the blood

SOMEBODY'S HERE AND I KNOW IT'S JESUS

Somebody's here and I know it's Jesus
Somebody's here and I know it is the
   Lord
Somebody's here and I know it's Jesus
Somebody's here and I know it is the
   Lord

I can feel Him in my heart and I know
   it's Jesus
I can feel Him in my heart and I know it
   is the Lord
I can feel Him working now, and I know
   it's Jesus
I can feel Him working now, and I know
   it is the Lord

WHEN I TAKE MY VACATION

So many are taking vacations
To the mountains, the lakes and the seas
To rest from their care and their worries
What a wonderful time that must be
But it seems not my lot to be like them
I must toil through the heat and the cold
Seeking out the lost sheep in the moun-
   tain
Bringing wanderers back to the fold

Chorus

When I take my vacation in Heaven
What a wonderful time that must be
Hearing concert from Gabriel's chorus
And the face of my Savior I see
Sitting down on the banks of the river
'Neath the shade of the evergreen tree
I shall rest from my burdens forever
Won't you take your vacation with me

Now some day I shall take my vacation
To the city John tells us about
With its foundation walls so precious
Where from gladness of heart I shall
   shout

Oh, no sight ever witnessed by mortal
Can compare with the glories up there
I shall spend my vacation with Jesus
In the place He went to prepare

There the weather will always be per-
fect
Not a cloud shall sweep o'er the sky
No earthquakes or cyclones shall
threaten
In the land of the sweet bye and bye
There is soon to be an excursion
I am booked for a ride in the air
You are invited to share my vacation
And the feast of our bridegroom to share

DOING ALL THE GOOD WE CAN
Whatever may be our station, high or
low it may be
There is an obligation that rests on you
and me
Let Jesus be our leader to guide us
through this land
Where the angels wait to welcome that
grand united band

Chorus
Doing all the good we can, doing all the
good we can
We all are missionaries
Doing all the good we can, doing all the
good we can
Doing all the good we can
We all are Missionaries, doing all the
good we can

We're taking in the outcast. We give the
widow aid
We're looking for salvation. For Jesus said
He paid
Fight until the Savior shall give the last
command
And this shall be our motto, doing all
the good we can

Moses was their leader, the meekest in
the land
He led the children of Israel from under
Pharaoh's cruel hand
God called him on Mount Nebo to view
the promised land
He was buried by a band of angels, and
not by human hand

SOW RIGHTEOUS SEED
There is coming a day when to judgment
we must go
There to reap as in life you have sown
Death eternal we will reap, if we sow to
the flesh
Heaven's joy will not be known

Every act you perform is a seed to some-
one
And the influence will never die
Be careful each day what you do and
what you say
You will reap it again bye and bye

Chorus
May we sow righteous seed for the reap-
ing
Which is coming to everyone
Oh, the joy on that day, when we hear
Jesus say
"Come, ye blessed, a crown you have
won"

NOBODY BUT YOU LORD
Who healed my wounded heart one
evening?
Nobody but You, Lord — nobody but
you
Who stopped my poor weary heart from
grieving?
Nobody but You, Lord — nobody but
You

167

Chorus

Nobody but You, Lord — nobody but You
Can keep me Holy and living true
When I'm in trouble, You carry me through
Nobody but You, Lord — nobody but You

Who can calm the ocean's wildest billows?
Nobody but You, Lord — nobody but You
Who can make down life's death pillows?
Nobody but You, Lord — nobody but You

Who gives peace for every trial?
Nobody but You, Lord — nobody but You
Who gives me joy and no denial?
Nobody but You, Lord — nobody but You

Who died to save the world from sorrow?
Nobody but You, Lord—nobody but You
Who gives us power for tomorrow?
Nobody but You, Lord—nobody but You

Through the year I keep on toiling
Toiling through the storm and rain
Watchfully and patiently waiting
Till my Savior comes again
I am waiting Lord, trusting in Thy word
Keep me from the paths of sin
Hide me in Thy love, write my name above
When the gates swing open, let me in

Prayer will keep me fit for service
Help me on every hand
I've stood many a trial
Some day I'll understand

I am praying, Lord, trusting in Thy word
Keep me from the paths of sin
Hide me in Thy love. Write my name above
When the gates swing open, let me in

Teach me how to love my neighbor
Teach me how to treat-my friends
Fill me with the Holy Spirit
Keep me humble to the end
Keep me humble, Lord, trusting-in Thy word
Keep me from the paths of sin
Hide me in Thy love. Write my name above
When the gates swing open, let me in

Tired of the load I am carrying
Tired of this world of sin
Angels in the kingdom beckon
Saying, "Weary soul come in"
I am coming, Lord, trusting in Thy word
Keep me from the paths of sin
Hide me in Thy love. Write my name above
When the gates swing open, let me in

I KNOW THE BIBLE'S RIGHT

You can get your Bible
And read through and through
Every time it says to be holy
It is talking to you

Chorus

I know the Bible's right
Well, there is somebody wrong
I know the Bible's right
Somebody is wrong

You read St. Matthew, one-twenty-one
The angel told Mary
She should bear a Son
I told you once, I tell you twice
That you can't go to Heaven

With a sweetheart and a wife
Some preachers come to your house
You ask him to rest his hat
The next thing that he wants to know
Sister, where is your husband at
Some preachers are given to have two
    wives
And if you spring the question
You see their temper rise

HAVE YOU ANY TIME FOR JESUS
Have you any time for Jesus
While the fleeting moments roll?
Is this mortal life so busy
That you cannot save your soul?

Chorus
Soon the summons from the portal
From the mansion in the skies
It may be sounding your departure
You must then take time to die

Time for business, time for pleasure
Time to revel on in sin
Will you not take time for Jesus?
Oh, invite Him to come in

Have you any time for Jesus?
Can it be life's journey through
That you have no time for Jesus
Who has spent His life for you?

If you have no time for Jesus
And you pass beyond the blue
In the resurrection morning
He will not have time for you

LOYALTY TO CHRIST
From over hill and plain
There comes a signal strain
'Tis loyalty, loyalty, loyalty to Christ
It's music rolls along
The hills take up the song
'Tis loyalty, loyalty, loyalty to Christ

Chorus
On to victory, on to victory
Cries the Great Commander on
We'll move at His command
We'll soon possess the land
Through loyalty, loyalty, loyalty to Christ

Come join our loyal throng
We'll rout the giant wrong
'Tis loyalty, loyalty, loyalty to Christ
Where Satan's banner floats
We'll send the bugle notes
Of loyalty, loyalty, loyalty to Christ

The strength of youth we lay
At Jesus' feet today
'Tis loyalty, loyalty, loyalty to Christ
His glory we'll proclaim
Throughout the world's domain
Of loyalty, loyalty, loyalty to Christ

JESUS, I'LL NEVER FORGET
Jesus, I'll never forget, when away down
    in Egypt land
How you brought me out, with a mighty
    outstretched hand
Broke the bonds of sin, and set me free
Gave me joy, peace and liberty

Chorus
Jesus, I'll never forget what You've done
    for me
Jesus I'll never forget how You set me
    free
Jesus, I'll never forget how You brought
    me out
Jesus, I'll never forget no, never

Jesus, I'll never forget how You stood by
    me
When I lost all help and was in misery
You strengthened my poor soul and bid
    me live
Now a consecrated life to Thee I'll give

WHAT HE DONE FOR ME
He sanctified me with the Holy Ghost
What He done for me
(Repeat twice)
I shall never forget what He done for me

Chorus
Oh, Oh, Oh, Oh, what He done for me
(Repeat twice)
I never shall forget what He done for me

He took my feet out of the miry clay
What He done for me
(Repeat twice)
I never shall forget what He done for me

He baptized my soul with the Holy Ghost
What He done for me
(Repeat twice)
I never shall forget what He done for me

I MEAN TO WORK UNTIL
THE DAY IS DONE
I mean to work until the day is done
I mean to work until the day is done
To cease from sorry, there'll be no tomorrow
I mean to work until the day is done

I mean to work until the victory is won
To fast and pray all along the way
Not run but not wear out, though tossed and driven about
I mean to work until the day is done

SINGING IN MY SOUL
I'm so glad somehow I've got salvation
It keeps the Spirit moving in my soul
Every day I find it's peace and joy in mind
It keeps me singing in my soul

Chorus
I'm singing, oh I'm singing in my soul
When the troubles roll

I sing from morn till night
It makes my burdens light
I'm singing in my soul

Every now and then there's something speaks within
And often tells me when I'm doing wrong
Then I steal away and bow my head and pray
My heart rings out a triumph song

I SHALL KNOW HIM
When my life's work is ended and I cross the swelling tide
When the bright and glorious morning I shall see
I shall know my Redeemer when I reach the other side
And His smile will be the first to welcome me

Chorus
I shall know Him (repeat)
And redeemed by His side I shall stand;
I shall know Him (repeat)
By the prints of the nails in His hands

Oh, the soul-thrilling rapture when I view His blessed face
And the luster of His kindly gleaming eye
How my heart will praise Him for His mercy, love and grace
That prepared for me a mansion in the sky

Oh, the dear ones in glory, how they beckon me to come
And our parting at the river I recall
To the sweet veils of Eden they will sing my welcome home
To the sweet veils of Eden they will sing my welcome home

HONEY IN THE ROCK
Like honey in the rock
Like honey in the rock
Yes it tastes like honey in the rock
Oh taste and see that the Lord is good
Oh it tastes like honey in the rock

MY RECORD WILL BE THERE
In a day that is not far, at the blazing
  judgment bar
Even now the awful summons I can hear
I must meet the mighty God
I must face His holy sword
I must stand before the judgment bar

Chorus
Oh, my record will be there, be its pages
  dark or fair
When I stand before the judgment bar
Oh, the book shall open wide in that
  morning bye and bye
My record, oh, my record will be there

We shall meet each broken vow that we
  hold so lightly now
Every heartache we have caused, each
  sigh or tear
Time cannot erase, we shall meet it face
  to face
We shall stand before the judgment bar

Every sinful deed and thought, then shall
  be to judgment brought
When the Lord in all His glory shall appear
All the deeds of darkest night shall come
  out to meet the light
When I stand before the judgment bar

I must meet my cankered soul, for whose
  greed my life was sold
It shall mock me in the judgment's lurid
  glare

Saying, "Ye have sold for naught, all the
  Savior's blood has bought
And you stand before the judgment bar"

Let us turn and seek the Lord. Let us trust
  His holy Word
Let us bow and call upon Him while He
  is near
Then my record I shall face. He will an-
  swer in my place
When I stand before the judgment bar

NOTHING SHALL MOVE ME
Nothing shall move me, nothing shall
  move me
Nothing shall move me from the word
  of God
Nothing shall move me, nothing shall
  move me
Nothing shall move me from the word
  of God

Trials won't move me, trials won't move
  me
Trials won't move me from the word of
  God
Trials won't move me, trials won't move
  me
Trials won't move me from the word of
  God

I'M PRESSING ON
ON ALL I KNOW
I'm pressing on, on all I know
I'm pressing on, everywhere I go
I'm pressing on, to that city
Where the mansions are prepared for me

Oh the press is on everywhere I go
I have some faith, but I'm asking for more
I'm pressing on, to that city
Where the mansions are prepared for me

I'M SO GLAD SO GLAD TODAY
I'm so glad the word is right
Now Jesus keeps me day and night
And if you let him he your guide
He will keep you sanctified

Chorus
I'm so glad, so glad today
That Jesus took my sins away
Oh He's my all, my all and all
I will answer to His call

I'm so glad, I'm saved from sin
Jesus so sweetly dwell within
You to Him I recommend
He'll go with you to the end

PRECIOUS MEMORIES
Precious memories, unseen angels
Sent from somewhere to my soul
As they linger ever near me
And the sacred past unfold

Chorus
Precious memories how they linger
How they ever flood my soul
In the stillness of the midnight
Precious sacred scene unfold

In the stillness of the midnight
Echoes from the past I hear
Old-time singing gladness ringing
From the lonely somewhere

As I travel on life's pathway
Know not what the years may hold
As I ponder, hope grows fonder
Precious memories flood my soul

LET'S GO ON
Let's go on, let's go on
Talking about that good old way
Let's go on, let's go on
Talking about the Lord

Feeling so much better
Talking about that good old way
Feeling so much better
Talking about the Lord

COME BY HERE GOOD LORD, COME BY HERE
Come by here good Lord, come by here
Come by here good Lord, come by here
Come by here good Lord, come by here
Oh Lord come by here

Somebody needs you Lord, come by here
Somebody needs you Lord, come by here
Somebody needs you Lord, come by here
Oh Lord, come by here

I KNOW THE BLOOD HAS MADE ME WHOLE
I know the blood has made me whole
I know the blood has made me whole
I have touched the hem of His garment
I know the blood has made me whole

King Jesus blood has made me whole
King Jesus blood has made me whole
I have touched the hem of his garment
King Jesus blood has made me whole

LITTLE BOY
When this little boy had made them re-member
That He was born on the twenty-fifth of December
The lawyers and doctors stood and amazed
But they had to give the little boy all the praise

Chorus
Little boy how old are you?
Little boy how old are you?
Little boy how old are you?
I'm only twelve years old

When the little boy began to grow older
His father and mother took him along
Returning from the feast they were near
They looked for the boy but the boy was
    gone

The lawyers and doctors began to won-
    der
Just like their heads were struck with
    thunder
To see the little boy was the youngest
And all the wise men had to come un-
    der

This little boy was a loving little child
In his mouth you find no guile
He died for you and He died for me
Just like He was we all must be

The lawyers and doctors were so high
They didn't know the little boy was so
    wise
They had studied multiplication
But the boy had to die for the whole
    generation

When the boy had given the key
They all wondered Who was He
The head of the council could plainly
    see
You had better let that little boy be

When the boy grew strong and old
Upon His shoulders was the government
The key of David placed in His hand
He had to die for every man

This little boy was Jesus Christ
He died to give the world eternal life
All who own Him do believe
A blessed comfort to receive

DON'T YOU WANT TO BE
A LOVER OF THE LORD
Don't you want to be a lover of the Lord
Of the Lord of the Lord
Don't you want to be a lover of the Lord
Don't you want to go to heaven when
    you die ?

EVERYTHING IN YOU
GOT TO COME OUT
Everything in you got to come out
Everything in you got to come out
If you want to go back with Jesus when
    He comes
Everything in you got to come out

If lying is in you, it's got to come out
If lying is in you, it's got to come out
If you want to go back with Jesus when
    He comes
Everything in you got to come out

If envy is in you, it's got to come out
If envy is in you, it's got to come out
If you want to go back with Jesus when
    He comes
Everything in you got to come out

If hatred is in you it's got to come out
If hatred is in you it's got to come out
If you want to go back with Jesus when
    He comes
Everything in you got to come out

MY LORD AND I
I have a friend so precious so very dear
    to me
He loves me with such tender love, loves
    me so faithfully
I could not live apart from Him, I love
    to feel Him nigh
And so we dwell together, my Lord and I

He knows how I am longing some precious soul to win
Back to the ways of righteousness from
the weary path of sin
He bids me tell His wondrous love, and
why He came to die
And so we walk together, my Lord and I

Chorus
My Lord and I (repeat)
And so we dwell together, my Lord and
I
My Lord and I (repeat)
And so we dwell together my Lord and I

SINCE THE COMFORTER
HAS COME
He'S taken me out from under the law
Yes, He did — yes, He did
And placed me in the number that I
John saw
Yes, He did — yes, He did

Chorus
You can tell the world about this
You can tell the nations I'm blessed
Tell them what Jesus has done, since the
comforter has come
And bring joy, joy, joy to my soul

My Lord has done just what He said
Yes, He did — yes, He did
He healed the sick and raised the dead
Yes, He did, — yes, He did

My Lord knew what I needed the most
Yes, He did — yes, He did
He filled my soul with the Holy Ghost
Yes, He did — yes, He did

I DON'T KNOW WHAT I'D DO
WITHOUT THE LORD
I am married to Jesus
And we never have been apart

I have a telephone in my bosom
I can ring Him from my heart
I can get Him on the air
Down on my knee in prayer
I don't know what I'd do without the
Lord

Sometimes I feel discouraged
And think my life's in vain
But since this mighty hand
With me has never changed
I have held to His mighty hand
Traveling on to the promised land
I don't know what I'd do without the
Lord

Chorus
I don't know what I'd do without the
Lord
I don't know what I'd do without the
Lord
When I look around and see what the
Lord has done for me
I don't know what I'd do without the
Lord

I CAME TO GLORIFY HIS NAME
He has set me free
He brought my liberty
He paid the price with His own precious
blood
On the cross of Calvary

Chorus
I came to glorify His name
I came to glorify His name
I came to glorify the name of the Lord
I came to glorify His name

He arose saying, "All Hail
I have triumphed over the grave
All power in heaven and earth I have
The keys of death and hell in my hand"

174

IF THIS AIN'T THE HOLY GHOST

If this ain't the Holy Ghost I don't know
It just suits me
If this ain't the Holy Ghost I don't know
It just suits me
If this ain't the Holy Ghost I don't know
I never felt this way before
And it just suits me

WALK WITH ME LORD
WALK WITH ME

Walk with me, Lord, walk with me
Walk with me, Lord, walk with me
All along this pilgrim journey
I want Jesus to walk with me

Be my guide, Lord, be my guide
Be my guide, Lord, be my guide
All alone this pilgrim journey
I want Jesus to walk with me

I'M SO GLAD JESUS LIFTED ME

I'm so glad, Jesus lifted me
I'm so glad, Jesus lifted me
I'm so glad, Jesus lifted me
Glory, Hallelujah, Jesus lifted me

Satan had me bound, but Jesus lifted me
Satan had me bound, but Jesus lifted me
Satan had me bound, but Jesus lifted me
Glory, Hallelujah, Jesus lifted me

THERE IS SOMETHING
WITHIN ME

Oh preachers and teachers have made
their appeal
Just fighting like soldiers on life's battlefield
And when to their pleading, my poor
heart did yield
All I could say, "Praise God there is
something within"

Chorus

There is something within me that's just
holding the reins
There is something within me that just
banishes pain
There is something within me more than
I can explain
All I can say, "praise God, there is some-
thing within"

Oh, have you that something, that burn-
ing desire?
Have you that something, that never
does tire?
Now if you have it, that heavenly fire
Then, let the world know, there is something within

THERE'S NO CONDEMNATION
IN MY LIFE

There is therefore now no condemnation
There is therefore now no condemnation
There is therefore now no condemnation
No condemnation in my life

I can testify, there's no condemnation
I can testify, there's no condemnation
I can testify, there's no condemnation
No condemnation in my life

I feel alright, there's no condemnation
I feel alright, there's no condemnation
I feel alright, there's no condemnation
No condemnation in my life

WHEN WE ALL GET TO HEAVEN

Sing the wondrous love of Jesus
Sing His mercy and His grace
In the mansions bright and blessed
He'll prepare for us a place

Chorus
When we all get to heaven
What a day of rejoicing that will be
When we all see Jesus
We'll sing and shout victory

While we walk the pilgrim pathway
Clouds will over-spread the sky
But when traveling days are over
Not a shadow, nor a sigh

I LOVE JESUS
I love Jesus (So do I)
I love Jesus (So do I)
I love Jesus (So do I)
I love Jesus (So do I)
I love Jesus He's my Savior
And He smiles and He loves me too

Glory Hallelujah (Praise the Lord)
Glory Hallelujah (Praise the Lord)
Glory Hallelujah (Praise the Lord)
Glory Hallelujah (Praise the Lord)
I love Jesus He's my Savior
And He smiles and He loves me too

SAVED AND I KNOW I AM
I'm saved and I know I am
Saved and I know I am
Saved and I know I am
I'm saved and I know I am

My sins are all under the blood
My sins are all under the blood
My sins are all under the blood
My sins are all under the blood

I don't have to sin no more
I don't have to sin no more
I don't have to sin no more
I don't have to sin no more

CALL ON JESUS
Call on Jesus. He will answer prayer
Call on Jesus. He will answer prayer
Call on Jesus. He will answer prayer
Call on Jesus. He will answer prayer

He's a prayer hearing Savior. He'll answer prayer
He's a prayer hearing Savior. He'll answer prayer
He's a prayer hearing Savior. He'll answer prayer
He's a prayer hearing Savior. He'll answer prayer

I WILL TO KNOW
I will to know if He will welcome me there
I do not want to be denied
I want to meet Him in that city above
And with Him, I'll ever abide

They tell me of a home beyond the blue skies
A home where no dark clouds shall rise
Oh they tell me of a home in the skies
And with Him, I'll ever abide

GOD'S CALLING
God's calling, why don't you come
God's calling, why don't you come
God's calling, why don't you come
Don't stay away

Make up your mind to go with Jesus
Make up your mind to go with Jesus
Make up your mind to go with Jesus
Don't stay away

SEEKING FOR ME
Jesus, My Savior, from Bethlehem came
Born in a manger, of suffering and shame
Oh it is wonderful, blessed be His name
He's seeking for me, for me

Chorus

Seeking for me, yes He's seeking for me
Oh it is wonderful. How can it be?
He's seeking for me, for me

I WANT TO BE LIKE JESUS

I want to be like Jesus, I want to be like
    Jesus
Oh how I long to be like Him
I'm on my journey, from earth to glory
Oh how I long to be like Him

I want to be like Jesus, I want to be like
    Jesus
Oh how I want to be like Him
So meek and lowly, so humble and holy
Oh how I want to be like Him

COME AND GO WITH ME

No confusion up there in my Father's
    house
In my Father's house, in my father's house
There's no confusion up there in my
    Father's house
There is peace, peace, peace

Chorus

Come and go with me to my Father's
    house
To my Father's house, to my Father's
    house
Come and go with me to my Father's
    house
There is peace, peace, peace

Joy and peace over there in my Father's
    house
In my Father's house, in my Father's
    house
Joy and peace over there in my Father's
    house
There is peace, peace, peace

AT THE CROSS

Alas, and did my Savior bleed?
And did my Sovereign die
Would He denote that sacred head
For such a worm as I?

Chorus

At the cross, at the cross, where I first
    saw the light
And the burden of my heart rolled away
It was there by faith I received my sight
And now I am happy all the way

Was it for crimes that I have done
He groaned upon the tree?
Amazing pity, grace unknown
And love beyond degree

But drops of grief can ne're repay
The debt of love I owe
Here Lord, I give myself away
'Tis all that I can do

ENDNOTES

Introduction

1.   With the rise of Black Theology in the later 1960s, scholars, particularly black schol-
     ars, began to study religion as one of the most important aspects of ethnic identity
     in American culture. Slowly it became apparent through the 1970s that black holi-
     ness-pentecostalism is a major part of the diversity with the black religious experi-
     ence and that William J. Seymour, Azusa Street pioneer; C. H. Mason, of the Church
     of God in Christ; H. L. Fisher of the United Holy Church; W. E. Fuller, Fire Bap-
     tized Church; and G. T. Haywood, Pentecostal Assemblies of the World play criti-
     cal roles in that diversification. Cf. Leonard Lovett, "Black-Holiness Pentecostalism:
     Implications for Ethics and Social Transformation" (Ph.D. Diss., Emory University,
     Candler School of Theology, 1978).
2.   James Baldwin, "White Racism or World Community?" (Paper presented at the
     Fourth Assembly of the World Council of Churches, Uppsala, Sweden, July 1968).

Chapter 1

1.   Bishop Charles H. Pleas was not only Mason's first convert (Asia Baptist Church,
     Natchez, Mississippi, 1896), but he was a founding charter member of the Church
     of God in Christ. In the early years of the twentieth century, he was part of the great
     migration from Mississippi to Kansas. He pioneered the Church of God in Christ in
     the State of Kansas, succeeded D. J. Young as the overseer and later bishop of Kansas
     where he served for almost fifty years. Cf. Charles H. Pleas, *Fifty Years of Achieve-*

ment: *A History of the Early Years of the Church of God in Christ* (Kansas City, KS: privately published, 1955).

2. Charles H. Pleas, *Fifty Years of Achievement: Church of God in Christ* (Kansas City, KS: privately published, 1955), 4.

3. Ibid., 2.

4. See Pleas, *Fifty Years of Achievement.*

5. The initial and oft reproduced biography of Charles H. Mason was first reduced to writing and revised by Professor W. Courts in 1918. It was revised in 1924. Mason's second daughter Mary, who passed away in 1951, reprinted it. Cf. Mary Mason, *The History and Life Work of Bishop C. H. Mason, Chief Apostle and His Co-laborers* (Memphis, TN: Church of God in Christ, 1931), 1-12. Mason died in 1961 at the age of ninety-five and was buried on the grounds of his massive (10,000 seats) Mason Temple, the first such burial allowed in the city. Cf. *The 1966 Official Convocation Program* (Memphis: Church of God in Christ, 1966), 61.

6. Otho Cobbins, *History of Church of Christ (Holiness) U.S.A. 1895-1965* (New York: Vantage Press, 1965), 428-429.

7. Cf. J. H. Green's Introduction to C. P. Jones, *Appeal to the Sons of Africa* (Jackson, MS: Truth, 1902).

8. Cf. Cobbins, *History*, 23.

9. Ibid., 428-429.

10. Ibid., 27-28.

11. Melvin Dieter, *The Holiness Revival.* See also Bob Parrott, *Albert Outler: The Preacher* (Nashville, TN: Abingdon Press, 1988), 264.

12. Cf. Albert C. Outler, ed., *The Works of John Wesley.* Vol. 3, Sermons III, Sermon 85:4 (Nashville, TN: Abingdon Press, 1986), 533. See also Parrott, ed., *Albert Outler: The Preacher* (Nashville, TN: Abingdon Press, 1988), 262-264.

13. Patrick H. Thompson, *Negro Baptists in Mississippi* (Jackson, MS: H. W. Bailey Printing, 1898), 33-36.

14. Professor Lee Williams, Sr., who has taught at Jackson State University for over forty years, has been a member of Mt. Helm Baptist Church of Jackson, Mississippi since 1935, and authored *A Short History of Mt. Helm.* Cf. Lee W. Williams, *Mt. Helm Baptist Church 1835-1988: The Parade of Pastors 1864-1988* (Jackson, MS: Mt. Helm Baptist Church, 1988), 22-25.

15. Cf. Cobbins, *History*, 28.

16. E. C. Morris, *Sermons, Addresses, Reminiscences and Important Correspondence, 1901* (Reprint. New York: Arno Press, 1980).

17. Cf. *The Southern Reporter.*

18. Cf. Vinson Synan, *The Holiness-Pentecostal Movement in the U.S.* (Grand Rapids, MI: William B. Eerdmans, 1971).

19. Timothy Smith, Donald Dayton and Melvin Dieter, various works by title. Cf. Timothy L. Smith, *Called Unto Holiness* (Kansas City, KS: Nazarene, 1962). See also Donald Dayton, *The American Holiness Movement: A Bibliographic Essay* (Wilmore, KY: B. L. Fisher Library, Asbury Theological Seminary, 1972).

20. Melvin E. Dieter, *The Holiness Revival of the Nineteenth Century* (Metuchen, NJ: Scarecrow Press, 1980), 174, 256, 273.

21. For a detailed account of Morris and his role among black Baptists, see James Melvin Washington, *Frustrated Fellowship: The Black Baptist Quest for Social Power* (Macon: Mercer University Press, 1986), 161, 174-175, 178, 181, 185, 191, 193.

22. On the resources of the slave church tradition, see Albert V. Raboteau, *Slave Religion: The "Invisible Institution" in the Antebellum South* (New York: Oxford University Press, 1978), 211-288.

23. Cf. William C. Turner Jr., "Black Evangelicalism: Theology, Politics, Race." *Journal of Religious Thought,* 45, no. 2 (Winter-Spring 1989), 40-56. Gayraud Wilmore and Henry Mitchell, two black church scholars, transcend this bias. Cf. Gayraud S. Wilmore, *Black Religion and Black Radicalism* (Maryknoll, NY: Orbis Books, 1983), 26-27. See also Henry H. Mitchell, *Black Belief* (New York: Harper & Row, 1975), 56-57.

24. Cf. Joseph R. Washington, *Black Religion* (Boston: Beacon Press, 1964). Cf. Sidney Ahlstrom, *The Religious History of the American People* (New Haven, CT: Yale University Press, 1972). Cf. Milton C. Sernett, *Black Religion and American Evangelicalism* (Metuchen, NJ: Scarecrow Press, 1975), 22. On the transformation white "evangelicalism," see Donald Dayton, *Discovering an Evangelical Heritage* (New York: Harper & Row, 1976). On black church "evangelicals," see William Pannell, "The Religious Heritage of Blacks," *The Evangelicals,* eds. David F. Wells and John D. Woodbridge (Nashville, TN: Abingdon Press, 1975), 96-121.

25. Cf. Lee W. Williams, *Mt. Helm Baptist Church 1835-1988: A Short History,* 22-25.

26. See Clifton H. Johnson, ed., *God Struck Me Dead* (New York: Pilgrim Press, 1969).

Chapter 2

1. Albert Raboteau recalled, "The shout would start with a leader calling out a verse of a spiritual while the shouters responded by walking around in a circle," in his *Slave Religion: The "Invisible Institution" in the Antebellum South* (New York: Oxford University Press, 1978), 245. For a discussion of the "Slave-Circle Culture" see Sterling Stuckey, *Slave Culture: Nationalist Theory and the Foundation of Black America* (New York: Oxford University Press, 1987), 3-97.

2. Cf. Zora Neale Hurston, *The Sanctified Church* (Berkeley: Turtle Island Press, 1983), 103-107.

3. Charles Price Jones, *Jesus Only* (Nashville: Baptist Publishing House, 1901). From 1897-1906 Jones printed the periodical, *The Truth*, first from his home, and after 1901 from the Office of Christ Temple in Jackson, Mississippi.

4. James Delk, *He Made Millions Happy* (Hopkinsville, KY: Privately Published, 1950).

5. Ibid., 6-11.

6. The Sanctified Church, led by the United Holy Church of America that was first founded at Method, North Carolina, by C. M. Mason, H. L. Fisher et al. in 1886 and the Church of God in Christ Inc., founded in 1896 and incorporated in 1897, proliferated into over twenty-five national and regional church bodies between 1886-1950.

7. When members of the Church of God in Christ enter Memphis, Tennessee, for their annual holy convocation in November, signs on billboards, in the airport, on the buses, and on bumper stickers announce, "The Saints are Coming."

8. Quoted in Cheryl Gilkes' "Power Among the Powerless: 'The Sanctified Church' and the Reorganization of Black Religion," a paper presented at the Society for the Scientific Study of Religion (22 October 1982), 16.

9. Douglas J. Nelson, "For Such a Time as This: The Story of Bishop William J. Seymour and the Azusa Street Revival, a Search for Pentecostal/Charismatic Roots," (Ph.D. diss, University of Birmingham, England, May 1981), 196-199.

10. J. O. Patterson, German Ross, and Julia Atkins, eds., *History and Formative Years of the Church of God in Christ, Excerpts and Commentary from the Life and Works of Bishop C. H. Mason* (Memphis, TN: Church Of God In Christ Publishing House, 1969), 17. See also Lawrence Neale Jones, "The Black Pentecostals" in *The Charismatic Movement*, edited by Michael P. Hamilton (Grand Rapids, MI: William B. Eerdmans, 1975), 145-158.

11. For a detailed account of the relationship of scores of white churches to the Church of God in Christ and the more than 300 white clergypersons ordained by C. H. Mason, see H. Vinson Synan, *The Holiness-Pentecostal Movement in the United States* (Grand Rapids, MI: William B. Eerdmans, 1971), 169-172.

12. Cf. José Comblin, *The Holy Spirit and Liberation* (Maryknoll, NY: Orbis Books, 1989), 2-3.

13. Ibid., 8-9.

14. Gayraud Wilmore, *The Black Church and Black Radicalism*, 210-213. Emphasis is mine.

15. Cf. Sydney Ahlstrom, *The Religious History of the American People* (New Haven, CT: Yale University Press, 1972), 1063.

16. Such narrow conclusion might be drawn from some social scientific studies, for example, I. M. Lewis, *Ecstatic Religion* (New York: Penguin, 1971) and especially a recent Columbia University dissertation in sociology of religion by Robert Mapes Anderson, *Vision of the Disinherited: The Making of American Pentecostalism* (New

York: Oxford University Press, 1979). For a better general assessment of ecstatic movements in Christianity, and one sensitive to these sociological studies, see Donald L. Gelp, *Pentecostalism: A Theological Viewpoint* (New York: Deus Books, 1971).

17. Cf. Sterling Stuckey, *Slave Culture: Nationalist Theory and the Foundation of Black America* (New York: Oxford University Press, 1987), 3-97.

18. Cited in David M. Tucker, *Black Pastors and Leaders: Memphis, 1819-1972* (Memphis, TN: Memphis State University Press, 1975), 93.

19. Hurston, *The Sanctified Church*, 103.

20. Cf. Stuckey, *Slave Culture*, 97. See also James Baldwin's *Go Tell it on the Mountain* (New York: Dell, 1952), 14-15.

21. One preacher, W. D. Welch, played the violin as the Saints danced in the Spirit. Welch was taught to play the violin by former slaves. He founded one of the first Church of God in Christ congregations in the Memphis, Tennessee area. Interview with the late Bishop O. M. Kelly (January 1982). Cf. Stuckey, *Slave Culture*, 370, note 159.

22. Black Baptist and Methodist churches began to introduce the drums into their church services with the rise of gospel music following World War II. Until the social and cultural revolution of the 1960s, the Baptist and Methodist churches experienced much tension over the use of drums. Elderly members angrily protested, "This is not a holy roller church!" Younger members did not see a problem.

23. Synan, *Holiness-Pentecostal Movement*.

24. Cf. Cheryl Gilkes, "Power Among the Powerless: 'The Sanctified Church' and the Reorganization of Black Religion," paper presented at the Society for the Scientific Study of Religion, (22 October 1982), 16.

25. Tucker, *Black Pastors and Leaders*, 92.

26. Cornel West does a superior task of organizing significant aspects of the African-American past by delineating four ideal types that embody distinct historical traditions of thought and action. They are the exceptionalist, the assimilationist, the marginalist, and the Afro-American humanist traditions. Cf. Cornel West, *Prophesy Deliverance* (Philadelphia: Westminster Press, 1982), 69-91.

27. Ibid., 71.

28. Cf. James Baldwin, *Notes to a Native Son*.

29. Baldwin, *Go Tell It on the Mountain*, 14-15.

30. Arthur Paris has provided us with the best critical survey of the vast body of sociological and anthropological literature on the black holiness-pentecostal churches. Cf. Arthur Paris, *Black Pentecostalism*, chapter 4.

31. Cf. Solomon Poll, *The Hasidic Community of Williamsburg: A Study in the Sociology of Religion* (New York: Schocken Books, 1962), 3.

32. Ibid. Quoted by Cheryl Gilkes in "Power Among the Powerless: 'The Sanctified Church' and the Reorganization of Black Religion," paper presented at the annual

meeting for the Scientific Study of Religion (Providence, RI: 22 October, 1982), 43-44.

33. Cf. Gilkes, "Power Among the Powerless," 44.

34. Minutes of the 12th Annual Holy Convocation, Church of God in Christ, Memphis, Tennessee (November 1919), 13-14. Files of Geraldine Wright, Southfield, Michigan.

35. This author was the first black pentecostal to attend Union Theological Seminary in New York City from 1952-1956.

36. Cf. Roswith Gerloff, "Theory and Practice of the Holy Spirit," *Quaker Religious Thought*, vol. 16, no. 3 (Summer 1975), 2-17. On the fundamentalization of the white pentecostal Assemblies of God, see Gerald T. Sheppard, "Word and Spirit in the Pentecostal Tradition," AGORA 1/4 (1978), 4-5, 17-22 and 2/1 (1978), 14-19.

37. Cf. James S. Tinney, "Black Origins of the Pentecostal Movement," *Christianity Today*, 16, no. 1 (8 October 1971).

38. Ibid., 4.

39. Walter Hollenweger, the preeminent scholar of pentecostalism, inspired a whole generation of historians and theologians, including James Tinney. Cf. Walter Hollenweger, "Black Pentecostal Concept." "Interpretations and Variations," *Concept*, Special Issue No. 30 (June 1970), 9. See also Hollenweger, *The Pentecostals* (Minneapolis, MN: Augsburg Press, 1972). This quote is from Tinney, "Black Origins," 4.

40. Church-sect dynamic is a sociological formulation of religion that has received an enormous amount of serious analysis. It is an omnibus distinction that covers everything from ministry to membership, from theology to ritual, from social class origins to attitudes toward the surrounding society. On each dimension, the "church" holds up one end while the "sect" see-saws on the other. Church-sect refers to two organizational models that are classic polar types. Cf. Ernst Troeltsch, *The Social Teaching of the Christian Churches*, vol. 2, Translated by Olive Wyon (New York: Macmillan, 1932). Actually Max Weber rarely touched on church-sect distinction. He gives credit to Troeltsch, his student and protegé. Cf. Max Weber, *The Protestant Ethic and the Spirit of Capitalism*, translated by Talcott Parsons (New York: Scribner, 1928; paperback ed. 1958), 255. Ernst Troeltsch's church-sect typology applied to European Christianity. Niebuhr saw in it a way to skillfully probe and critique the dynamics of denominationalism that are unique to American Christianity. Cf. Sidney Mead, *The Lively Experiment*.

41. H. Richard Niebuhr, *The Social Sources of Denominationalism* (New York: Holt, Rinehart & Winston, 1929), 3.

42. Ibid., 225.

Chapter 3

1. The most complete survey of bibliography related to pentecostal historiography is by a holiness scholar, Charles Edwin Jones, *A Guide to the Study of the Pentecostal Movement,* vol. 2, parts III and IV (Metuchen, NJ: Scarecrow Press, 1983). For the most objective discussion of pentecostal origins, see Cecil M. Robeck, Jr., "Pentecostal Origins From a Global Perspective" (Paper presented at conference, Brighton, England, July 1991).

2. Douglas C. Nelson, "For Such a Time as This: The Story of Bishop William J. Seymour" (Ph.D. Diss., University of Birmingham, England, May 1981). See also James. S. Tinney, "Black Origins of the Pentecostal Movement" (*Christianity Today,* 10 October 1971). This article predated H. Vinson Synan, *The Holiness-Pentecostal Movement in the U.S.* (Grand Rapids, MI: William B. Eerdmans, 1971).

3. Iain MacRobert, *The Black Roots and White Racism of Early Pentecostalism in the U.S.A.* (London: Macmillan, 1988).

4. H. Vinson Synan, *The Holiness-Pentecostal Movement in the United States* (Grand Rapids, MI: William B. Eerdmans, 1971), see especially 178-184.

5. Nelson, "For Such a Time," 300.

6. Ibid., 299. See the more detailed analysis of Seymour's theology in Robeck, "Pentecostal Origins." ("Evangelist is Arrested," San Antonio Right, 7/21/09).

7. Nelson, "For Such a Time," 150-181.

8. Ibid., 31.

9. Ibid., 181-192. There are two primary eyewitness accounts, one by J. C. Van Zandt, "Speaking in Tongues" (Portland, OR: privately published, n.d.); also Arthur C. Osterberg, "I Was There" (FGBFI Voice, May 1966).

10. Nelson, "For Such a Time," 197.

11. Such cases occurred frequently. Nelson offers the case of G. B. Cashwell, a white participant at Azusa Street, who experienced a "change of heart" toward blacks. "For Such a Time," 198.

12. Frank Bartleman, *How Pentecost Came to Los Angeles* (Los Angeles: privately published, 1925), 52.

13. Mary Esther Mason, *The History and Life Work of Elder C. H. Mason and His Co-Laborers.* (Memphis, TN: privately published, 1933), 14. See also David M. Tucker, *Black Pastors and Leaders: Memphis 1819-1972* (Memphis, TN: Memphis State University Press 1975), 98. Tucker used the out-of-date escapist aberration theory to explain the rise of the Church of God in Christ, but his book gives valuable insight to the social, economic, and political conditions in Memphis between 1819-1972.

14. Synan, *The Holiness-Pentecostal Movement,* 110.

15. Nelson, "For Such a Time," 208-211.

16. Ibid., 208.

17. *Everlasting Gospel*, 72-73 cited in Nelson, "For Such a Time," 238, n. 134.

18. Nelson, "For Such a Time," 209.

19. Ibid., 216.

20. Ibid., 218.

21. Personal conversation with Bishop C. H. Mason, Norfolk, Virginia, 1948.

22. Personal conversation with Bishop C. H. Mason.

23. Nelson, "For Such a Time," 246-252.

24. Allen L. Clayton, "The Significance of William Durham for Pentecostal Historiography" (Paper presented at the Society for Pentecostal Studies, 1979), 3. Clayton argues that Durham was closer to the Zinzedorfian view of sanctification than the Wesleyan view. Zinzedorf's view was: "All our perfection is in Christ, all Christian perfection is faith in the blood of Christ. The whole of Christian perfection is imputed, not inherent. We are perfect in Christ; never in ourselves. The moment someone is justified, he is sanctified wholly." See also Nelson's chronicle of events and arguments with their racial and leadership overtones and undertones in "For Such a Time," 246-252, 277-278.

25. For a thorough and insightful account of how the exciting twentieth-century pentecostal movement was compromised, see Roswith Gerloff, "Theory and Practice of the Holy Spirit," *Quaker Religious Thought*, 16, no. 3 (Summer 1975), 2-17. See also Ithiel Clemmons, "Pentecostal Hopes and Historical Realities," Presidential Address at the Society for Pentecostal Studies (12 November 1981), published in *Pneuma* 4, no. 1 (Spring 1982).

26. Jon Michael Spencer, *Protest and Praise: Sacred Music of Religion* (Minneapolis, MN: Fortress Press, 1990), 157.

27. Spencer thoroughly examines the thirteen issues of *The Apostolic Faith* (September 1906-May 1908). For the conflict with Parham, see "The Endowment of Power," in *The Apostolic Faith* 1/4 (December 1906), 2.

28. Nelson, "For Such a Time," actually provides concrete evidence to support a position already discovered by his mentor, Walter J. Hollenweger. See Hollenweger, *The Pentecostals* (Minneapolis, MN: Augsburg Press, 1971), xvii.

29. By prophetic social consciousness, I specifically envision people who are brought together regardless of class, caste, and race, with a sensitivity to making life more human. Cf. Douglas J. Nelson and Ithiel Clemmons, "A Brief History of the Church of God in Christ" (North Carolina: unpublished brief, 1983), 21-22.

30. Nelson, "For Such a Time," 31.

31. For a detailed study of the dynamics of black holiness-pentecostalism, see these three important doctoral dissertations: Arthur Paris, *Black Pentecostalism: Southern Religion in an Urban World* (Amherst: University of Massachusetts Press, 1982); Leonard Lovett, "Black-Holiness Pentecostalism: Implications for Ethics and Social Transformation" (Ph.D. diss. Emory University, Candler School of Theology, 1979);

and William C. Turner, "The United Holy Church: A Study in Black-Holiness Pentecostalism" (Ph.D. diss. Duke University, 1984), esp. 184-190.

32. Turner, "The United Holy Church," 189-190.

33. Ibid., 190.

34. Ibid.

35. The United Holy Church of America was organized in 1886 in Method, North Carolina.

Chapter 4

1. Frank Bartleman, *Azusa Street* (reprint of Bartleman, *How Pentecost Came to Los Angeles*, 1925, Plainfield, NJ: Logos International, 1980), 54.

2. Cf. Mary Mason, *The Life and Work of Bishop C. H. Mason and His Co-laborers* (Memphis, TN: privately published, 1931), 24-25.

3. Mason, *Life and Work*, 25.

4. See Gerald T. Sheppard, "Pentecostalism and the Hermeneutics of Dispensationalism: The Anatomy of an Uneasy Relationship," *Pneuma* 6/2 (1984), 5-33. Also, C. I. Scofield, the nineteenth-century lawyer and Bible teacher, gives extensive evangelical commentary on Acts, chapter 2.

5. Cf. H. Vinson Synan, *The Holiness-Pentecostal Movement in the U.S.A.* (Grand Rapids, MI: William B. Eerdmans, 1971), 92-93.

6. For a detailed account of the debate that divided the Church of God in Christ in August 1907, see my essay "The Church of God in Christ and the Initial Evidence Controversy" (Memphis, TN: The Church of God in Christ Publishing House, 1990).

7. Cf. Cornel West, *Prophetic Fragments* (Grand Rapids, MI: William B. Eerdmans, 1988), x-xi.

8. While this statement is not an historical observation but a homiletic statement, from one of my sermons, it represents an effort at articulating what the founding mothers and fathers were saying. It is the task of teachers to rationalize intuitions, create paradigms, and articulate existential behaviorisms for the community.

9. Cf. Lucille J. Cornelius, *The Pioneer History of the Church of God in Christ* (San Francisco: privately published, 1975), 19.

10. Cf. Synan, *The Holiness-Pentecostal Movement*, 149-151.

11. Cornelius' indication of this factor finds confirmation from many leading scholars. See Cornelius, *Pioneer History*, 19. Donald Weeks, in his unpublished history of the Church of God in Christ, writes: "I want to make it perfectly clear, that in the archives of the Assemblies of God or from any other materials I gathered, there is no sign of personal racism found in the founders of the Assemblies of God. Cf. Weeks, "History of the Church of God in Christ" (Oakland, CA: unpublished paper, 1989).

Chapter 5

1. For an in-depth review and analysis of the "Circle of Culture" among the African diaspora and its influence upon African-American Christianity, see Sterling Stuckey, *Slave Culture: Nationalist Theory and the Foundations of Black America* (New York: Oxford University Press, 1987), 3-97.

2. In their definitive work on the black church, C. Eric Lincoln and Lawrence Mamiya have accurately pinpointed the fact that the Church of God in Christ had some unusual beginnings that break from the norm. Cf. C. Eric Lincoln and Lawrence H. Mamiya, *The Black Church in the African-American Experience* (Durham, NC: Duke University Press, 1990), 76-91.

3. For an excellent description of the annual summer or fall revival among black Baptists, see Mechal Sobel, *Travelin' On: The Slave Journey to an Afro-Baptist Faith* (Westport, CT: Greenwood Press, 1979). As a young person growing up in rural Arkansas, Mason loved the yearly revival meeting. Cf. Mary Mason, *Life and Labors of C. H. Mason*, op. cit., 14. Professor William C. Turner has given possibly the best description and the best analysis of the structure and meaning of the annual holy convocation among black holiness-pentecostal churches. Cf. Turner, "The United Holy Church," 147-177.

4. Cf. Gayraud S. Wilmore, *Last Things First*, 77-96. See especially pages 82 and 89 for perspectives in black holiness-pentecostalism generally and specifically the Church of God in Christ.

5. For an excellent analysis of how black Christianity in America, especially black holiness-pentecostalism, took the message of liberation in the Old and New Testaments and welded them to the base of African spirituality and to fading but still vital elements of the African worldview, cf. Wilmore, *Last Things First*, 76-96. See especially pages 82 and 89 for perspectives on black holiness-pentecostalism generally and specifically the Church of God in Christ.

6. Turner, "United Holy Church," 147.

7. Ibid., 157.

8. U.H.C. Yearbook, 1936, 29.

9. Ibid., 151.

10. In the early years of the "black holiness" or "sanctified" churches, followers suffered ridicule, arrest, and imprisonment for public preaching and witnessing.

11. For an in-depth discussion of the meaning of "sacred time," see Wilmore, *Last Things First*, 73-76.

12. Cf. David M. Tucker, *Black Pastors and Leaders: Memphis 1819-1972* (Memphis, TN: Memphis State University Press, 1975), 94.

13. In these sessions are discerned the retention and revitalization of African-American as opposed to Anglo-American culture.

14. Tucker, *Black Pastors*, 92.
15. Vittorio Lanterari, *The Religions of the Oppressed: A Study of Modern Messianic Cults* (New York: Knopf, 1983), 4, quoted in Tucker, *Black Pastors and Leaders*, 87.
16. Turner, "United Holy Church," 159.
17. Ibid., 161.
18. Today, the rapid growth of the Church of God in Christ has necessitated jurisdictions. There are in a geographical state several convocations under the leadership of a bishop. (While the Church of God in Christ uses episcopal language, its strong Baptist roots makes it structurally more "representative" in government.) In New York State, for example, six jurisdictions hold convocations.
19. This writer, who presides over ninety-five congregations of the Church of God in Christ in Eastern New York First Jurisdiction, holds a spring conference and annual holy convocation that draws about ten thousand persons.

Chapter 6

1. In 1895, W. H. Tolman said, "We are now a nation of cities," cf. W. H. Tolman's *Municipal Reform Movement in the U.S.* (New York: publisher, 1895), 35. The venerable Lyman Abbott queried, "What shall we do with our great cities? What will our great cities do with us?" These are two questions that confront every American. The city is not all bad nor all good. It is humanity compressed, the best and the worst combined, in a strangely composite community. Cf. Arthur Meier Schlesinger, *The Rise of the City* (New York: Macmillan, 1933), 1, cf. Arthur M. Schlesinger and Dixon Ryan Fox, Eds. *A History of American Life*, Vol. 10 in *The Rise of the City*, (New York: MacMillan, 1933), 78-120.
2. C. Eric Lincoln, *Sounds of the Struggle: Persons and Perspectives in Civil Rights* (New York: Morrow, 1971), 51.
3. Ibid., 229.
4. Louis R. Harlan, "Booker T. Washington and the Politics of Accommodation," in John Hope Franklin and August Mear, eds., *Black Leaders of the Twentieth Century* (Urbana, IL: University of Illinois Press, 1982).
5. Cf. Lincoln, *Sounds*, 228.
6. Cf. "America's Black Population," Census Bureau, 1. See also, C. Eric Lincoln and Lawrence H. Mamiya, *The Black Church in the African American Experience* (Durham, NC: Duke University Press, 1990), 119; see also Robert Michael Franklin, *A Church Transforming the City: The Urban Witness of the Church of God* in Christ (unpublished paper).
7. Cf. Lincoln and Mamiya, *The Black Church*, 112.
8. Cf. Howard N. Rabinowitz, *Race Relations in the Urban South, 1885-1890* (New York: Oxford University Press, 1978), 22-23.

9. Cf. Robert M. Franklin, *A Church Transforming the City: The Urban Witness of the Church of God in Christ* (unpublished paper, 1990).

10. Franklin, *A Church Transforming the City*, 1.

11. Mary Magnum Johnson, assisted by Inez Cole Barber, *The Life and Works of Mother Mary Magnum Johnson: Founder of The Church of God in Christ in the State of Michigan*, Detroit, Michigan. n.p., n.d. 14. Mother Johnson died in 1935 at the age of ninety.

12. The Evening Lights Saints were holiness people of the Winebrunner movement. These white people defied the segregation laws of the South to worship and fellowship with the black saints. They were the formative group of the Church of God, Anderson, Indiana. For an in-depth look at their work, see my book on the life of Bishop O. M. Kelly, Ithiel Clemmons, *Profile of a Churchman* (New York: K & C Publishers, 1978).

13. Lincoln and Mamiya, *The Black Church*, 119.

14. Benjamin Mays and Joseph Nicholson, *The Negro's Church* (New York: Russell and Russell, 1969, reissue).

15. Cf. Clair Drake and Horace Cayton, *Black Metropolis: A Study of Negro Life in the North* (New York: Harper & Row, 1945, revised 1962), vol. 2, 670. Professors Lincoln and Mamiya have perceptively pointed out that much more historical work needs to be done on the period of the migrations. Mays, Nicholson, Drake, Cayton, and E. Franklin Frazier did most of their work in Chicago, trained by the Chicago School of Sociology. Fortunately, young scholars, like Robert M. Franklin, trained at the Chicago Divinity School and who have interdisciplinary credentials, are uncovering previously overlooked evidence that leads to more sophisticated conclusions.

16. Interview with Bishop Samuel M. Crouch who served as the Bishop of the Churches of God in Christ on the West Coast from 1933 to 1977. This interview was by Rose Marie McDuff. Cf. Rose Marie McDuff, "An Ethnohistory of Saints Home Church of God in Christ," an unpublished M. A. thesis in anthropology (Sacramento: California State University, 1979), 20.

17. Ibid., 149-150.

18. Ibid., 27.

19. Ibid., 42.

20. This writer was intimately acquainted with E. R. Driver, Jr., the third son of E. R. Driver, Sr. E. R. Driver, Jr., born in 1907, became a successful pastor. He related this to me in 1973.

21. Cf. Franklin, *The Church Transforming the City*, 3.

Chapter 7

1. Dr. Adrienne M. Israel is an associate professor of history and intercultural studies at Guilford College in Greensboro, North Carolina, and a member of the Church of God in Christ. She earned a doctorate degree in history from the Johns Hopkins University and holds a master's degree in African studies and a bachelor's degree in English from Howard University. A native of Massillon, Ohio, she has worked as a journalist and freelance writer. Her current work in progress is a biography of nineteenth century Methodist holiness evangelist Amanda Berry Smith.

2. Monroe N. Work, ed., *Negro Yearbook 1911: Annual Encyclopedia of the Negro* (Nashville, TN: Sunday School Union Print, 1912), 84.

3. Ibid., 86.

4. Ibid., 85.

5. Georgia Harkness, *Women in Church and Society* (Nashville, TN: Abingdon Press, 1972), 129-130.

6. Nineteenth century holiness leaders such as Phoebe Palmer, John Inskip, and Amanda Smith frequently used the terms "heart purity" and "entire sanctification." Smith, an ex-slave who became a world renowned evangelist-missionary, influenced C. H. Mason through her autobiography, *An Autobiography: the Story of the Lord's Dealings with Mrs. Amanda Smith, the Colored Evangelist,* reprint, (Chicago: Afro-Am Press, 1969).

7. See Nancy Hardesty, *Women Called to Witness: Evangelical Feminism in the Nineteenth Century* (Nashville, TN: Abington, 1984).

8. C. Eric Lincoln and Lawrence H. Mamiya, *The Black Church in the African American Experience* (Durham, NC: Duke University Press, 1990), 227.

9. Jean O'Barr, "African Women in Politics," *African Women South of the Sahara,* Margaret J. Hay and Sharon Stichter, eds., (London: Longman Group, 1984), 143.

10. Ibid.

11. Pearl T. Robinson, "New Conflicts," *The Africans: a Reader,* eds., Ali A. Mazrui and Toby K. Levine (New York: Praeger Publishers, 1986), 136.

12. Ibid.

13. See David Sweetman, *Woman Leaders in African History* (Portsmouth, NH: Heinemann Educational Books, Inc., 1984).

14. See Sterling Stuckey, *Slave Culture: Nationalist Theory and the Foundations of Black America* (New York: Oxford University Press, 1987).

15. Ibid., 278.

16. Cheryl Townsend-Gilkes, "Together and in Harness: Women's Traditions in the Sanctified Church," *Signs: Journal of Women in Culture and Society,* vol. 10, no. 4, 1985.

17. Dorothy W. Exumé, Clyde Young, et al., *From the Beginning of Bishop C. H. Mason and the Early Pioneers of the Church of God in Christ* (Memphis, TN: Church of God in Christ, 1991), 36.

18. Donald Weeks, "The History of the Church of God in Christ," unpublished Ph.D. dissertation, Oakland, CA: 1992, 107.

19. According to a biographical sketch, in 1881 she married Henry Holt, her first husband, who subsequently died. Her second husband was William Woods. See Sherry Sherrod DuPree, ed. and comp., *Biographical Dictionary of African-American Holiness Pentecostals, 1880-1990* (Washington, DC: Middle Atlantic Regional Press, 1989), p. 231.

20. Evelyn Brooks Higginbotham, *Righteous Discontent: The Women's Movement in the Black Baptist Church 1880-1920* (Cambridge, MA: Harvard University Press, 1993), 98.

21. Ibid., 99.

22. Mother Lizzie Roberson, "History of the Bible Band," reprinted from *Christian Hope Magazine*, April 1937, in the program of the Forty-Third Annual Woman's International Convention, Church of God in Christ, Inc., 326.

23. Exumé, 36.

24. Charles H. Pleas, *Fifty Years of Achievement from 1906-1956: a Period in History of the Church of God in Christ*, (Memphis, TN: Church Public Relations, n.d.), 12.

25. Roberson, 326.

26. DuPree, 231.

27. Ibid.

28. Pleas, 13.

29. Cheryl Townsend-Gilkes, "The Role of Women in the Sanctified Church," *The Journal of Religious Thought*, vol. 32, no. 1, 31.

30. Jacquelyn Grant, "Womanist Theology: Black Women's Experience as a Source for Doing Theology, with Special Reference to Christology," *African American Religious Studies* (Durham, NC: Duke University Press, 1989), 219.

31. Pleas, 15.

32. Roberson, 326.

33. Ibid.

34. DuPree, 232.

35. Pleas, 14.

36. Weeks, 108.

37. Vinson Synan, *The Holiness-Pentecostal Movement in the United States* (Grand Rapids, MI: William B. Eerdmans Publishing Company, 1971, reprinted, 1989), 61-68.

38. Bureau of Census, *Negro Population, 1790-1915* (Washington, DC: Government Printing Office, 1918), tables six and seven, 36.

39. Ibid., 60.

40. Lucille J. Cornelius, "The Pioneer: History of the Church of God in Christ" (n.p., 1975), 22.

41. Lillian Brooks-Coffey, compl., *Yearbook of the Church of God in Christ for the Year 1926*, re-copied by Elder Jerry R. Ramsey (1991), 77-78.

42. *Handbook for the Women's Department* (Memphis, TN: Church of God in Christ Publishing House, 1980), 21.

43. DuPree, 232.

44. Lizzie Roberson, General Supervisor, Omaha, NE, and Lillian B. Coffey, Asst. Supervisor, Chicago, IL, Notice from the Office of the National Supervisor of Women's Work, Church of God in Christ, Incorporated, Headquarters, Memphis, TN: n.d., from the private papers of Carrie Cantrell, Illinois State Supervisor.

45. Dupree, 56.

46. Lillian S. Calhoun, "Woman on the Go for God," *Ebony,* May 1963, 80-81.

47. Lillian Brooks-Coffey, "This is My Story," *From the Beginning of Bishop C. H. Mason and the Early Pioneers of the Church of God in Christ* (Memphis, TN: Church of God in Christ, 1991), 38.

48. Calhoun, 81.

49. Ibid., 84.

50. Ibid.

51. Ibid.

52. Coffey, *From the Beginning,* 39. Also see DuPree, 56.

53. Calhoun, 80.

54. Ibid.

55. Ibid., 86.

Chapter 8

1. For a definition and description of the Sanctified Church Movement in the U.S., see the most recent volume of Cheryl J. Sanders, *Saints in Exile: The Holiness-Pentecostal Experience in African-American Religion and Culture* (New York: Oxford University Press, 1996). Professor Sanders' work builds on the prolific essays on the Sanctified Church done by Cheryl Townsend-Gilkes beginning in 1980. See also the Ph.D. dissertation by David Douglas Daniels, "The Cultural Renewal of Slave Religion: Charles Price Jones and the Emergence of the Holiness Movement in Mississippi, 1895-1905" (New York: Union Theological Seminary, 1992). See also the Ph.D. dissertation of Thomasina Neely, "Belief, Ritual, and Performance in a Black Pentecostal Church: The Musical Heritage of the Church of God in Christ" (Bloomington, IN: Indiana University, 1993).

2. There are several encyclopedias and dictionaries of American religion generally, and of the holiness-pentecostal movement and African-American religion in particular, that have extensive entries on the Church of God in Christ and its founder. See Stanley M. Burgess and Gary B. McGee, *Dictionary of Pentecostal and Charismatic Movements* (Grand Rapids, MI: Zondervan Publishing House, sixth printing, 1993).

3. Cf. Joseph R. Washington, *Black Sects and Cults* (Garden City, NY: Doubleday/Anchor Books, 1973).

4. The Rev. German R. Ross and Julia Mason Atkins, eds., *History and the Formative Years of the Church of God in Christ* (Memphis, TN: COGIC Publishing House, 1969), 80-130.

5. Cheryl Townsend-Gilkes, "Cultural Constituencies in Conflict: Religion, Community Reorganization, and the Rise of the Saints," a paper delivered at Boston University in 1982. Cheryl Gilkes' paper is one of the most important documents of the origins and growth of the Church of God in Christ.

6. Cf. Robert Michael Franklin, "My Soul Says Yes, The Urban Ministry of the Church of God in Christ" in Clifford J. Green, ed., *Churches, Cities, and Human Community: Urban Ministry in the United States, 1945-1985* (Grand Rapids, MI: William B. Eerdmans Publishing Co., 1996), 77-96. loc. cit., 81. See also Marie Simmons, *Down Behind the Sun: The Life and Work of Dr. Arenia C. Mallory* (Lexington, MS: privately printed, 1980).

7. Professor Alonzo Johnson of Columbia, South Carolina, a COGIC pastor with a Ph.D. from Union Seminary, New York, coined the phrase "restorationist vision" that defined Bishop Ford's ministry, focus, and purpose. His assessment of Bishop Ford's brief tenure has been part of the dialogue this author had with him, Dr. David Daniels of McCormick Seminary, and Dr. Robert Franklin of the Ford Foundation, Bishop Ford's son in the gospel over the past two years.

8. Robert Michael Franklin, "My Soul Says Yes," op. cit., 91.

9. Ibid., 91.

10. In 1945, during the 38th Annual Holy Convocation at Memphis, Tennessee, Mother Lizzie Roberson, the National Mother, gave her final message before passing away during the meeting. Her final message to the saints was "stay out of worldly politics, stay out of lodges."

11. Robert Michael Franklin, "My Soul Says Yes," op. cit., 94.

12. Ibid., 94.

13. Robert Michael Franklin, "My Soul Says Yes," op. cit., 94.

14. Cf. Cheryl J. Sanders, *Saints in Exile,* op. cit., 50.

15. For an enlightening discussion of the holiness-pentecostal dialectic of being in the world but not of the world, see chapter one of Cheryl J. Sanders' excellent study, *Saints in Exile,* op. cit.

16. Cf. Walter Brueggemann, *Hope Within History* (Atlanta, GA: John Knox Press, 1987), 107.

17. Walter Brueggemann, *Living Toward a Vision: Biblical Reflections on Shalom*. Note especially the chapter "Shalom for Haves and Have Nots" (Philadelphia: United Church Press, 1976); *Hope Within History* (Atlanta, GA: John Knox Press, 1987); *Hopeful Imagination: Prophetic Voices in Exile* (Philadelphia: Fortress Press, 1986).

18. Cheryl J. Sanders, *Saints in Exile*, op. cit., 128.

19. Cf. Conversations with Harvey Cox. Regent University, April 24, 1995.

20. Cheryl J. Sanders, *Saints in Exile*, op. cit., 130.

21. Cited in *Saints in Exile*, 141.

22. During his time as presiding bishop of the Church of God in Christ, Bishop J. O. Patterson often repeated this exchange between Bishop Mason and Rev. Amos.

23. Ibid., 95.

Appendix B

1. Thelma L. Williams, and Earline Nelson, *100 COGIC Old Time Congregational Songs and Choruses* (Memphis, TN: Pentecostal Temple Church of God in Christ, 1956).

Glossary

1. For a detailed explanation of these theological distinctions in the holiness origins of pentecostalism, see Donald W. Dayton, *The Theological Roots of Pentecostalism* (Grand Rapids, MI: Francis Asbury Press of Zondervan, 1987), 15-28.

2. See William Pannell, "The Religious Heritage of Blacks," 96-107, and especially, William Bentley, "Bible Believers in the Black Community," 108-121, in *The Evangelicals: What They Believe, Who They Are, Where They Are Changing*, eds. David F. Wells and John D. Woodbridge (Nashville, TN: Abingdon Press, 1975), and James Washington, "The Origins of Black Evangelicalism and the Ethical Function of Evangelical Cosmology," *Union Seminary Quarterly Review*, 32/2 (1977) 104-116.

3. See Gerald T. Sheppard, "Word and Spirit: Scripture in the Pentecostal Tradition," AGORA, 1/4 (1978) 4-5, 17-22 and 2/1 (1978) 14-19, and his "Biblical Hermeneutics: The Academic Language of Evangelical Identity," *USQR*, 32/2 (1977) 81-94.

4. In the 1830s, two sisters, Sarah Larkford and Phoebe Palmer, members of New York City Methodist churches, organized a weekly prayer meeting that lasted into the 1900s. The "Tuesday Meeting," as it was called, became the center of revival within Methodism (and beyond) of the original Wesleyan teaching of sanctification as a second crisis in the Christian life in which the believer gained victory over sin. Phoebe Palmer left her own distinctive cast on this doctrine by emphasizing that all Christians should immediately enter this experience. See Donald Dayton, *The*

American Holiness Movement: A Bibliographic Introduction (Wilmore, KY: Asbury Theological Seminary, 1971).

5.   Cf. Frederick Dale Bruner, *A Theology of the Holy Spirit* (London: Hodder & Stoughton, 1970), 7; H. Vinson Synan, *The Holiness Pentecostal Movement in the United States* (Grand Rapids, MI: William B. Eerdmans, 1971), 13; Melvin E. Dieter, "Wesley-Holiness Aspects of Pentecostal Origins," in Vinson Synan, ed., *Aspects of Pentecostal-Charismatic Origins* (Plainfield, NJ: Logos International, 1975), 62-69; Iain MacRobert, *The Black Roots and White Racism of Early Pentecostalism in the U.S.A.* (New York: St. Martin's Press, 1988), 88-42; C. Eric Lincoln and Lawrence Mamyia, *The Black Church in the African-American Experience* (Durham, NC: Duke University Press, 1990).

6.   Cf. Roswith Gerloff, "Theory and Practice of the Holy Spirit," in *Quaker Religious Thought,* 16/3 (Summer 1975), 2-4.

7.   Many brilliant contemporary theologians, historians, and ethicists – both black and white – have written about this unusual phenomenon. See Eugene D. Genovese, *Roll, Jordan, Roll: The World the Slaves Made* (New York: Pantheon, 1972). For the best full-length treatment of Slave Religion, however, see Albert J. Raboteau, *Slave Religion: The "Invisible Institution" in the Antebellum South* (New York: Oxford University Press, 1978).

GLOSSARY

Church vs. *sect* - Typically a church-type social configuration manifests a highly prescribed, predictable, and ritualized worship; a professional priesthood or clergy-laity distinction in a hierarchical organizational structure; and a tendency toward relative rather than absolute ethics that recognizes possible conflicts and compromises with other ethical demands.

By contrast, a sect-type congregation features spontaneous worship with more unpredictable liturgical permutations, a lay ministry with strong professional distinctions for clergy, an explicitly non-bureaucratic organizational structure, and a rigorous ethical code that is not to be compromised and which extends its influence to the members' most mundane activity.[1]

Cult - An insular group, uncooperative with others, that shows an ethically irresponsible attitude toward "outsiders" and is often controlled by strong, manipulative leadership. A pentecostal church under normal circumstances would never qualify under these terms as a cult.

Evangelicals or *evangelicalism* - The peculiarly American, mainly white, post-fundamentalist movement represented by the National Association of Evangelicals and magazines such as *Christianity Today*. While the confessional position of most black pentecostals would be orthodox enough to be called "evangelical" in the older, Reformation sense, blacks have not identified readily with American evangelicalism of the type I have described.[2]

In the 1920s and 1930s, fundamentalists regularly condemned all pentecostals as sub-Christian or unorthodox. Many white pentecostal groups, such as the Assemblies of God, countered this charge by joining the National Association of Evangelicals from its inception in 1942. Consequently, they may well deserve criticism for letting fundamentalists and conservative evangelicals dictate much of their doctrinal and social agenda.[3] Black pentecostals did not establish such a connection with what appeared to them to be a predominately white evangelical movement, conservative both theologically and politically.

Glossolalia or *speaking in tongues* - Taken from New Testament Greek, this refers to the speaking of an unknown language or language-like speech "of men or angels" (1 Corinthians 13:1).

Speaking in tongues may also be done in private or public worship to let the Holy Spirit pray through the believer to God about needs that the believer may not know how to express. A message in tongues may be given in public in anticipation of an inspired prophetic "interpretation," usually given by someone other than the one speaking in tongues.

Holiness or *sanctified* - Synonyms for describing persons or churches who emphasize, from the Wesleyan tradition, that one should have a second experience of sanctification after conversion.

Pentecostals - Since the turn of this century, people who call themselves pentecostals are identified as Christians who view speaking in tongues as a sign that someone has received the baptism of the Holy Spirit with empowerment like that of the disciples at Pentecost.

Perfectionalists - Those who believe in a special action of the Holy Spirit within an individual either against the tendency to sin or, in some circles not so common among black holiness-pentecostal churches, it might be thought to ensure actual perfection so that one will never sin again.

While all sanctified people are *perfectionist* in their aim, only the latter sort are theologically called *perfectionalists* in a strict sense. In practice, an experience of sanctification usually signified a spiritually-aided capacity to be committed to the ideal of a sinless life, often exhibited by radical conformity to implicit rules against behavior perceived by the group as worldly or sinful.

Before the period of glossolalic pentecostalism, the experience of sanctification was commonly called "Holy Spirit baptism" or the "baptism of the Holy Spirit." John Wesley was unquestionably the great Protestant preacher of Christian perfection. The Methodist church that Wesley founded was the bearer of the doctrine of Christian perfection in the United States in the first half of the nineteenth century.[4]

By the mid-nineteenth century, perfectionism was linked to abolitionism as well as revivalism. At the turn of the century, however, many sanctified people felt they had not yet received the power to do what Jesus and the disciples did in their day. The empowerment they sought came to be associated with a third experience, which included speaking in tongues or glossolalia as a sign of such a spiritual baptism as on the day of Pentecost in the New Testament (cf. Acts 2).

Many holiness people and whole church denominations suddenly became "holiness-pentecostal," for example, the Church of God in Christ. Others thought of sanctification as belonging to conversion and so were "pentecostals" without the same Wesleyan holiness emphasis, for example, as seen often in the Assemblies of God. Most scholars agree that the roots of pentecostalism lie not only in the black American understanding and practice of Christianity but to some degree also in the Wesleyan perfectionist thought of the American holiness movement.[5]

Pneumatology - The theory of the Holy Spirit, as used in this book, goes beyond theological reflection on the person and work of the Holy Spirit. Pneumatology and spirituality are related dialectically. Pneumatology is spirituality in reflection; spirituality is pneumatology in action. In pentecostal theological thought, pneumatology is the reflection of spiritual spontaneity.

"Practice and activity of the Spirit can (and should) be traced in manifold aspects of human life and thought – in the openness to the Spirit's operations outside the established churches, in the struggles for liberation from oppressive and dominating structures . . ."[6]

Slave Religion[7] - An institution peculiar to the slaves in the southern United States. The slaves – the African diaspora in the United States – did not simply become Christian, nor did they uncritically accept the Eurocentric interpretation of biblical and theological thought. Laboring in torrid heat on land owned and ruled by white American Christians, they struggled to understand their lives and servitude in light of the biblical texts they heard preached, the Protestant hymns they heard sung, the personal Christian testimonies that often appeared irreconcilable to their day-to-day experiences.

Their biblical and theological reflection both built upon and departed from their earlier African, non-Christian, but deeply spiritual theological reflection. The most durable and adaptable constituents of the slave's culture, linking the African past and the American present, was his or her religion. The slaves' unique biblical and theological reflection gave rise to a remarkably indestructible, autonomous institution: the black church. It evolved from secret meetings, held away from the jaundiced eyes of oppressors, "an invisible institution," to independent churches separate and apart from white control. In that institution slaves creatively fashioned a Christian tradition that was a biblical, theological reflection upon their unique experiences. They also read the biblical texts in light of their ordeal as slaves.

BIBLIOGRAPHY

Ahlstrom, Sydney E. *A Religious History of the American People*. New Haven: Yale University Press, 1972.

Baldwin, James. *Go Tell it on the Mountain*. New York: Dell, 1952.

———. *Notes of a Native Son*. New York: Bantam, 1972. Orig. 1925.

Bartleman, Frank. *How Pentecost Came to Los Angeles: As It Was in the Beginning, Old Azusa Street From My Diary*. Privately printed 3rd edition, 1925.

Berger, Peter L., and Thomas Luckman. *The Social Construction of Reality*. Garden City, NY: Doubleday, 1967.

Berger, Peter L., and John Richard Neuhaus. *To Empower People: The Role of Mediating Structures in Public Policy*. Washington, DC: American Enterprise Institute for Public Policy Research, 1977.

Blassingame, John. *The Slave Community: Plantation Life in the Antebellum South*. New York: Oxford University Press, 1972.

Brauer, John C., ed. *The Impact of the Church Upon Its Culture: Reappraisals of the History of Christianity*. Chicago: University of Chicago Press, 1968.

Brooks-Coffey, Lillian. *Yearbook of the Church of God in Christ for the Year 1926*. Memphis, TN: Recopied by Elder Jerry R. Ramsey, 1991.

Brooks-Coffey, Lillian, Dorothy W. Exumé, Clyde Young, et al. *From the Beginning of Bishop C. H. Mason and the Early Pioneers of the Church of God in Christ*. Memphis, TN: Church of God in Christ Publishing House, 1991.

Brown, Robert McAfee. *Is Faith Obsolete?* Philadelphia: Westminster Press, 1974.

Brueggemann, Walter. *Hope Within History*. Atlanta, GA: John Knox Press, 1987.

————. *Hopeful Imagination: Prophetic Voices in Exile*. Philadelphia: Fortress Press, 1986.

————. *Living Toward a Vision: Biblical Reflections on Shalom*. Philadelphia: United Church Press, 1976.

Burgess, Stanley M., and Gary B. McGee, eds. *Dictionary of Pentecostal and Charismatic Movements*. Grand Rapids: Zondervan, 1987.

Burkett, Randall K. *Garveyism as a Religious Movement: The Institutionalization of a Black Civil Religion*. ATLA Monograph Series, no. 13. Metuchen, NJ: Scarecrow Press, 1978.

Burkett, Randall, and Richard Newman, eds. *Black Apostles: Afro-American Clergy Confront the Twentieth Century*. Boston: G. K. Hall, 1978.

Cada, Lawrence, et al. *Shaping the Coming Age of Religious Life*. New York: Seabury, 1979.

Calhoun, Lillian S. "Woman on the Go for God." *Ebony*, May 1963.

Campbell, C. *Theologies Written from Feminist Perspectives: An Introductory Study*. New York, NY: Office of the General Assembly, Presbyterian Church, 1987.

Childs, Brevard. *Memory and Tradition in Israel*. Naperville, IL: A. R. Allenson, 1962.

Church of God in Christ. "Celebrates 50th Anniversary," *Ebony* (March 1958).

————. *Official Manual with the Doctrines and Discipline*. Memphis: Church of God in Christ, 1973.

Comblin, José. *The Holy Spirit and Liberation*. Maryknoll, NY: Orbis, 1989.

Cone, James H. *Black Theology and Black Power*. New York: Seabury, 1969.

Cone, Cecil M. *Identity Crisis in Black Theology*. Nashville: AME Church, 1975.

Cornelius, Lucille J. "The Pioneer: History of the Church of God in Christ." n.p., 1975.

Corum, Fred T., ed. *Like As of Fire: A Reprint of the Azusa Street Documents*. Wilmington, MA: Privately printed, 1981.

Cotton, Mother Emma. "Inside Story of the Outpouring of the Holy Spirit, Azusa Street 1906." *Message of the Apostolic Faith*. 1, no. 1 (April 1939).

Dayton, Donald H. *The American Holiness Movement: A Bibliographic Introduction*. Wilmore, KY: B. L. Fisher Library. Asbury Theological Seminary, 1971.

————. *Theological Roots of Pentecostalism*. Grand Rapids: Francis Asbury Press, 1987.

Delk, James. *He Made Millions Happy*. Hopkinsville, KY: Privately printed, 1950.

Demerath, N. J., and P. E. Hammond. *Religion in Social Context*. New York: Random House, 1969.

Dieter, Melvin E. *The Holiness Revival of the Nineteenth Century*. Metuchen, NJ: Scarecrow Press, 1980.

Douglas, M., and S. M. Tyson, eds. *Religion and America*. Boston: Beacon Press, 1982.

Drake, St. Clair, and Horace Cayton. *Black Metropolis: A Study of Negro Life in the North*. New York: Harper & Row, 1962.

DuBois, W. E. B. *The Souls of Black Folk*. New York: New American Library, 1969.

Dugas, Paul D. *The Life and Writings of Elder G. T. Haywood*. Stockton, CA: Apostolic Press, 1968.

Ellis, J. Delano, ed. *A Brief Historical, Doctrinal and Structural Report on the Church of God in Christ*. Memphis: Church of God in Christ, 1983.

FBI File, War Department Correspondence, obtained under the Freedom of Information Act, c. 1916-18.

Fidler, Richard L. "Historical Review of the Pentecostal Outpouring in Los Angeles at the Azusa Street Mission in 1906." *International Outlook* (January-March 1963).

Franklin, Robert Michael. *Liberating Visions*. Philadelphia: Fortress Press, 1990.

——. "My Soul Says Yes, The Urban Ministry of the Church of God in Christ," in Clifford J. Green, ed., *Churches, Cities, and Human Community: Urban Ministry in the United States, 1945-1985*. Grand Rapids, MI: William B. Eerdmans Publishing Company, 1996.

Frazier, E. Franklin. *The Negro Church in America*. New York: Schocken Books, 1964.

Gerlach, Luther P., and Virginia H. Hine. *People, Power and Change Movements of Social Transformation*. Indianapolis: Bobbs Merrill, 1970.

Gerloff, Roswith. "African Survivals in West and Afro-American Pencostalism," unpublished typescript. Privately printed, n. d.

——. "Theory and Practice of the Holy Spirit." *Quaker Religious Thought*, vol.16, no. 3 (Summer 1975).

Gottwald, Norman K. "Sociology of Ancient Israel," in 6 volumes of *Anchor Bible Dictionary*. Garden City, NY: Doubleday Publishers, 1992.

Grant, Jacqueline. "Womanist Theology: Black Women's Experience as a Source for Doing Theology, with Special Reference to Christology," *African American Religous Studies*. Durham, NC: Duke University Press, 1989.

Gutiérrez, Gustavo. *We Drink From Our Own Wells: The Spiritual Journey of a People*. Maryknoll, NY: Orbis, 1984.

Hamilton, Michael P., ed. *The Charismatic Movement*. Grand Rapids: William B. Eerdmans Publishing Company, 1975.

Handy, Robert T. *A History of the Churches in the United States and Canada*. New York: Oxford University Press, 1977.

Harkness, Georgia. *Women in Church and Society*. Nashvile, TN: Abingdon Press, 1972.

Harris, James H. *Black Ministers and Laity in the Urban Church: An Analysis of Political and Social Expectations*. New York: University Press of America, 1987.

Hartoock, Nancy C. M. *Money, Sex and Power*. Boston: Northeastern University Press, 1985.

Hauerwas, Stanley with Richard Bondi and David Burrell. *Truthfulness and Tragedy*. Notre Dame: University of Notre Dame Press, 1987.

Heschel, Abraham J. *Israel: An Echo of Eternity*. New York: Farrar, Straus & Giroux, 1967.

Higginbotham, Evelyn Brooks. *Righteous Discontent: The Women's Movement in the Black Baptist Church 1880-1920*. Cambridge, MA: Harvard University Press, 1993.

Holland, Joseph and P. S. J. Henriot. *Social Analysis: Linking Faith and Justice*. Maryknoll, NY: Orbis, 1983.

Hollenweger, Walter J. "Black Pentecostal Concept," *Concept*. Special Issue, no. 30 (June 1970). Geneva: World Council of Churches.

——————. *The Pentecostals: The Charismatic Movement in the Churches*. Minneapolis: Augsburg, 1972.

——————. *Pentecost Between Black and White: Five Case Studies on Pentecost and Politics*. Belfast: Christian Journals Ltd., 1974.

Hurston, Zora Neale. *The Sanctified Church: The Folklore Writing of Zora Neale Hurston*, 1923. Reprint. Berkley, CA: Turtle Island Press, 1981.

Jackson, Joseph H. *A Story of Christian Activism: The History of the National Baptist Convention, U.S.A. Inc*. Nashville: Townsend Press, 1980.

Johnson, Mother Mary Magnum. *The Life and Works of Mother Mary Magnum Johnson: Founder of Church of God in Christ in the State of Michigan*. Privately printed, n.d.

Jones, Charles Edwin. *A Guide to the Study of the Pentecostal Movement*. Vol. 2, pts. 3 and 4. Metuchen, NJ: Scarecrow Press, 1983.

Lanterari, Vittorio. *The Religions of the Oppressed: A Study of Modern Messianic Cults*. New York: Knopf, 1963.

Lemann, Nicholas. *The Promised Land: The Great Black Migration and How it Changed America*. New York: Knopf, 1991.

Lincoln, C. Eric. *Race, Religion and the Continuing American Dilemma*. New York: Hill & Wang, 1984.

Lincoln, C. Eric, and Lawrence H. Mamiya. *The Black Church in the African-American Experience*. Durham, NC: Duke University Press, 1990.

Lovett, Leonard. "Black Holiness-Pentecostalism: Implications for Ethics and Social Transformation." Ph.D. diss., Emory University, Candler School of Theology, 1978.

Mays, Benjamin E., and Joseph William Nicholson. *The Negro's Church*. New York: Arno, 1969.

Mbiti, John S. *African Religion and Philosophy*. Garden City, NY: Doubleday/Anchor Books, 1970.

McKenna, David. *Renewing Our Ministry*. Waco, TX: Word Books, 1986.

McLemore, Richard, and Aubrey and Nannie Pitts McLemore. *The History of the First Baptist Church of Jackson, Mississippi*. Jackson, MS: Hederman Brothers, 1976.

Naisbitt, John. *Megatrends*. New York: Warner Books, 1982.

McDuff, Rose Marie. "The Ethnohistory of Saints Home Church of God in Christ." M.A. diss., California State University, 1973.

Mead, Sidney E. *The Lively Experiment: The Shaping of Christianity in America*. New York: Harper & Row, 1963.

Meier, August. *Negro Thought in America, 1880-1915: Racial Ideologies in the Age of Booker T. Washington*. Ann Arbor, MI: University of Michigan Press, 1969.

Middleton, Harris with Morris Levitt, Roger Furman, and Ernest Smith. *The Black Book*. New York: Random, 1974.

Mitchell, Henry. *Black Belief: Folk Beliefs of Blacks in America and West Africa*. New York: Harper & Row, 1975.

Morris, E. C. *Sermons, Addresses and Reminiscences and Important Correspondence*, 1901. Reprint. New York: Arno, 1980.

Nelson, Douglas J. "For Such a Time as This: The Story of Bishop William J. Seymour and the Azusa Street Revival, A Search for Pentecostal/Charismatic Roots." Ph.D. diss., University of Birmingham, England, May 1981.

Niebuhr, H. Richard. *The Social Sources of Denominationalism*. 1927. Reprint. New York: World, 1972.

——————. *The Social Sources of Denominationalism*. New York: Holt, Rinehart & Winston, 1929.

O'Barr, Jean. "African Women South of the Sahara," Margaret J. Hay and Sharon Stichter, eds. London: Longman Group, 1984.

Outler, Albert C., ed. *John Wesley*. New York: Oxford University Press, 1964.

Otto, Rudolf. *The Idea of the Holy*. New York: Oxford University Press, 1967.

Paris, Arthur E. *Black Pentecostalism: Southern Religion in an Urban World*. Amherst, MA: University of Massachusetts Press, 1982.

Paris, Peter. *The Social Teaching of the Black Churches*. Philadelphia: Fortress Press, 1985.

Patterson, J. O., German Ross, and Julia Atkins, eds. *History and Formative Years of the Church of God in Christ: Excerpts and Commentary from the Life and Works of Bishop C. H. Mason*. Memphis: Church of God in Christ, 1969.

Payne, Daniel A. *Recollection of Seventy Years, with a new Preface by Benjamin Quarles*. New York: Arno, 1969.

Piepkorn, Arthur Carl. "Holiness and Pentecostal" in vol. 3 of *Profiles in Belief: The Religious Belief Bodies of the United States and Canada*. New York: Harper & Row, 1979.

Pleas, Charles H. *Fifty Years of Achievement from 1906-1956: a Period in History of the Church of God in Christ*. Memphis, TN: Church of God in Christ Public Relations, n.d.

Poll, Solomon. *The Hasidic Community of Williamsburg: A Study in the Sociology of Religion*. New York: Schocken Books, 1962.

Pope, Liston. *Millhands and Preachers*. 2nd ed. New Haven, CT: Yale University Press, 1965.

Reuther, Rosemary, and E. McLaughlin, eds. *Women of the Spirit: Female Leadership in the Jewish and Christian Traditions*. New York: Simon & Schuster, 1979.

Roberson, Lizzie. "History of the Bible Band," *Christian Hope Magazine*, April 1937.

Roberts, J. Deotis. *Black Theology Today: Liberation and Contextualization*. New York and Toronto: Edwin Mellen Press, 1983.

Robertson, Roland. *The Sociological Interpretation of Religion*. New York: Schocken Books, 1970.

Robinson, H. Wheeler. *The Christian Experience of the Holy Spirit*. London: Oxford University Press, 1915.

Robinson, Pearl T. "New Conflicts," *The Africans: a Reader*, eds., Ali A. Mazrui and Toby Levine. New York: Prager Publishers, 1986.

Roboteau, Albert. *Slave Religion: The "Invisible Institution" in the Antebellum South*. New York: Oxford University Press, 1978.

Ross, German R. and Julia Mason, eds. *History and the Formative Years of the Church of God in Christ*. Memphis, TN: Church of God in Christ Publishing House, 1969.

Runyon, Theodore, ed. *Sanctification and Liberation*. Nashville: Abingdon, 1981.

Sandeen, Ernest R. *The Roots of Fundamentalism: British and American Millenarianism 1800-1830*, 1970. Reprint. Grand Rapids: Baker Book House, 1976.

Sanders, J. Oswald. *The Holy Spirit and His Gifts*, 1940. Reprint. Grand Rapids: Zondervan, 1976.

Schaller, Lyle E. *It's A Different World*. Nashville: Abingdon, 1987.

Segundo, Juan Luis. *The Liberation of Theology*. Maryknoll, NY: Orbis, 1976.

Sernett, Milton C. *Black Religion and American Evangelicalism*. Metuchen, NJ: Scarecrow Press, 1975.

Shopshire, James M. "A Socio-Historical Characterization of the Black Pentecostal Movement in America." Ph.D. diss., Northwestern University, 1975.

Shorter, Aylard, ed. *African-Christian Spirituality*. Maryknoll, NY: Orbis, 1978.

Smith, L. E. "An American Prophet: A Critical Study on the Thought of Howard Thurman," Ph.D. diss. Ann Arbor, MI: University Microfilms, 1982.

Smith, Timothy L. *Called Unto Holiness: The Story of the Nazarenes, The Formative Years*. Kansas City, MO: Nazarene, 1955.

————. *Revivalism and Social Reform in Mid-Nineteenth Century America*. Nashville: Abingdon, 1957.

Sobel, Mechal. *Trabelin' On: The Slave Journey to an Afro-Baptist Faith*. Westport, CT: Greenwood Press, 1979.

Soelle, Dorothy. *The Strength of the Weak*. Translated by Robert and Rita Kimber. Philadelphia: Westminster Press, 1984.

Southern, Eileen. *The Music of Black Americans: A History*. New York: Norton, 1971.

Spurgeon, Anne M. "From the Wellspring of Africa: African Spirituality in Afro-American Culture." Senior thesis, Northwestern University, 1986.

Steinberg, Stephen. *The Ethnic Myth: Race Ethnicity and Class in America.* Boston, Beacon Press, 1981.

Strauss, Claude Levi. *Structural Anthropology.* Translated by Clair Jacobson. New York: Basic Books, 1963.

Stuckey, Sterling. *Slave Culture: Nationalist Theory and the Foundations of Black America.* New York: Oxford University Press, 1987.

Synan, H. Vinson. *The Holiness-Pentecostal Movement in the United States.* Grand Rapids, MI: William B. Eerdmans Publishing Company, 1971, reprinted 1989.

Tinney, James S. "Black Origins of the Pentecostal Movement," *Christianity Today,* vol. 16, no. 1 (8 October 1971).

————. "Competing Theories of Historical Origins for Black Pentecostalism." Paper read at the American Academy of Religion, New York City, 16 November 1979.

Townsend-Gilkes, Cheryl. "Cultural Constituencies in Conflict: Religion, Community Reorganization, and the Rise of the Saints." Paper delivered at Boston University, 1982.

————. "Power Among the Powerless: 'The Sanctified Church' and the Reorganization of Black Religion." Paper presented to the Society for the Scientific Study of Religion, session on "Black Religion, Power, and Social Change," Providence, RI, 22 October 1982.

————. "The Role of Women in the Sanctified Church," *The Journal of Religious Thought,* vol. 32, no. 1.

————. "Together and in Harness: Women's Traditions in the Sanctified Church," *Signs: Journal of Women in Culture and Society,* vol. 10, no. 4, 1985.

Toynbee, Arnold J. *A Study of History.* Abridgment of volumes 1-4 by D. C. Somervell. London: Oxford University Press, 1946, 1956.

Troeltsch, Ernst. *The Social Teachings of the Christian Churches.* Vol. 2. Translated by Olive Wyon. New York: Macmillan, 1932.

Tucker, David M. *Black Pastors and Leaders: Memphis 1819-1972.* Memphis: Memphis State University Press, 1975.

Turner, William C. "The United Holy Church: A Study in Black-Holiness Pentecostal Churches." Ph.D. diss., Duke University, 1983.

Washington, James M. *Frustrated Fellowship: The Black Baptist Quest for Social Power.* Macon, GA: Mercer University Press, 1986.

Washington, Joseph R. *Black Sects and Cults.* Garden City, NY: Doubleday/Anchor Books, 1973.

Weber, Max. *The Protestant Ethic and the Spirit of Capitalism.* Translated by Talcott Parsons. New York: Scribner's, 1928.

————. *The Sociology of Religion.* Translated by E. Fernhoff. Introduction by T. Parsons. Boston: Beacon Press, 1963.

————. *On Charisma and Institution Building.* Selected papers by S. N. Eisenstadt. Chicago: University of Chicago Press, 1968.

Weeks, Donald. "The History of the Church of God in Christ." Oakland, CA: Unpublished Ph.D. dissertation,1992.

West, Cornel. *Prophesy Deliverance.* Philadelphia: Westminster Press, 1982.

————. *Prophetic Fragments.* Grand Rapids: William B. Eerdmans Publishing Company, 1988.

Whitehead, Alfred North. *Essays in Science and Philosophy,* 1947. Westport, CT: Greenwood Press, 1968.

Wiesel, Lei. "Of Hope and the Abyss," *The New York Times* (1 July 1987).

Williams, Melvin D. *Community in a Black Pentecostal Church: An Anthropological Study.* Pittsburgh, PA: University of Pittsburgh Press, 1974.

Williams, Thelma, and Earline Nelson. *100 COGIC Old Time Congregational Songs and Choruses.* Memphis, TN: Pentecostal Temple Church of God in Christ, 1956.

Wilmore, Gayraud S. *Black Religion and Black Radicalism.* New York: Doubleday, 1972.

————. *Last Things First.* Philadelphia: Westminster Press, 1982.

————. "Reinterpretations in Black Church History." *Chicago Theological Seminary Review* (Winter, 1983).

————. *Black Religion and Black Radicalism.* Garden City, NY: Doubleday/Anchor Books, 1973; Orbis, 1983.

Wilson, Bryan. *Sects and Society.* London: Heinemann, 1961.

Wimberly, Edward P., and Anne Streaty Wimberly. *Liberation and Human Wholeness: The Conversion Experiences of Black People in Slavery and Freedom.* Nashville: Abingdon, 1986.

Witvliet. *The Way of The Black Messiah: The Hermeneutical Challenge of Black Theology as a Theology of Liberation.* Translated by John Bowdin. Oak Park, IL: Meyer Stone Books, 1987.

Work, Monroe N., ed. *Negro Yearbook 1911: Annual Encyclopedia of the Negro.* Nashville, TN: Sunday School Union Printing, 1912.

Van Dusen, Henry P. *Spirit, Son, and Father: Christian Faith in Light of the Holy Spirit.* New York: Scribner's, 1958.

Yinger, Milton. *Religion in the Struggle for Power.* Durham, NC: Duke University Press, 1946.

OTHER BOOKS FROM
Pneuma Life Publishing

Opening the Front Door of Your Church
by Dr. Leonard Lovett
A creative approach for small to medium churches that want to develop a more effective ministry. *Opening the Front Door Of Your Church* is an insightful and creative approach to church development and expansion, especially for churches within the urban environment.

Why? Because You Are Anointed
by T.D. Jakes
Like the eternal nature of ocean tides, the question, why?, always comes back. There seem to be as many reasons to ask why as there are grains of sand on the beach. And yet, like the tide, God brings the answers and washes our questions away. *Workbook also available*

Water in the Wilderness
by T.D. Jakes
Just before you apprehend your greatest conquest, expect the greatest struggle. Many are perplexed who encounter this season of adversity. This book will show you how to survive the worst of times with the greatest of ease, and will cause fountains of living water to spring out of the parched, sun–drenched areas in your life. This word is a refreshing stream in the desert for the weary traveler.

The Harvest
by T.D. Jakes
God's heart beats for lost and dying humanity. The Church, however, has a tremendous shortage of sold-out, unselfish Christians committed to the salvation and discipleship of the lost. This disillusioned generation hungers for lasting reality. Are we ready to offer them eternal hope in Jesus Christ? Without a passion for holiness, sanctification, and evangelism, we will miss the greatest harvest of the ages. God has ordained the salvation of one final crop of souls and given us the privilege of putting in the sickle. Allow God to set you ablaze. Seize the opportunity of a lifetime and become an end-time laborer in the Church's finest hour! *Workbook also available*

Help Me! I've Fallen
by T.D. Jakes
"Help! I've fallen, and I can't get up." This cry, made popular by a familiar television commercial, points out the problem faced by many Christians today. Have you ever stumbled and fallen with no hope of getting up? Have you been wounded and hurt by others? Are you so far down you think you'll never stand again? Don't despair. All Christians fall from time to time. Life knocks us off balance, making it hard – if not

impossible – to get back on our feet. The cause of the fall is not as important as what we do while we're down. T.D. Jakes explains how – and Whom – to ask for help. In a struggle to regain your balance, this book is going to be your manual to recovery! Don't panic. This is just a test!

When Shepherds Bleed
by T.D. Jakes
Shepherding is a dangerous profession, and no one knows that better than a pastor. Drawing from personal encounters with actual shepherds in Israel and years of ministry, Bishop T.D. Jakes and Stanley Miller provide unique insight into the hazards faced by pastors today. With amazing perception, the authors pull back the bandages and uncover the open, bleeding wounds common among those shepherding God's flock. Using the skills of spiritual surgeons, they precisely cut to the heart of the problem and tenderly apply the cure. You'll be moved to tears as your healing process begins. Open your heart and let God lead you beside the still waters where He can restore your soul.

Becoming A Leader
by Myles Munroe
Many consider leadership to be no more than staying ahead of the pack, but that is a far cry from what leadership is. Leadership is deploying others to become as good as or better than you are. Within each of us lies the potential to be an effective leader. *Becoming A Leader* uncovers the secrets of dynamic leadership that will show you how to be a leader in your family, school, community, church and job. No matter where you are or what you do in life this book can help you to inevitably become a leader. Remember: it is never too late to become a leader. As in every tree there is a forest, so in every follower there is a leader. ***Workbook also available***

This is My Story
by Candi Staton
This is My Story is a touching autobiography about a gifted young child who rose from obscurity and poverty to stardom and wealth. With a music career that included selling millions of albums and topping the charts came a life of brokenness, loneliness, and despair. This book will make you cry and laugh as you witness one woman's search for success and love.

The African Cultural Heritage Topical Bible
The African Cultural Heritage Topical Bible is a quick and convenient reference Bible. It has been designed for use in personal devotions as well as group Bible studies. It's the newest and most complete reference Bible designed to reveal the Black presence in the Bible and highlight the contributions and exploits of Blacks from the past to present. It's a great tool for students, clergy, teachers — practically anyone seeking to learn more about the Black presence in Scripture, but didn't know where to start.
The African Cultural Heritage Topical Bible contains:
• Over 3**95** easy to find **topics**
• **3,840 verses** that are systematically organized

• A comprehensive listing of Black Inventions
• Over **150 pages** of Christian Afrocentric articles on Blacks in the Bible, Contributions of Africa, African Foundations of Christianity, Culture, Identity, Leadership, and Racial Reconciliation written by Myles Munroe, Wayne Perryman, Dr. Leonard Lovett, Dr. Trevor L. Grizzle, James Giles, and Mensa Otabil.
Available in KJV and NIV versions

The God Factor
by James Giles
Is something missing in your life? Do you find yourself at the mercy of your circumstances? Is your self-esteem at an all-time low? Are your dreams only a faded memory? You could be missing the one element that could make the difference between success and failure, poverty and prosperity, and creativity and apathy. Knowing God supplies the creative genius you need to reach your potential and realize your dream. You'll be challenged as James Giles shows you how to tap into your God-given genius, take steps toward reaching your goal, pray big and get answers, eat right and stay healthy, prosper economically and personally, and leave a lasting legacy for your children.

Making the Most of Your Teenage Years
by David Burrows
Most teenagers live for today. Living only for today, however, can kill you. When teenagers have no plan for their future, they follow a plan that someone else devised. Unfortunately, this plan often leads them to drugs, sex, crime, jail, and an early death. How can you make the most of your teenage years? Discover who you really are – and how to plan for the three phases of your life. You can develop your skill, achieve your dreams, and still have fun.

Strategies for Saving the Next Generation
by Dave Burrows
This book will teach you how to start and effectively operate a vibrant youth ministry. This book is filled with practical tips and insight gained over a number of years from working with young people from the street to the parks to the church. Dave Burrows offers the reader vital information that will produce results if carefully considered and adapted. It's excellent for pastors and youth pastors as well as youth workers and those involved with youth ministry.

Five Years To Life
by Sam Huddleston
"One day in jail, Sam's life changed. 'Jesus used my daddy, not to scare the hell out of me, but to love it out of me.'" *Five Years To Life* is the moving account of the power of unconditional love from an earthly father and from the heavenly Father. It's the story of a man who learned to make right choices because his heart had been dramatically changed.

The Biblical Principles of Success

Arthur L. Mackey Jr.

There are only three types of people in the world: People who make things happen, People who watch things happen, and People who do not know what in the world is happening. *The Biblical Principles of Success* will help you become one who makes things happen. Success is not a matter of "doing it my way." It is turning from a personal, selfish philosophy to God's outreaching, sharing way of life. This powerful book teaches you how to tap into success principles that are guaranteed – *the Biblical principles of success!*

Flaming Sword

by Tai Ikomi

Scripture memorization and meditation bring tremendous spiritual power, however many Christians find it to be an uphill task. Committing Scriptures to memory will transform the mediocre Christian to a spiritual giant. This book will help you to become addicted to the powerful practice of Scripture memorization and help you obtain the victory that you desire in every area of your life. *Flaming Sword* is your pathway to spiritual growth and a more intimate relationship with God.

Four Laws of Productivity

by Dr. Mensa Otabil

Success has no favorites, but it does have associates. Success will come to anyone who will pay the price to receive its benefits. *Four Laws of Productivity* will give you the powerful keys that will help you achieve your life's goals. You will learn how to discover God's gift in you, develop your gift, perfect your gift, and utilize your gift to its maximum potential. The principles revealed in this timely book will radically change your life.

Beyond the Rivers of Ethiopia

by Mensa Otabil

Beyond the Rivers of Ethiopia is a powerful and revealing look into God's purpose for the Black race. It gives scholastic yet simple answers to questions you have always had about the Black presence in the Bible. At the heart of this book is a challenge and call to the offspring of the Children of Africa, both on continent and throughout the world, to come to grips with their true identity as they go *Beyond the Rivers of Ethiopia.*

Single Life

by Earl D. Johnson

A book that candidly addresses the spiritual and physical dimensions of the single life is finally here. *Single Life* shows the reader how to make their singleness a celebration rather than a burden. This positive approach to singles uses enlightening examples from Apostle Paul, himself a single, to beautifully portray the dynamic aspects of the single life. The book gives fresh insight on practical issues such as coping with sexual desires, loneliness, and preparation for your future mate. Written in a lively style, the author admonishes singles to seek first the kingdom of God and rest assured in God's promise to supply their needs... including a life partner!

Leadership in the New Testament Church
by Earl D. Johnson
Leadership in the New Testament Church offers practical and applicable insight into the role of leadership in the present day church. In this book, the author explains the qualities that leaders must have, explores the interpersonal relationships between the leader and his staff, the leader's influence in the church and society and how to handle conflicts that arise among leaders.

The Call of God
by Jefferson Edwards
Since I have been called to preach, now what? Many sincere Christians are confused about their call to the ministry. Some are zealous and run ahead of their time and season of training and preparation while others are behind their time neglecting the gift of God within them. *The Call of God* gives practical instruction for pastors and leaders to refine and further develop their ministries and tips on how to nourish and develop others with God's call to effectively proclaim the gospel of Christ. *The Call of God* will help you to have clarity from God as to what ministry involves; be able to identify and affirm the call in your life; determine which stage you are in your call from God; remove confusion in relation to the processing of a call or the making of the person; understand the development of the anointing to fulfill your call.

Come, Let Us Pray
by Emmette Weir
Like an ocean, prayer is so vast that we will never plumb its depths. Are you content to walk along the shore, or are you ready to launch out into the deep? No matter what your stage of spiritual development, you can learn to pray with greater intimacy, gratitude, and power. Discover the secrets of personal prayer in *Come Let Us Pray*.

Mobilizing Human Resources
by Richard Pinder
Pastor Pinder gives an in-depth look at how to organize, motivate, and deploy members of the Body of Christ in a manner that produces maximum effect for your ministry. This book will assist you in organizing and motivating your troops for effective and efficient ministry. It will also help the individual believer in recognizing their place in the body, using their God given abilities and talents to maximum effect.

The Layman's Guide to Counseling
by Susan Wallace
The increasing need for counseling has caused today's Christian leaders to become more sensitive to raise up lay-counselors to share this burden with them. Jesus' command is to "set the captives free." *The Layman's Guide to Counseling* shows you how. A number of visual aids in the form of charts, lists, and tables are also integrated into this reference book: the most comprehensive counseling tool available. *The Layman's Guide to Counseling* gives you the knowledge you need to use advanced principles of Word-based counseling to equip you to be effective in your counseling ministry. **Topics Include** Inner

Healing, Parenting, Marriage, Deliverance, Abuse, Forgiveness, Drug and Alcohol Recovery, Youth Counseling, Holy Spirit, Premarital Counseling

The 1993 Trial on the Curse of Ham
by Wayne Perryman
Is the Black race cursed? This trial, attended by over 450 people, was the first time in over 3,000 years Ham had an opportunity to tell his side of the story and explain exactly what took place in the tent of his father, Noah. The evidence submitted by the defense on behalf of Ham and his descendants was so powerful that it shocked the audience and stunned the jury. Evidence presented by the defense was supported by over 442 biblical references.

The Church
by Turnel Nelson
Discover God's true intent and purpose for His Church in this powerful new release by Pastor Turnel Nelson. This book speaks to the individual with an exciting freshness and urgency to become the true Bride of Christ.

The Minister's Topical Bible
by Derwin Stewart
The Minister's Topical Bible covers every aspect of the ministry providing quick and easy access to Scriptures in a variety of ministry related topics. This handy reference tool can be effectively used in leadership training, counseling, teaching, sermon preparation, and personal study.

The Believer's Topical Bible
by Derwin Stewart
The Believer's Topical Bible covers every aspect of a Christian's relationship with God and man, providing biblical answers and solutions for many challenges. It is a quick, convenient, and thorough reference Bible that has been designed for use in personal devotions and group Bible studies. With over 3,800 verses systematically organized under 240 topics, it is the largest devotional-topical Bible available in the New International Version and the King James Version.

Daily Moments With God
by Jacqueline E. McCullough
As you journey into God's presence, take this volume with you. Evangelist Jacqueline E. McCullough has compiled her very own treasury of poetry, punctuated phrases, and sermonettes to inspire you to trust, love, and obey the Lord Jesus Christ. *Daily Moments With God* will direct your thoughts toward God, shed insight on the Scriptures, and encourage you to meditate on life-changing truths. As your spirit soars in prayer, praise, and worship, the presence and power of God will transform you.

God's Glorious Outpouring *Video*
Hosted By: Tim Storey, Leon Isaac Kennedy and Carlton Pearson.
A must viewing for every Christian leader. In 1906, within a former horse stable, then converted into Azusa Missions, ordinary people met with an extraordinary God! Relive

this outpouring which has been termed by church scholars as God's greatest outpouring of the 20th Century! Listen as today's outstanding church historians Dr. Vinson Synan, Dr. Cecil Roebeck, and others relate how this outpouring swept throughout the world and has now encompassed over 350 million people! Reflect as the only known witnesses relate how it really was! Be inspired as those who were there tell how the Lord is. He will soon do it again!

Tragedy to Triumph *Video*
Hosted By: Tim Storey and Leon Isaac Kennedy.
He dared to follow God. The results – he was a catalyst that helped change the world! A must viewing for every Christian leader. Most have never heard of William Seymour, yet Yale Church historian Sydney Ahlstrom remarks, "Seymour exerted a greater influence upon American Christianity than any other black leader." Within one year, not only the United States but fifty other nations were touched as 312 Azusa Street became one of the most famous addresses in the world! Listen as today's outstanding church historians Dr. Vinson Synan, Dr. Leonard Lovett, presiding Bishop Ford of the Church of God in Christ, Dr. Cecil Roebeck, Jim Zieglar and others relate how this outpouring swept throughout the world and has now encompassed over 350 million people!

Available at your local bookstore
or by contacting:

Pneuma Life Publishing
P.O. Box 10612
Bakersfield, CA 93389-0612

1-800-727-3218
1-805-324-1741

For Additional Copies of

BISHOP C. H. MASON
and the Roots of the Church of God in Christ

Call 1-800-727-3218